DEAL ME IN

DEAL ME IN

Twenty of the World's Top Poker Players
Share The Heartbreaking and Inspiring Stories
of How They Turned Pro

Marvin Karlins and Stephen John

Phil's House Publishing, Inc.
Las Vegas, Nevada

Deal Me In. Copyright 2009 © Phil's House Publishing, Inc.

Phil's House Publishing, Inc.,
3910 Pecos McLeod, I.C., Suite C-100
Las Vegas, NV 89121

www.philshousepublishing.com
www.pokerbrat.com

Printed and bound in China by Global PSD

Book design by Kimberly Welch, I Design
www.idcreativegroup.com

Edited by William Carver

Photo credits on page 287

FIRST EDITION

Library of Congress Control Number: 2009904081

ISBN: 978-0-9824558-0-7

In Fond Memory of

Stu Ungar, David "Chip" Reese, Benny Binion,
Walter "Puggy" Pearson, and Johnny Moss

Any list of the greatest poker players in the world would certainly include, in addition to the players profiled in this book, T. J. Cloutier, Erick Lindgren, John Juanda, Gus Hansen, David Oppenheim, John Hennigan, Patrick Antonius, David Benjamine, Ted Forrest, "Amarillo Slim" Preston, Huck Seed, Mike Matusow, David Chiu, and Barry Greenstein.

Within the pages of *Deal Me In* are twenty amazing stories from all over the globe, filled with inspiration, hope, failure, and the will to succeed. Sometimes the player found the game, and sometimes the game found the player.

DEAL ME IN

CONTENTS

ACKNOWLEDGMENTS

From the beginning, this book has been a passion project shared amongst a small group of people committed to gathering and presenting the personal and inspirational stories of many of the world's best poker players.

Both writers, Marvin Karlins and Stephen John, have captured the color and passion of the world's best, and both went to great lengths to secure interviews, even if it meant, for example, Steve waking up at 2 a.m. to catch Johnny Chan outside the poker room at the Bellagio! Bill Carver contributed meticulous edits, and Chris Jodry provided general support in a thousand different ways.

Shannon Reiter, the president of Phil's House Publishing, has overseen everyone and everything in *Deal Me In*, from initial concept to final printing. Shannon, your commitment and enthusiasm are nothing short of awesome.

Kimberly Welch of I Design, continues to amaze us with her creativity, which is on full display in the brilliant cover and chapter layouts; it's astonishing that this is her first full color book! And Aric Meidl, as always, has provided solid support by managing our online presence and web stores.

Steven Goff's team at Global PSD has been quick and resourceful in getting the book printed, under pressures of time and in an efficient and environmentally friendly fashion.

The "advisers," Elliott Wolf of Peanut Butter Publishing, and Dan Friedberg and Ryan Straus of Crest Law Group, have all been remarkably useful, positive and always forward thinking.

Steve Banks and Darren Weis of S and S Enterprises are great poker fans and industrious managers of the warehouse and shipping. Steve, we know you'll get that Omaha bracelet one of these days!

Justin Marchand and Mary Hurbi and the entire team at CardPlayer have been nothing short of fabulous enriching this project with beautiful photos and marketing expertise. And Larry Grossman was more than generous to share with us some very special, personal photos from the earlier days of the game.

A special thanks goes, of course, to all of the poker players gathered in this book. Your patience, often through multiple interviews and drafts, is deeply appreciated. Your stories are inspiring, and your accomplishments are mighty indeed.

Phil Hellmuth deserves special recognition for his unwavering commitment, financial support and endless enthusiasm for bringing this project to fruition. Phil, we are all so lucky to have you as a colleague and a friend.

Finally, everyone involved wants to thank Bob Soderstrom for coming up with the idea of writing this book, and for his tireless energy and iron will when it comes to "Getting Stuff Done!"

Global Printing, Sourcing & Development (Global PSD), in association with American Forests and the Global ReLeaf programs, will plant two trees for each tree used in the manufacturing of this book. GlobalReLeaf is an international campaign by American Forests, the nation's oldest nonprofit conservation organization and a world leader in planting trees for environmental restoration.

introduction

JACK M^CCLELLAND

Poker tournaments are my life as well as my career. In the early 80's I was playing hundreds of small tournaments a year in Las Vegas. I constantly complained to my late wife Alma about how poorly the tournaments were conducted. Alma, who was a very sharp lady (and sometimes sharp-tongued), said to me, "If you're such a genius, why don't you go and run them yourself."

Along the way I have seen many great players pass by. I will never forget the steely stare of Johnny Moss, or the beautiful grin of David "Chip" Reese as he happily stacked your chips in front of him. And who could forget the meteoric rise and fall and amazing comeback of Stu Ungar?

Twenty-six years and thousands of tournaments later, I still love my job.

While reading the first-person accounts in *Deal Me In*, I'm struck by the distance that many of the great players have traveled to find the game of poker. For most of the players in this book, poker on the nearest laptop simply did not exist when they first became intrigued by the game. "Finding a game" in those days meant traveling long distances and subjecting yourself to colorful and sometimes dishonest and dangerous players. Today, the game comes into your living room and finds you. In earlier years, you went out into the world and found a game.

In his account, the great Johnny Chan talks about traveling in the late 70's as a 16-year-old from Houston to Las Vegas, Phil Hellmuth shares stories of how he traveled the State of Wisconsin in search of bigger games, and recalls the number of times he traveled to Vegas (ten) before he had a single winning trip. Howard Lederer slept on a cot in the Chess Club of New York, cleaned the poker room there, and delivered sandwiches to the players—all so he could be close to the game and afford the nightly buy-ins!

Many of these journeys were made in the face of relentless family pressure, which was focused on the gambling aspect of the game. And then there were the social stigmas too, all swirling around the sophisticated, rigorous, and elegant game we love called poker.

It's also interesting to see in these accounts so many similar themes and tips for the player with pro aspirations. Money management, a critical theme, is addressed by players like Erik Seidel, Phil Ivey, and Chris Ferguson, as is the ability to step down in limits when you need to get your game back on track. And, of course, to avoid "leaking" your winnings from a skill game like poker into non-skill house games like roulette.

I was particularly moved by Annie's and Jennifer's unique journeys as women in a man's world. And I'd be remiss if I didn't mention the amazing, emotional stories of the Vietnamese players, Scotty Nguyen and Chau Giang, who immigrated to the United States without a penny in their pockets, but enormous talent in their brains and dreams in their hearts.

From a personal standpoint, the year 1989 turned out to be an amazing one at the World Series of Poker. Optimism was high in our own household. I had finished at the final table of the Seven-Card Stud World Championship in1988, and that same year, a disciplined Johnny Chan won his second consecutive WSOP Main Event by flopping the nut straight and trapping poker newcomer Erik Seidel by checking twice. My late wife Alma watched the tape of Chan's trap over-and-over.

Early into the 1989 WSOP, the Ladies World Championship event was held. The game was Seven-Card Stud. Alma ended up at the final table in spite of the fact that she had lost a large pot on a decision (made by her husband, the tournament director, me), that an opponent's hand was still retrievable.

The dinner break wasn't much fun for the two of us.

Several hours later, though, playing heads up, Alma began a hand with three queens. Her opponent, Adrienne Zoia, made open jacks on the fourth card and began betting. With each card, Adrienne's hand kept improving. I was announcing the action, and my mind was racing with the possibilities, and the feeling that Alma was in trouble. After the last card was dealt, she slowly double-checked her hole cards and calmly raised. Adrienne called all-in and Alma showed four queens to win her WSOP bracelet. She looked up and said to me, "I did it just like Johnny Chan." She then looked across the room to a table where Jack Binion was playing and shouted, "Jack Binion, you owe me a gold bracelet!" That was one of my proudest moments.

For the past eight years I have been fortunate to work at the Bellagio along with my partner, Doug Dalton, Director of Poker Operations. As a team we helped develop the World Poker Tour in 2002. In the process, we have seen our venue gain a reputation as the premiere poker room worldwide, and it remains the cornerstone of the WPT. This new, exciting, made-for-TV tour, dreamed up by Lyle Berman and Steve Lipscomb, took the world by storm.

The combination of (1) the audience now having the ability to see the players' hole cards, (2) the explosion of Internet poker, and (3) the chance

Jack MCCLELLAND

of hitting the lottery like Chris Moneymaker, who happened to turn $40 into millions, intensified the expanding interest in poker. Although the incomparable Doyle Brunson continued to win fortunes playing poker, an influx of new stars like Daniel Negreanu, Erick Lindgren, Phil Ivey and Allen Cunningham have hit the scene. All of a sudden it was "cool" to play poker. As poker tournaments grow larger and millions of dollars flow like water, the poker craze continues. Superstars like Carlos Mortensen, Scotty Nguyen, and Joe Hachem have increased their fame by winning titles on both the World Poker Tour and the World Series of Poker.

Most of the players who tell their stories in this book recognized very early in their lives that they had a special faculty for the game, and this in turn motivated them to follow their talent to each new challenge. Everyone here quickly beat up their home game in their hometown—the kind of game most of us have struggled through every Thursday night for decades—and went searching for the next big game in the next big city, until they ended up at a final table in the WSOP or WPT. This book is about how these supremely talented people became some of the world's greatest professional poker players, one win at a time.

I have been very blessed and lucky throughout my career. With the unending love and support of my wonderful wife Elizabeth, I expect to remain in the game a little longer still.

I am honored to write this introduction. Shuffle up and READ!

Jack McClelland

Director of Poker Tournament Operations

Bellagio Casino
Las Vegas, NV

BIG GUNS

♣ ♥ ♠ ♦

CHAPTER ✦ ONE

doyLε BRUNSON

Everything is super-sized in the Lone Star State, and when it comes to poker legends, none are bigger than "Texas Dolly" Brunson, the godfather of the green felt. For nearly four decades this man has remained center-stage in the poker world, chalking up victories wherever the biggest tournaments and cash games are contested. During this time he wrote a book (Super/System) that remains the most influential treatise on poker to this day.

He won both WSOP and WPT titles, he has been inducted into the Poker Hall of Fame and Walk of Fame, and he had a poker hand named in his honor (10-2, the starting hand he played to win two consecutive WSOP championship titles). Known as a fierce competitor, and at the same time recognized for his strong sense of honor and commitment to his family, Doyle has been an outstanding ambassador of goodwill for poker worldwide.

His goal to be remembered as "someone who loved poker and did everything I could to promote the game" has already been achieved in his own lifetime. His legacy assured, he will continue to inspire future generations of players as long as cards are shuffled and poker hands are dealt.

I grew up in a small town of around a hundred people or so. My parents were kind, God-fearing people. My dad was a farmer and managed a cotton gin. He played poker as well, though you'd never much know it to be around him. There were only a few boys my age around, and a couple of them became my good friends. We would all end up all-star athletes. Ours was a very poor farming town, and we knew that the only way we'd ever get out of there was to get an athletic scholarship and go to college, so that's what we strove to achieve. If we failed, we were resigned to the fact that we'd have to become farmers ourselves. None of us liked that idea much. So it was basketball and track that got the lion's share of my attention as a youth, not poker.

♣ ♥ ♠ ♦

Although I had played poker once or twice as a senior in high school and enjoyed the experience, it wasn't until my freshman year in college that I fell in love with the game. I remember the night it happened: I had returned to my dormitory room after a date and there was a poker game being played. I played all night long and right through my classes the next morning. We had a track meet that afternoon and I was the star miler, but I didn't feel like running. I was really tired. So I called my coach: "Coach, I'm sick, I don't think I can run today."

He said, "What's wrong?"

"I think I have the flu, or something," I replied.

So he said, "OK," and hung up. I thought, "I guess I got away with it."

After the call I went to my room and got into bed. I was just falling asleep when there was a bang on the door. It was my coach. He said: "Hey, let's go to the doctor."

CHAPTER ⬥ ONE

I said: "No, I'm not that sick. I'll be alright."

He insisted: "No, I want to take you to the doctor."

I looked at him and I could see he knew what had happened. So I said, "OK, I'll go run." And he said, "I figured you might, so I brought your uniform."

So I put the uniform on and went over to the track. One of the first events was the half-mile, an event I did not run for the team. I was stretched out under a bench trying to sleep and a kid comes over and says, "The coach wants you." I walked over to where he was standing and he said, "Go in there, I want you to run the half mile." "It's not my event," I pointed out, "I don't run the half mile, coach." That didn't change his mind. "Today, you do run the half-mile," he declared, and he put me in there. I just knew I'd be sick. I won the race. I surprised everyone, especially myself. I ran one of my best half miles ever. After the thrill of the race was over, I began to feel pretty run down again quickly. I decided to celebrate my stunning and unexpected win with a victory nap under the bleachers. I had just fallen asleep when this kid comes up again and says, "The coach wants you to run in the mile."

♣ ♥♠♦

Although I had played poker once or twice as a senior in high school and enjoyed the experience, it wasn't until my freshman year in college that I fell in love with the game.

♣ ♥♠♦

I returned to the track and reminded the coach I had just run the half mile. My legs were still rubbery. He told me, "You'll be all right. Go ahead and run anyway." This time I was up against much tougher competition. Unbelievably, I ran one of my best times again, and won that race too. I was whipped, though, exhausted. I went back to the bench to lie down once again. That same annoying kid came back a third time and said the coach wanted me run yet again, this time to anchor the mile relay. I was still winded from the other races and my sides were hurting. I felt like I

doyLe brunson

was going to throw up. But I did what I was told and I ran that race, too. We didn't win that race, though, and I learned a valuable lesson—don't mess with the coach. He put me through it that day, but it didn't dampen my desire to play sports. The card game the night before got me very excited about poker too. I've always loved competition, and athletics and poker both fulfilled that need in me.

I went to Hardin-Simmons University in Abilene, Texas, on an athletic scholarship. I planned to be a professional basketball player and then, when my playing days were over, come back home as a teacher and a coach. The Minnesota Lakers had already been to my games and had been scouting me in my junior year. I was a 6-foot-3 shooting guard, which was virtually unheard of at the college level in those days. That year I was named the most valuable player in my conference. The Lakers told my coach they were considering drafting me after my senior year. Life was sweet.

♣ ♥♠♦

I planned to be a professional basketball player and then, when my playing days were over, come back home as a teacher and a coach.

♣ ♥♠♦

I thought basketball was going to provide me with all the opportunities I could hope to have. But fate would intervene. I had a hard-labor summer job after my junior season. I was working at a plant one day and suffered a severe injury when a load of sheetrock fell on me and crushed my leg. It snapped my leg like a twig. Just like that, my professional basketball aspirations had ended.

Fortunately, the school honored my athletic scholarship for my senior year. With an athletic career now out of reach, I knew that I had to reassess my career direction. I'd decided that I needed to earn a master's degree, which would help me land a good teaching job. I had a problem, though. I had no scholarship or money for graduate school. I also had no job. What I did have, however, was good poker skills. I began playing poker around the dormitories to pay my tuition. There was no shortage of games around college campuses, and from the beginning it was pretty

obvious that I was better than most of my opponents. Through athletics, I had made friends at many universities around Texas, so I started going to different campuses on the weekends and playing in games throughout the state. Consequently, I 'played' my way through graduate school with poker winnings.

Once I earned my master's degree, the next objective was to get a job. At this point I had not considered poker as a career, and even when I didn't find a teaching position that appealed to me, I did not turn to poker. Instead, I took a job as a sales representative for the Burroughs Corporation, a manufacturer of bookkeeping machines. It would be the only "real job" I would ever have. I stayed with them a few months, dutifully sat through their training program, and accepted an assignment as the representative for the north side of Fort Worth, Texas. I began making sales calls with as many clients as I could. During many of the sales visits, I noticed that poker games were being played in the back rooms. I thought to myself, "What better way to build a relationship with some my clients than to sit down for a friendly game of poker. I could play some poker, bond with the employees and maybe make some sales." So I sat down and played in some of the games.

♣ ♥ ♠ ♦

*I was making more money beating the employees in poker than I was
trying to sell them my products. So I quit my job and
started playing poker full-time.*

♣ ♥ ♠ ♦

As it turns out, if you beat the decision-makers out of their money, they are less likely to buy your product. I was making more money beating the employees in poker than I was trying to sell them my products. I enjoyed the poker and hated the sales. It didn't take a rocket scientist to see that it was time for me to make a change. So I quit my job and started playing poker full-time.

The north side of Ft. Worth was a very tough neighborhood. The

DOYLE BRUNSON

stockyards were there and a lot of violent people were drawn to the area. The place was filled with outlaws, tough guys, and other seedy characters, but the environment made for great money games. Being a better poker player wasn't enough to assure you of winning money, however. Some of the games were crooked, and you had to keep a constant eye out for cheaters. Even if you managed to avoid being cheated, you also had to dodge the police, who were constantly raiding the illegal games in the area. And even if you did win money and avoid arrest, there was always the issue of collecting your winnings. Cashing in without being robbed or shot was an adventure itself. There were some poor losers out there, and violence was a way of life for many of the players in the games.

♣ ♥ ♠ ♦

Sometime during the evening, this guy just walks in, puts a gun up to the head of the man sitting next to me, pulled the trigger and spattered his brains all over the back wall.

♣ ♥ ♠ ♦

I personally saw five people get killed for various reasons. One man was sitting right next to me at the poker table when it happened. It was in the back of a pool hall and there were two games going. The man, who was someone I knew from poker, worked at the local meat-packing plant. We were not great friends but still, he was someone I knew. Sometime during the evening, this guy just walks in, puts a gun up to the head of the man sitting next to me, pulls the trigger, and splatters his brains all over the back wall.

Two seconds earlier, my acquaintance had been laughing and joking. In an instant he was stone dead right beside me. That kind of thing can shake you up. Later, I heard that the two men had an issue over a woman. At that particular moment, I could have cared less. I only cared about getting out of there before any more bullets started flying. I remember we all ran out the back door and through a creek. We didn't want to have to talk to the police about it.

I stayed in the North Fort Worth area for a couple of years and then

CHAPTER · ONE

started playing downtown with a more respectable clientele. From there, I began playing in games all around Texas and into neighboring states. Of course, you had to be invited to play in those games, but you became well-known pretty quickly back in those days—if you could play. It was during this time that I teamed up with Sailor Roberts and Amarillo Slim and we traveled together and looked out for each other. It helped to have a friend watching your back. Even then I can't tell you how many times I ended up getting robbed in those early days. It was dangerous back then.

♣ ♥ ♠ ♦

♣ ♥ ♠ ♦

The robber cocked both barrels of his shotgun and put it right between my eyes and said 'I'm going to ask you one last time— who runs this poker game?'

♣ ♥ ♠ ♦

I remember one incident in particular. We were at a guy's house in Austin playing in a big game. There were several tables going. Suddenly I heard this loud sound. It was glass breaking and a bunch of guys wearing ski masks came through the windows carrying shotguns. They lined us all up against the wall and made us drop our pants down to our ankles. One of the gunmen said, "We want all the money you have, and we don't have time to strip search each of you to find it. So we're going to pick a few of you out to search, and if we find you're hiding anything we're going to blow your leg off." Right away one guy standing a few feet from me says, "Hey good buddy, I've got $400 in my pocket." Another player hollered, "Don't forget this $600 in my shirt."

Then one robber with a double-barreled shotgun walked up to me, turned me around, and asked, "Who runs this poker game?" I'm no

♣ ♥ ♠ ♦

snitch, so I answered, "I don't know." He wasn't happy with that answer, so he took his shotgun and hit me in the stomach with it. Then he repeated the question: "Who runs this poker game?" My principles prohibited me from saying anything other than, "I don't know." That made him even madder and he took his shotgun and hit me right upside the head. "Now do you know who runs this poker game?" He snarled. Stubbornly, I repeated, "I don't know." The robber then cocked both barrels of his shotgun and put it right between my eyes and said "I'm going to ask you one last time—who runs this poker game?" And I said, "That guy right over there!"

There's brave, and then there's stupid.

Sometimes, when I see young poker players sitting in the comfortable, safe surroundings of a fancy casino, I wonder if they ever could imagine some of the things we had to go through to play poker back in the early days. Actually, I'd like the younger guys to appreciate where we came from. If we hadn't gone through all those tough times, I don't think poker would ever have got to where it is today, because it would never have materialized out here in Las Vegas.

♣ ♥ ♠ ♦

There was nothing they could do – the cancer was terminal.
They gave me three months to live.

♣ ♥ ♠ ♦

After several years of playing poker, I faced a life-threatening event. I was diagnosed with cancer. Five doctors examined me. The cancer had spread from my head into my body. The outlook was bleak. I was 28 at the time, and like most guys my age, I felt my whole life was in

CHAPTER ONE

front of me. Surgery was scheduled. The doctors opened me up to get a better idea as to the extent of the problem. They took one look and just sewed me up, telling me there was nothing they could do—the cancer was terminal. They gave me three months to live. Understandably, I was crushed, devastated.

Three weeks later, I decided to go to the best cancer hospital in Houston to seek a second opinion, but I was not very optimistic. I was not going down without a fight, however, and wanted to explore every last option. The doctors in Houston decided to open me up again and take a peek. What they discovered was nearly unbelievable to them. The cancer had disappeared completely—it was gone.

At first I believed the original doctors must have been incompetent—there must not have been cancer to begin with. Not so, the Houston doctors told me. They had my x-rays right there and confirmed that the radiographs showed advanced cancer. They explained to me that, rarely, a spontaneous remission occurs and the cancer fades. That was 47 years ago.

♣ ♥ ♠ ♦

In fact, when I played in Texas, not only was poker illegal, you were thought of as a gangster, an undesirable, a thug, or some other seedy type of character.

♣ ♥ ♠ ♦

I think my case is actually in some medical journal or record book somewhere. It was a miracle—there's no other word for it. God was not in my life at that point, but I really believe that He intervened. I am convinced this was a divine intervention.

I remember leaving the hospital and noticing things I had never noticed before: things like how blue the sky was, and how beautiful the flowers were. I ended up with a general appreciation of life that I really didn't have before—I had just taken things for granted. And that's the point where I realized I was going to spend the rest of my days enjoying life by doing what I wanted to do, and that was poker. Poker was, in

doyLe ♦ bRunson

♣ ♥ ♠ ♦

my mind, the only thing I had ever experienced that made it impossible for me to tell if I was working or playing.

Without the cancer scare, I suspect I probably would have returned to the workforce and found a 'real job.' My wife wanted me to do something 'legitimate.' I had promised her I would. But after my illness she accepted the fact that I was going to pursue a poker career, and it was not long after that when we moved to Las Vegas and began to raise our family there. I think she finally became comfortable with the decision once I began making good money at the tables. She realized I could support my family playing the game.

♣ ♥ ♠ ♦

Is a poker career for everybody? No. Like any profession, I believe you need the right attitudes and skills if you're going to succeed.

♣ ♥ ♠ ♦

Even after the brush with death convinced me to become a poker professional I didn't 'go public' with the information—not at first, anyway. In today's world it is prestigious to be a professional poker player. But it wasn't always that way. In fact, when I played in Texas, not only was poker illegal, you were thought of as a gangster, an undesirable, a thug, or some other seedy type of character. Poker players were looked down upon by the general public and viewed as 'second-class citizens.' One of my old college roommates even crossed the street to avoid saying 'hello' to me, all because he knew I was playing poker for a living.

That made quite an impression on me. After that, I didn't discuss my profession with anybody outside of my family; I even tried to hide it from my neighbors, because I wanted to shield my wife and children from

being harassed or humiliated.

At Hardin-Simmons University where I played basketball, I was denied a spot in their athletic hall of fame because my occupation as a poker player was not up to their moral standards. For thirty years they rejected me. Finally, I got a letter saying they had inducted me into the hall of fame.

Today, of course, I can't go to the bathroom without someone wanting an autograph, or a photo with me, so the mentality has certainly changed, but it took a long time getting there.

♣ ♥ ♠ ♦

I clearly remember the incident that finally allowed me to feel comfortable telling people I played poker for a living. It involved the World Series of Poker championship in the early seventies. We were down to three players: myself, Puggy Pearson, and Amarillo Slim. At that point, a barrage of reporters and television crews showed up. That had never happened before. I called a break and told the other guys I didn't want the publicity. I was afraid of what would happen to my family once the news reached Texas. I didn't want them to suffer because of me. Puggy didn't want the publicity either. Slim said, "I do." We spoke with the tournament director, Jack McClelland, and he agreed to let me withdraw. I made up an excuse that I was sick, and got to keep the $40,000 in chips I had accumulated. Slim ended up with the title, which was a good thing because he was such a great ambassador for poker. He did all the talk shows, which I wouldn't have done, had I won. The most interesting thing about this whole incident was what happened when I got home. I told my wife and kids about my decision to withdraw to save them from embarrassment and they said, "Oh, you shouldn't have done that. We would have been proud of you had you won and gotten all

that publicity." So at that point I realized my family had really accepted what I was doing, and I told them that next time I had a chance at the title, I'd go for it.

♣ ♥ ♠ ♦

*I like to equate a poker career to a cloud in the sky
floating around — that's how free you are.*

♣ ♥ ♠ ♦

It's still hard for me to realize how far poker has come. Players have gone from being second-class citizens to being celebrities. I take these changes with a grain of salt. I don't consider myself a celebrity—just a poker player. I think a lot of these young guys fancy themselves as celebrity entertainers, and I think it takes away from the essence of the game. When it comes to poker, I guess you could call me a purist: I think people should play poker for the competition, and not to put on a show so they can get more TV time.

Some people ask me if, looking back on my life, I regret my decision to play professional poker full time. The answer is no. I have always loved the competitive aspect of poker and, unlike athletics, where people can only compete at the highest levels for a small portion of their lives, poker gives people a chance to compete for as long as they can sit at the tables and keep their wits about them. Poker has given me the chance to satisfy my need to compete. It has also allowed me a tremendous amount of freedom. With poker, you are your own boss. You play when you want to, when you feel like it. I like to equate a poker career to a cloud in the sky, floating around—that's how free you are. One cannot ignore the money that can be made, either. Today, playing tournament or cash poker can be very lucrative, plus there's money to be made away from the table as well. Top players can market themselves and make serious money with endorsement deals and poker-related business ventures. Poker has also given me insight on how to deal with life. It's taught me you've got to play the hand you're dealt. It might not be the hand you want, but you need to learn to play it to the best of your ability and hope for a positive outcome.

CHAPTER ONE

Even though I have experienced many benefits from my years at the tables, I don't mean to imply that a poker career is problem-free. One major drawback involves interpersonal relationships: to become a really great player you have to devote so much time and energy to the game that it leaves little time for family and friends. My major regret as a poker player was that I spent so much time playing that I neglected my family. There is also the poker lifestyle to consider. Poker players have to deal with constant temptations, particularly if they get well known. Drugs, women, gambling, non-stop action – it's just hard to keep your personal life from spinning out of control. I've lost several good friends to drug addiction. The risks are always there. And, of course, there's the problem of handling losses at the tables. Even the best players can experience dry spells, and they need to handle the tough times without 'steaming' and going broke.

♣ ♥ ♠ ♦

Is a poker career for everybody? No. Like any profession, I believe you need the right attitudes and skills if you're going to succeed. In poker, the right attitudes involve a love of the game, a passion to play, a competitive spirit and the desire to win. I know that my devotion to the game and my competitive nature have helped me become a better poker player. As far as skills are concerned: a great memory is critical to poker success.

All the great players have a recall ability that less skilled opponents lack. In my case, I can remember hands I played back 40 or 50 years ago. I remember what happened and why, and it helps me play those hands more successfully when they show up again. In addition to

doyLε bɹunson

having great recall, great poker players have the skill to cope with pressure situations. The same holds true with great athletes. Being able to think clearly and act effectively when the game is on the line separates the champions from the runner-ups. I've always handled myself in pressure situations better than most people, and I've seen the same behavior in the best poker professionals I've played against.

I plan to keep playing poker as long as I can remain competitive at the tables. It's been a great fifty years: poker has been good to me, and I hope I have been good for poker. In the end, I would like to be remembered as someone who loved the game, played longer at the highest levels than anyone else, emphasized the importance of honor and trust in conducting oneself at the tables, and did everything possible to promote poker in a positive way. ♠

CHAPTER ONE

You can visit and play poker with Doyle at Doyle's Room (doylesroom.net). Doyle supports the American Cancer Society (www.cancer.org) which is a nationwide, community-based voluntary health organization dedicated to preventing cancer, saving lives, and diminishing suffering through research, education, advocacy, and service.

doyle BRUNSON

CHAPTER 🦅 two

JOHNNY CHAN

JOHNNY CHAN

Johnny Chan is one of the most legendary, colorful and recognizable characters in poker. He has already earned credentials ranking him among the best poker players of all time, and he still has many years ahead of him.

A fierce competitor, Chan captured back-to-back World Series of Poker Main Event titles in 1987 and 1988, and amassed ten WSOP bracelets over the course of three decades. In addition to his legendary tournament performances, Chan has been a consistent winner in the world's toughest, ultra-high-stakes cash games, and is an imposing presence at the tables.

Johnny's Hold'em skills were highlighted in the Hollywood poker film, "Rounders", which featured his classic 'trap play' against Erik Seidel on the final hand of the 1988 WSOP championship event. In 2002, Johnny's contributions to the game were publicly recognized with his induction into the Poker Hall of Fame.

Bob Stupak, owner of Vegas World Casino (now the Stratosphere), once hosted a tournament called the America's Cup. At the final table, I knocked out nine players in just two hours to win the tournament. Afterward, Bob came up to me and said, "Johnny, you ran over those players like they weren't even there. You were like the *Orient Express.*" From that point on, this became not only my nickname, but an expression of my playing style—a style that has enabled me to become one of the most successful poker players in the world.

♣ ♥♠♦

Perhaps the most important thing I learned was the value of money – earning it, investing it and protecting it. Money is hard to come by and easy to lose. And when you lose it, getting it back is even harder.

♣ ♥♠♦

Though I have accomplished a great deal in poker, I'll never forget my humble beginnings. My family moved from Hong Kong to the United States in 1968, when I was 11 years old, settling in Phoenix, Arizona. My parents owned a restaurant there, but none of us spoke English. The only two words I knew were 'yes' and 'no.' They were my responses to anything said to me, even though I didn't have the slightest idea what was being asked, or whether those responses were appropriate. You can imagine how it looked when someone said to me, "Johnny, what was it like growing up in Hong Kong?" And I would say, "Yes."

I was the only Chinese student in a school of over a thousand youngsters. I felt isolated. It was difficult at first, having to learn English. Other kids looked at me strangely, made fun of my accent, and picked on me because I was different. You'll not hear me complain, though. The experience toughened me. Despite the language barrier, I enjoyed school and got good grades. My best subject was math. Numbers are universal and don't require fluent English.

In 1973 we moved to Houston. The Asian community there was larger and Houston was growing. My parents opened a larger restaurant

called *Hoe Sai Gai,* which means, in English, *Great Whirl.* In Asian culture the children traditionally work in the family business, and I was no exception. I worked long hours and did whatever was required of me: mopping the floor, cleaning toilets, bussing tables, and even doing the cooking at times. Everyone in the family pitched in. I knew right away that this was not going to be my life's profession, although the hard work taught me a number of life lessons that I carry with me today. Perhaps the most important thing I learned was the value of money—earning it, investing it, and protecting it. Money is hard to come by, and easy to lose. And when you lose it, getting it back is even harder.

I worked at the family restaurant all through high school and while attending the University of Houston. I studied hotel management, although, I must admit, that I think I always knew that this was not the direction my life was going to take.

Our restaurant is also where I first learned to play poker. Many of today's younger players learn poker from competing online. When I first started playing, there was no such thing as online. My training ground was games played on weekends, after business hours at the restaurant—dealer's choice, $.50–$1 limits. We played everything: Dr. Pepper, baseball, Mexican square, Hold'em, and Omaha. Learning different kinds of poker from the beginning was the major reason I'm comfortable playing a variety of games in different kinds of professional tournaments today.

The people who played in our game were restaurant customers, employees, and friends. On a good night you could win twenty bucks, which was pretty big for a teenager back then. The games would often go all night, and when dawn broke we'd quit and go to Denny's for breakfast. The winner would pay for the meal. It was quite the happy time for the winner, who picked up the check like a badge of honor. It wasn't long before the games spread from the restaurant to other spots around Houston, including private homes. I began playing more frequently and more seriously. The stakes progressed from small change and bragging rights to playing for real money.

JOHNNY CHAN

I recall thinking, "Wow, you really can make money playing poker!" I was winning pretty steadily and I began building a bankroll. Somewhere along the line, I became aware of a company that organized junkets and represented the Landmark Hotel in Las Vegas. They were offering special deals on trips to Las Vegas, where they required you to gamble as a condition of the trip. For a 16-year old, it was a pretty big deal just to fly on a plane, much less stay in a nice hotel and have people treat

you like a VIP. This was a three-night, four-day junket. To qualify, you had to put up $2,500 up front and, in return, you received a free round trip air ticket and an RFB comp: room, food, and beverage, on the house. I used my poker winnings to help sponsor the trip, and I went with a group of friends.

When I arrived at the Landmark I was given my own personalized name tag, which identified me as a junket player. . . I mean VIP. I stuck the tag on my shirt, walked into the casino, and approached the blackjack tables. A pit boss glanced my way, spotted my name tag, and asked, "Mr. C, how much

♣ ♥ ♠ ♦

money would you like?" He did not check my age or ask for identification. In those days the casinos were not concerned with your age. The only number they were interested in was the number of dollars you were prepared to gamble. We're talking about old Vegas—the seventies. "You have money but no ID? No problem. Come right this way." When he asked me how much money I needed, I said, "Well, give me the limit," which turned out to be the $2,500 front money I had deposited in the cage.

I sat down at the blackjack table around 7:00 p.m. It didn't go so well. Fifteen minutes later I moved to craps, and the result was equally bad. By

7:30 p.m. my entire $2,500 was gone—poof, vanished.

Now I was broke in Las Vegas. I was busted emotionally as well as financially. I felt angry, frustrated, embarrassed, and humbled. As you might imagine, when you have no money, your status as a VIP becomes pretty tenuous as well. The whole thing was a huge mess, and did not go at all as I had planned. Worse, I still had three days left on the trip. I decided to take a walk—the only thing left I could afford to do. I walked from my hotel all the way downtown, in the heat of the Las Vegas summer day. It didn't matter. I was not paying attention to the weather. It could have started to snow, and I doubt I would have noticed.

♣ ♥♠ ♦

I started to leave. Little did I know at the time, the casino management had a different plan. It seems that the casinos in Las Vegas frown on the idea of a player actually leaving the casino with a wad of money.

♣ ♥♠ ♦

I ended up at the Golden Nugget and went inside. I was instantly blown away. I spotted guys playing poker! I didn't know there *were* poker games in the casinos. I thought there were only traditional casino games like blackjack, craps, and roulette. I remember thinking that if I had known this I wouldn't have blown my money at the Landmark. I watched the game for a while and thought I could beat it. The players were really bad. I was kicking myself for blowing my money on games I didn't know when I just knew I could own everyone at the table I was watching. I was dying to get into that game. You remember my little problem, though, right? I had no money. I was desperately trying to think of some creative way to get into that game, when it dawned on me that I had a MasterCard with a $200 limit. But how would I turn that into cash? I had never heard of a cash advance on a credit card, but I went to the cashier thinking I would use my charm and salesmanship to negotiate some arrangement.

"Excuse me, Miss," I said, "I have this credit card and. . ." The cashier cut me off. She said, "Would you like the limit?" It was just that easy. The credit card company informed me that there would be a 19 percent interest charge plus this fee and that fee, etc. I barely heard the number. I couldn't have cared less. If it were 100 percent interest I would have taken the money.

♣ ♥♠ ♦

I firmly believe that the best way to become a true winner is to first understand what it is like to be a loser. I think you have to know what it is like to lose it all before you can truly appreciate what you've won.

♣ ♥♠ ♦

I got the $200 and went directly to the poker table. It was a $10–$20 limit Hold'em game. I bought in for two stacks of reds ($5 chips) and started playing. I played for three days, almost nonstop, and cashed in for $30,000! It was hard for me to contain my feelings. Just imagine being a teenager in the seventies with $30,000 in cash in your pocket. Mentally, I had already started thinking about the car, the jewelry, and other things I would buy. I was anxious to get back home and tell my parents and friends what had happened.

I started to leave. Little did I know at the time, the casino management had a different plan. It seems that the casinos in Las Vegas would frown on the idea of a player actually leaving the casino with a wad of money. They were not about to let me just walk out the door without providing me with an 'opportunity' to stay and gamble some more. The pit boss said, "Mr. Chan, we've got you a big suite, food, a limo, and tickets to any show you want to see." With my VIP status, and my dignity, fully restored, I took them up on their offer. I had beaten the odds once. Doing it again shouldn't be a problem, right? *Wrong.*

I enjoyed it while I could, but I was a sucker, a youngster who did not understand the value of money. I lost every dollar I had won, and went home broke and deeply discouraged. I knew I was better than the other players at the poker tables. I was furious with myself that I had lost. The worst part of this experience is that I did not learn my lesson. I lost money on several other junkets before I began to realize that my biggest problem was self-control. To this day, I firmly believe that the best way to become a true winner is first to understand what it is like to be a loser.

CHAPTER two

I think you have to know what it's like to lose it all before you can truly appreciate what you've won.

After this experience I flew home to Houston—high school, working at the restaurant, and of course, playing poker games around town. But things were different, a *lot* different. I had won big money, and that experience had changed the way I thought about life. Even though Vegas had sucked me dry, I knew that there was big money to be made in that town, and I knew I was going to win more than my fair share of it. It was just a matter of when and how.

♣ ♥ ♠ ♦

When my parents enrolled me at the University of Houston to study hotel management, I didn't last long. Now that I had had that taste of the big money, school was the furthest thing from my mind. I figured it would take me a year working in the hotel management business to make $30,000. I made that much in less than a week at the Nugget.

When I turned 21, I quit school and moved to the city that never sleeps, determined to be a professional poker player. I didn't want to work the rest of my life in the restaurant. I wanted to be my own boss. Besides, I liked the nonstop action and, of course, the lure of money. When I told my parents the news, they were devastated and angry. "Johnny, Las Vegas is sin city," they would say. "What are you thinking?" They didn't want me to be a gambler. They loved me and were worried, although at the time it felt as if they were trying to control me. They knew that very few gamblers survived in Las Vegas. I remember my dad telling me, "Once you leave, don't ever come back." Those words really hurt. I knew he was trying to protect me from harm, but it always hurts to realize that you have disappointed your family. Deep down, I knew they could be right. Las Vegas has ruined the lives of more than one person. How many people go to Las Vegas each year with hopes of striking it rich, only to crawl back home, with their heads down and tails tucked between their legs? The number has to be in the thousands. Would I be another notch in the belt? It was possible. Still, I was determined to try. I believed this was my shot at the brass ring.

♣ ♥♠♦

I remember my dad telling me, 'Once you leave, don't ever come back.' Those words really hurt. I knew he was trying to protect me from harm but it always hurts to realize that you have disappointed your family.

♣ ♥♠♦

There was no way I would've backed down from my parents at that point. "Dad, you'll regret saying that," I told him. "One day I'll be a world champion and I'll be rich. I'm going to make it. That's what I want to do." I hopped in my car and headed to Las Vegas, hoping my old Camaro would survive the trip. I never looked back.

When I first arrived in Las Vegas, things were difficult. I had bad habits. I'd win at the poker tables but then give it all back playing blackjack or dice, or betting on sports events. Or I'd play too long, lose my temper, and make bad decisions. In poker, temper can destroy your game faster than your toughest opponent. I knew full well that if I was ever going to conquer this game, I'd first have to conquer and control my own temperament. But saying it is easier than doing it. I slipped many times before I finally learned to get hold of my emotions, instead of letting them control me.

After going broke several times, I had to get a regular job to bring in money. At one time I worked as a chef at the Fremont Casino downtown. It's very tough to stand in a kitchen tossing salads when what you want is to be at the poker table tossing chips. After my shift I'd go right from the kitchen to the poker room, where they held a $3–$6 limit Hold'em game. When I was low on cash, the $3–$6 game was a good way to

CHAPTER two

rebuild my bankroll. My goal was to win $50–$100 per session and save enough money to join the higher-limit games.

It took me a while to get my emotions and my game under control. I learned a lot of expensive lessons about surviving as a poker professional in Vegas. You have to develop the right mental attitude at the table: the ability to keep cool, handle the inevitable losing streaks, and not go on tilt. I discovered that it was the calm and collected players who usually ended up with the money.

♣ ♥ ♠ ♦

One day I didn't go broke. I don't remember exactly when it was, but that day was a milestone. I made money the next day too, and the next. Before I knew it, the Orient Express had left the station and was heading down the track, full-steam ahead. I won my first gold bracelet in 1985, beating out 300 to 400 other players. I won about $185,000 and my career took off. It was at that moment that I knew I had made it.

When it was obvious that my success was not a flash in the pan, my parents had a change of heart and gave me their support and approval. When I won the WSOP main event in 1987, the Houston newspapers picked up the story, and my parents were telling people, "That's our son!" After that, every time I'd come to Houston for the holidays they'd call their friends and relatives and say, "Johnny's home. Hey, let's all have dinner."

I also learned that winning at the Vegas poker tables wasn't enough. You had to hold onto the money and avoid the temptations that could bust you. If I can give others any advice, it would be to learn this lesson: once you win the money, protect the money. I warn young players that

JOHNNY CHAN

Las Vegas is full of temptations. If you don't watch yourself, you can go broke overnight. It's not just casino games that are the only problem, either.

Las Vegas is a betting town. Gamblers are in movie theaters, bars, restaurants, and shopping malls. You might be at a restaurant, and your dinner mate says, "I'll bet you a hundred bucks that this guy's going to hit a home run," or some similar kind of wager. The next thing you know you're betting hundreds of thousands of dollars on all kinds of different prop bets. I see people making million-dollar prop bets on how many bracelets they're going to win this year or next year. It's not a good idea. I do my best when I focus on poker and stay away from the horses, the crap tables, and the prop bets. Do what you do well, and avoid getting sucked into stupid things.

Playing professional poker in Vegas also taught me the importance of good physical fitness. When I first came to Nevada, keeping physically fit was not high on my priority list. It took me years to realize that my poor physical condition was limiting my ability to play my best. Poker is a game that takes a lot of concentration, for many hours at a time, and my body wasn't in proper shape to handle it. Back in the seventies it seemed everyone smoked, drank alcohol, ate poorly, and had poor exercise habits. I was right there with them. Years of living like that really wore me down. The smoking, poor diet, and lack of exercise really affected my play in these long tournaments. So I decided to make a major change in my lifestyle. I gave up a four-pack-a-day cigarette habit, stopped drinking, ate healthier foods, and began exercising regularly. It worked, and the slimmer, healthier, happier Johnny Chan was able to elevate to a higher level. To this day I continue to work out, make sure I get enough sleep, and watch what I eat and drink. In fact, I've been so impressed with the benefits of a healthy lifestyle that I started a business that produces the *All In Energy Drink*. It's particularly good for today's poker player who needs to keep sharp while playing in grueling, fourteen-hour-a-day no-limit Hold'em tournaments.

Almost everyone who has met me over the last several years has asked

CHAPTER   two

me about the movie "Rounders." Poker has been a big money game for many years, but a lot of people see "Rounders" as the thing that put no-limit Texas Hold'em on the national map. Before "Rounders," Johnny Chan was a well-known and respected name within the poker community. But I could walk around in Seattle or Pittsburgh, and no one would know who I was. And if they found out, the news might merit a curious glance, but little more. After "Rounders" came out, people all over the world knew Johnny Chan, whether they followed poker or not. People who never played poker in their lives might come up to me and say, "Aren't you the guy who plays Texas Hold-*up*?"

The movie changed my life. I became a rock star overnight. It opened up doors for endorsements, personal appearances, and charity events. When they approached me about using video footage of my victory over Erik Seidel I was happy to oblige, under one small condition; I wanted to be in the movie. To accommodate me, they actually added a scene near the end of the movie where Matt Damon's character challenges me heads up at the poker table.

♣ ♥ ♠ ♦

The movie "Rounders" changed my life. I became a rock star over night. It opened up doors for me. When they approached me about using video footage of my victory over Erik Seidel I was happy to oblige with one small condition.

♣ ♥ ♠ ♦

I have six children, and I value my reputation as a good father even more than my reputation as a poker player. None of my children play professionally. They play online, and we sometimes play at the family table—just for fun. I've never told them that they should or should not play poker. I've left it up to them. I have, however, stressed the importance of education. My oldest son is a real estate broker and runs my energy drink business. If he ever decided on his own that he wanted to become a poker player, of course I would teach him. But so far, he has not shown interest, and I would never ask him to change his life. He's happy.

JOHNNY CHAN

I believe history will remember me as a player whose accomplishments have withstood the test of time. I've won ten bracelets over three decades, and my name is among the most recognized in poker. But withstanding that test of time is no easy feat. If you don't believe me, you can ask guys like Chris Moneymaker and Jamie Gold. Both guys have risen to the very top of the poker world and won major tournaments. Since then they have found out that while getting there is very difficult, staying there is even harder.

Guys like Doyle Brunson, Phil Hellmuth, and I have withstood the test of time. Daniel Negreanu, Allen Cunningham, and Phil Ivey are examples of the younger players who are no-brainers to be named to the Poker Hall of Fame. They are consistent, good players who know how to play. They stay focused, keep their cool, and manage their money.

Looking back on my 30 years as a professional poker player, I have few regrets. The game has been good to me. Professional poker has given me the personal freedom to be my own boss, and also the chance to mingle with players from all walks of life. I love to travel. I love to shop. I love to eat at nice restaurants, and to swim and work out. I still love poker as much as I always have, but it's not an obsession with me—it's not something I feel the need to do seven, six, five, or even four days a week. I now choose the tournaments I want to play in very carefully, and if I don't feel like playing, I don't feel bad passing them up. Sometimes, players will come up to me and ask what they can do to play better. I tell them, "Find a game you can beat. Handicap yourself when you sit down to play. Determine whether you're a favorite or an underdog at the table. Then you have to ask yourself: if you're an underdog, why are you playing? . . . and if you're a favorite, why are you quitting?" ♣

CHAPTER two

You can visit Johnny at JohnnyChan.com and AllInEnergy.com. Johnny supports the Andre Agassi Foundation (www.AgassiFoundation. org) which is dedicated to transforming U.S. public education for under served youth.

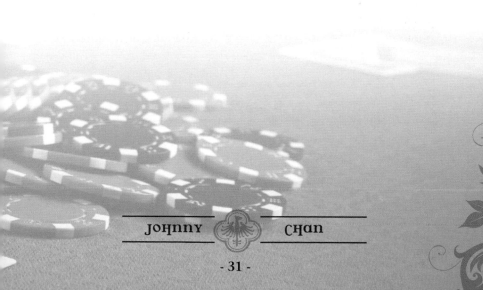

JOHNNY CHAN

CHAPTER THREE

JENNIFER HARMAN

Jennifer Harman

Jennifer Harman is one of the most successful high-stakes cash-game players in the world. For over a decade she has been a fixture in the $2,000–$4,000 "Big Game" at the Bellagio, winning millions of dollars and solidifying her reputation as one of the premier Texas Hold'em players in the world.

Although she prefers cash games to tournaments, Jennifer has managed to capture two WSOP titles—the only woman to accomplish such a feat in open events—and has amassed over $2 million in tournament earnings. Her first gold bracelet came in the 2000 WSOP, when she won the deuce-to-seven lowball event, a game she had never played until that tournament. She received five minutes of instruction from Howard Lederer just prior to the event.

She was also chosen to write the limit Texas Hold'em chapter in Doyle Brunson's Super System *2, considered by many to be the definitive book on poker. Jennifer and her husband, fellow poker player Marco Traniello, were married in 2000. They have twin sons who were born in November, 2007.*

I basically grew up playing poker, although my most memorable early experience of the game came as an observer rather than a participant. It happened when my mom, dad and their friends were on a road trip, traveling across Nevada in three separate motor homes. We stopped

off for the night in Tonopah and the adults relaxed around the kitchen table playing poker. I had a good view from a bunk bed overlooking the action. Just six years old at the time, I distinctly remember the unbelievable feeling that rushed over me as I watched the game. My imagination went crazy as I looked at the different colored chips, heard the distinctive sound they made, and stared at all the coins and dollar bills moving around the table. Even at that age I had an understanding of what money was, and seeing that much of it stacked up in the center of the

♣ ♥ ♠ ♦

table captured my attention. The whole experience was intense, and I was taking it all in. I had never played poker before, but that game— the sights, the sounds, the stacks of colored chips and money—left an everlasting impression on me.

By the time I was eight I had begun playing poker with my cousins. There were five or six of us playing regularly. My mom would deal the games to make sure we played correctly. The games usually lasted an hour or two—mostly five-card draw, with a little seven-card stud thrown in for good measure. We'd play for pennies, and I usually came out ahead. Mom didn't mind us playing for coins; in reality, we were mostly playing for fun. No one really cared about the money. By the time I was ten, our

game had expanded to include my girlfriends and their brothers. We still played primarily because we enjoyed the game, and certainly more for bragging rights than for actual money earnings.

During middle school I didn't play very often, but I did get involved in some sessions with my dad and his friends. When I was 13 I joined my father when he went to his friend's house to play in a neighborhood poker game. About an hour into the session he had lost most of his chips and asked me to sit in for him. Here I was, a teenage girl facing a table full of older men, and I was supposed to build my dad's chip stack back up. The first thing he did when I sat down was whisper in my ear, "Now, don't draw to any inside straights." I was slightly miffed at the inference. "I know," I responded, "I know how to play." And of course, I did. Before we left that night, I had brought my dad back to even.

♣ ♥♠ ♦

*I had never played poker before, but that game –
the sights, the sounds, the stacks of colored chips and money –
left an everlasting impression on me.*

♣ ♥♠ ♦

My dad had another good friend who was always bragging how good he was at poker—a real pro, he told me. When I was 15, he'd come to our house and challenge me to a little seven-card stud, a game he liked to play. We'd sit across from each other at the kitchen table and play one on one, but not for money. He just enjoyed teaching me the game. As we'd play, he'd continue to boast about his exceptional card skill, and tell stories about how he had won lots of money playing in the $1–$3 stud game at the casino.

It was just after my 16th birthday that I decided to see for myself just how good he really was. I'm not sure why I was so curious. Probably to see if he was as good as he represented. I had a fake ID, so I had no problem getting into the poker room. I sat behind him and watched him play, and I said to myself, "I can play this game." So, that's exactly what I decided to do.

JENNIFER HARMAN

The next day I brought twenty bucks with me to school. My plans were to finish classes and head to the casino for a shot at the tables. The problem was that I had an eye appointment scheduled earlier that afternoon. As part of the exam they dilated my eyes and I could barely see. Even though I knew that playing poker while partially blind was probably not the brightest thing to do, I was too excited about playing to change my plan, so I went anyway. I sat down in the $1–$3 stud game and realized almost immediately how right I was; playing poker in that condition was indeed a bad idea. My eyes were so dilated I couldn't read the cards. I had to quit. As I got up to leave, I noticed a really big table near the back wall, and wondered what was going on over there. I walked over and asked one of the players what game was being dealt. He said they were playing Texas Hold'em, a game I had never heard of before. The dealer explained the rules to me, and the bells in my head started to go off. I knew I had to give this game a shot.

♣ ♥♠♦

I was just a kid, and my mom didn't have any idea I was playing in the casino. I played for about an hour and lost some money, but not my enthusiasm for this new game.

♣ ♥♠♦

The next day I went back to the casino and took a seat in the game. It was $3–$6 limit, and I bought in for $40. I got dealt my very first Texas Hold'em hand, and I'll never forget it! I had A-K of clubs suited, in the hole. As I would later discover, my lone opponent had pocket queens. The flop came—three clubs with a queen. So I flopped the nut flush, dominating his three queens. Of course, I didn't know he had three queens, but I was pretty sure I had him beat. The turn card was another queen. He now had four queens, but I still thought I had him beat, so I bet six dollars. He could have wiped me out but instead took pity on me. He grabbed my hand and said, "Don't bet," and showed me his quad queens. The other players laughed. I was happy the guy stopped me from betting because it saved me money. I showed him my hand—the club-flush—and said, "Well, I guess this isn't any good" and threw it in the muck. I don't

remember much about the rest of my play that afternoon. I was just a kid, and my mom didn't have any idea I was playing in the casino. I played about an hour and I lost some money, but not my enthusiasm for this new game. I knew I'd be back.

After my first experience with Hold'em I returned to the casino two or three times a week to play in the $3–$6 game. By the time I was 17, I had become a regular and had come to know some of the players. Freddy Deeb was playing at the time, and we became friends. Deeb is a very good poker player, famous for wearing multi-colored shirts and, more recently, winning the $50,000 H.O.R.S.E. event at the 2007 World Series of Poker, cashing in for $2,276,832. One weekend I was playing in the $3–$6 game and Freddy, who was playing across from me, leaned over and said, "Let me put you in that $5–$10 game. I'll put up the money and you can play." I froze. The offer was very flattering, but I couldn't do it. I told him, "No, I'm sorry I can't. It's too high." I was too nervous to play in the $5–$10 game.

♣ ♥♠ ♦

Poker took my mind off my medical problems and helped get me through a very tough time, waiting for a kidney to become available as the clock was ticking.

♣ ♥♠ ♦

It was between my 17th and 18th birthdays that I became very ill, developing kidney failure. I was gravely familiar with this condition. My mom had died of it. It's a medical problem that runs in our family. I needed a kidney transplant, and had to undergo dialysis for four months while I waited for a donor to become available. The doctors told me that I had only months to live without a new kidney.

The days I wasn't on dialysis I went to the casino. Poker took my mind off my health problems, and helped get me through a very tough time. You can imagine the anxiety one feels waiting for a kidney to become available as the clock is ticking. I played between four and six days a week, gambling with money I had saved from jobs I held at Dairy Queen and Macy's. I lost more than I won during this time; I remember making

JENNIFER HARMAN

a lot of trips to the ATM machine. And when I finally had the transplant I took a leave from poker and went to college at the University of Nevada, Reno. I didn't return to the tables for three years, focusing my efforts on my studies and regaining my strength.

When I turned 21 I was hired as a cocktail waitress at Harrah's in Reno. My job was to fill in for other waitresses when they went on break, so I worked different areas of the casino, including the poker room. Because I had been playing poker for so many years, I already knew a lot of the players at the tables—they tipped really well. I was making good money cocktailing and after about a month on the job I began playing poker at the end of my shifts. I'd often play against the same people I was serving beers to a few hours earlier—and I was winning. In fact, I was making more money at the tables than I did at my job, and like I said, the cocktailing income was pretty good. Gaining confidence, I began playing in the higher limit games, $5–$10 and $10–$20. As I won more, the larger blinds became less intimidating. I had built up a decent bankroll, so I didn't have to play 'scared.' Nobody was backing me; I was playing strictly on my own money.

♣ ♥♠♦

A week after I discovered the Bicycle Club I remember
saying to myself, 'I'm home, this is where I belong.'

♣ ♥♠♦

Playing higher and winning more cash didn't eliminate the pain of losing, however. I remember dropping $200 during one session and being really upset about it. I had never lost that much before, and I was steamed. I took another $200 out of my pocket, walked into the casino and put it all down on one hand of blackjack. I was so nervous I was shaking. I won, picked up my money and left. I was even for the night. I didn't play blackjack again for a long time—and then only for fun.

I continued my dual job as a cocktail waitress/poker player in Reno before deciding to move to Los Angeles. I needed a change of venue, and some time to sort my life out. At one time I thought I wanted to be a doctor, but when I got sick, I just couldn't deal with the whole medical

scene, so I gave up that idea. The problem now was to decide just what I did want to do.

When I first arrived in Los Angeles, I had no idea California had legal card rooms. I ran into a poker acquaintance from Reno who told me about the Bicycle Club in nearby Bell Gardens. He thought I'd really do well there. I didn't take his advice at first. After a month he called me and said, "You really should come down here, the games are very, very good." So I went to the Bike and started playing $5–$10 limit Hold'em. It wasn't long before I was going there five or six days a week and playing eight to ten hours a day. The drive from my home in Marina Del Rey

♣♥♠♦

to the casino took about 30 minutes, and I usually started playing around 2:00 in the afternoon. Within six weeks I had moved up from $5–$10 to $30–$60 limits and was showing a profit. I still experienced losing sessions, of course, and they still disturbed me. One day I was buried in the $30–$60 game and I didn't want to quit at a loss, so I played for 30 hours straight. It was one of the longest sessions I have ever played. Everyone was having fun in the game except me, of course. I weighed around 98 pounds at the time, and everyone else at the table was tipping the scales at 300, so I was really squished from all sides. I could barely squeeze in to pick up my cards. Everyone around me was eating and having a good time, but I was having trouble breathing and *really* having trouble getting good cards. I ended up having to leave as a loser; I think I dropped around $2,000. I had never lost that kind of money before. It was at times like this I wondered what my father would think.

My father had been unaware for quite some time that I was playing poker to earn a living. He and I never really had an extremely close relationship, but even so the news that I was playing poker professionally only made things worse – much worse. When he finally found out, his reaction was not good at all. I was in my late 20s at the time. He told

me that I had a choice; I could quit playing poker for a living or he would disown me and strike me from his will. It was extremely emotional for me to have to face a decision like that but poker was what I knew, what I loved and it was what I was good at. I chose to continue to pursue poker despite the ultimatum and my father made good on his threat. In later years, after I had enjoyed some success, the relationship between my father and I began to heal. During the last few years of his life things were better between us. He died a few years ago.

♣ ♥♠ ♦

He told me that I had little choice; I could quit playing poker for a living or he would disown me and strike me from his will.

♣ ♥♠ ♦

I continued playing in the California card rooms for four years, keeping to a five days a week schedule on a regular basis. Even though I was supporting myself full-time on my poker earnings and playing 40 to 50 hours a week in the process, I never thought of myself as a poker professional, or as someone who was going to pursue poker as a career. I was just having fun. A week after I discovered the Bicycle Club I remember saying to myself, "I'm home, this is where I belong." But it wasn't as if I saw poker as a lifetime commitment. It was more like something I could enjoy doing while I figured out what to do with the rest of my life.

When I was 26 I met a poker player at the tables who lived back east. We fell in love and got married. He was from Maryland and wanted to live there, so we decided to move and start a new life. We had no jobs, however, so I took all the money I had won at the tables—about $60,000— and used it to purchase a dump truck for hauling coal. The business did not go well for us. After a year in the hauling business we ended up completely broke. Things were really bad for a while. I remember hitting a deer in the road and breaking the windshield, and we couldn't afford to replace the glass. It got so bad that his mother would bring us food to eat, because we didn't have enough money to buy groceries. We had little choice—poker was all we knew to get our lives back on track. We had to return to either Los Angeles or Las Vegas and rebuild our finances at the

poker tables. We decided on Las Vegas, but needed some money to get started again.

I tried to borrow money from my father, but because he wanted no part of me playing poker in Las Vegas, he turned me down. My grandmother, however, loaned me $20,000 and that's what we used to start this new chapter in our life.

Once we moved to Vegas we both got busy playing at the tables. It took a few months to pay my grandmother back and get ourselves out of debt. We bought a house and I've been in Vegas playing poker ever since. It's interesting in a way. I never made a conscious choice to become a professional poker player, and I certainly never thought I'd be playing the game for life. I always had it in the back of my mind that I'd be doing something else. The experience in Maryland and my time in Vegas changed all that. It made me realize that I had never found another job that gave me the financial rewards and enjoyment I found at the tables.

My first marriage would come to an end. After it ended, I nearly went broke again. I was making emotional decisions and they weren't turning out well. I am not bitter about it, though. I got back on my feet and started to win money at the tables. He and I are on good terms today.

Poker has not only provided me with financial opportunities but also enabled me to form strong personal friendships as well. One such person has been a tremendous friend for many years. Our first meeting, however, was a little unusual.

I had been dating Todd Brunson in the late 1990s. Todd is the son of the legendary Doyle Brunson and himself a pretty good poker player. Todd won a bracelet in the 2005 Omaha High-Low event at the World Series of Poker. Back in 1998, there was a fairly new player on the poker scene that few people knew. He and Todd were playing in a satellite tournament for the 1998 $2,000 Pot-Limit Hold'em Tournament at the Horseshoe Casino. The satellite payout was $1,500. When Todd and Daniel met heads up at the final table they decided to make a "save." The save was for $500, or a

third of the money at risk. The new guy caught fire and beat Todd to win the satellite.

He went to pay back Todd for the third that he owed him. Todd proposed that rather than accept the $500 in cash, he would take 33% of the new guy's action in the tournament instead. The new guy, who needed the cash, agreed and played in the tournament.

Todd, who barely knew the guy at all, came home that evening and told me, "Jennifer, why don't you go down to the Horseshoe and watch this Daniel *Niagra* guy. I have a cut of his action and I'd like you there to represent my interests." So, I went to the Horseshoe, played some cash games and checked in on this new guy, who I later found out was Daniel *Negreanu*, not *Niagra*.

I watched Daniel win the tournament that night. I walked up to him afterward, introduced myself and told him that I was there to look out for Todd's interests and congratulated him on his big win. We went to the bar to celebrate and ended up talking all night long. We have been the best of friends ever since – more like brother and sister, really.

♣ ♥ ♠ ♦

I still don't like to lose—who does?—but I have come to understand that learning how to lose is as important as learning how to win.

♣ ♥ ♠ ♦

Over the years we have shared a lot, about our personal lives and about poker. We frequently talked for hours and hours on end. When we go up against each other at the tables, I try as hard as I can to beat him, but if I have to lose my money, I feel a little better if I lose it to Daniel.

Daniel has gotten to know me extremely well; once he wrote an article for *Card Player Magazine* and decided to interview me. He actually wrote the whole article, including the answers to my questions without actually asking them to me. All I had to do was edit it and there wasn't much to edit.

Poker also allowed me to meet the true love of my life, but more indirectly. I met Marco downstairs in the Bellagio parking garage around

3:00 AM one night after a truly miserable day at the tables. There was a game earlier that day that I had really wanted to play. I raced to the game but it was shut out. I waited hours for them to start a second game, and when they did I lost $50,000. I was not in the best of spirits and decided to go home. When I got to the car, I met Marco. Our cars were parked next to each other, and we arrived at the same time. He started up a conversation – he said he was in Las Vegas on vacation. He asked me to go dancing. I

♣ ♥ ♠ ♦

said no. I don't even know why I told him, but I admitted I had just lost $50,000 in a poker game, and I was hardly in the mood for dancing. He was very charming and quite persistent, however, so we ended up dancing that night in a nightclub outside the casino. We dated the whole week he was on vacation. Then he went to Italy for three weeks and came back. We fell in love – a few weeks later we were married. It was fast. We got our marriage license at the local court house, called up a chapel on the strip late night, and got married at 11:00 PM in jeans and t-shirts.

In 2004, I took a year off from poker. I needed a second kidney transplant. It was even harder to deal with than the first surgery, because I was older and had gotten even sicker. For some reason the old kidney caused havoc on my blood pressure which had risen to a dangerously high level for weeks. I was so scared I was going to have a stroke; I remembered calling my family with instructions in case the worse happened. I did not want to be kept alive by a machine. As it turns out I was even sicker than I thought. The day I had my transplant I lost 35 pounds. My kidney's inability to function caused me to retain water and toxins.

After surviving two kidney transplants through organ donation, I did a charity event for the National Kidney Foundation. The organization's main purpose is to help victims of kidney disease and their families, and to raise money to fund research. Kidney failure affected both my sister

JENNIFER HARMAN

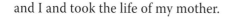

and I and took the life of my mother.

It's tragic that my mother never got to see me play professionally. She would have loved it. She played pinochle for money in the backrooms of various establishments. She was competitive. She would have been thrilled to have seen me play.

Today, when someone asks me why I play poker professionally, I tell them it's the love of the game. The longer I play, the greater the affection and satisfaction that goes along with it. To me, poker retains its appeal because it provides a never-ending challenge: you're always learning—stimulating your brain—when you're playing. The social aspect of the game is a big plus, too. I've met some wonderful people and developed some lasting friendships at the tables. Playing poker has also helped me deal with life more successfully. For example, the people reading skills I've developed at the tables help me deal more effectively with others, in whatever setting we meet.

If there's a downside to poker, it's the inevitable losing sessions that every player—no matter how skilled—will eventually encounter. I remember one personal loss in particular. I had just dropped $100,000 playing $1,000–$2,000 Hold'em in Vegas and was totally devastated. Ted Forrest, an outstanding poker professional, came up to me and asked what was wrong. I told him I had lost $100,000 and he just shrugged it off. "Hey, don't sweat it," he said, "you'll do that a million times." Well, that kind of put things in perspective.

I still don't like to lose—who does?—but I have come to understand that learning how to lose is as important as learning how to win, and in the long run the players who can manage themselves and their bankrolls in tough times will build their characters and be stronger and better for the experience. Hopefully, I won't have to build my character any further in the years to come! ♥

CHAPTER ✤ THREE

You can visit Jennifer at JenniferHarman.com and play poker with her at Full Tilt Poker (www.fulltiltpoker.net). Jennifer supports the National Kidney Foundation (www.kidney.org), a major voluntary nonprofit health organization that is dedicated to preventing kidney and urinary tract diseases, improving the health and well-being of individuals and families affected by kidney disease, and increasing the availability of all organs for transplantation. Jennifer also supports the Nevada Society for the Prevention of Cruelty to Animals (www.nevadascpa.org), a nonprofit organization that operates a no-kill animal sanctuary, promotes humane education, makes referrals for lower-cost spay/neuter and vaccination services and challenges people to be the best possible guardians for the companion animals in their care.

CHAPTER 🦅 FOUR

HOWARD LEDERER

HOWARD LEDERER

Howard Lederer is one of the most talented and respected players in the ranks of professional poker. Winner of two WSOP and WPT championships, "The Professor" is closing in on $5 million in tournament winnings. In addition to his success at the tables, Howard is an accomplished poker businessman and educator, helping players improve their game through instructional videos and personal seminars.

Howard begin his gaming career as a high school apprentice to an international grandmaster at the Chess Center of New York City, where small stakes poker was also played. He built his first bankroll by cleaning the Chess Center and delivering sandwiches to players, a humble beginning for a man who would later become one of the original minds behind the enormously successful website known as Full Tilt Poker

In recent years, Howard has used Zen-like wisdom to strengthen his performance as a formidable opponent in the biggest tournament and cash games played worldwide. And in the poker community he is a highly respected businessman, colleague and gentleman.

I guess you could say my poker career began on the living room floor. That's where my family spent a lot of time playing card games when I was growing up. My dad had a rack of old-style clay chips, and we'd battle to see who could win the most. It was during these sessions that I learned to cherish competition. It was OK – even honorable – to play hard, vanquish your opponent, and remain friends after the contest was over. I developed a love of competition from my father, who was fiercely competitive. When I was seven, he taught me chess, and in nine years he never let me win a game. At 16, I got serious about the game and finally beat him twice in a row. He never played me again. Instead, he pointed me to people in town who were better than he and could give me a higher level of competition.

♣♥♠♦

During my teen years I attended a private school. As a senior I was allowed to undertake one term of independent study. I decided to go to New York City for two months to study with an international chess master. I had just turned 18. My study plan included a lesson once a week with the master, and lots of homework studying chess literature. I played in weekend tournaments at the Chess Center of New York. When I visited the club I discovered that chess wasn't the only game being played: there was a small $.25–$1 limit poker game in the back room. I was completely into chess at the time, so at first the poker game didn't hold my interest. I remember sitting in a few times. I played mostly because I enjoyed competition, and socializing with the players. They were interesting characters with lots of great stories to tell. But I didn't understand what a great game poker is. I saw it more as a game of chance and not a test of skill.

CHAPTER · FOUR

At the end of my senior year I was accepted at Columbia University, but I decided to defer my education for a year and continue my independent study. I was going to rent a room at a hotel, get a temporary job, and become a chess professional—that was my goal. I moved to New York in mid-June with $2,000 in my pocket. When I returned to the Chess Center, however, I found myself more drawn to poker than to chess. I began playing in the backroom game on a regular basis, but within two weeks I was broke. I was disappointed, but I had a lot of pride and didn't want to return home with my tail between my legs. I had an idea. The July 4th weekend was approaching and the Chess Center was closing. Everyone was heading to the World Chess Open in Pennsylvania. I approached the owner of the Center and made him an offer: if he'd let me stay in the Club over the weekend while it was closed I'd clean the entire place, making it spotless by the time he returned. He agreed, and when he came back the Center was spotless. He was so pleased he said I could continue to live at the Center. In return, my job was to get the poker room cleaned and ready for play each night. In addition, I was to take food and drink orders from the players—which I would fill from the deli across the street. For this I received good tips. That money was used to play in chess tournaments on weekends and in buy-ins for nightly poker games. I lived at the Chess Center for almost half a year.

♣ ♥ ♠ ♦

I found myself more drawn to poker than chess. I began
playing in the backroom game on a regular basis.
Within two weeks I was broke.

♣ ♥ ♠ ♦

My life took on a routine. The poker games would start around 7:00 p.m., and by midnight I had made enough trips to the deli for coffee and sandwiches to earn the tip money I needed to buy into the game. At that time the game was $.50–$1, and it cost $15 to buy in. I'd sit down, lose the $15, and have to borrow two bucks to buy cigarettes and a sandwich, which would hold me over to the next day, when I could earn enough to pay back what I owed and get back in the game.

HOWARD LEDERER

I must have gone broke a hundred times trying to beat the table. It was so different back then. I knew Las Vegas existed, but didn't know there was a World Series of Poker or big-stakes professional poker players or a thriving poker scene in Nevada where great players showcased their skills. I didn't fully understand that there was much skill to the game at all. I was a bad player who loved to play. I was trying to get better, but I was basically just having fun.

♣ ♥♠ ♦

I didn't fully understand there was much skill to the game
at all. I was a bad player who loved to play.

♣ ♥♠ ♦

It took the better part of a year before I learned enough about playing the game to become a consistent winner at the table. I finally saved enough money to move out of the Center. I knew a guy who owned a one-bedroom apartment and I rented his living room for $150 a month. That gave me more independence and more time to play. I also moved to the Center's highest-limit table, a $2–$6 game with a $100 buy-in. Those games would start on Friday night and frequently not end until Sunday. At first, I played the entire marathon until I realized that if I left the game at a reasonable hour Friday night, got a good night's rest, and then came back on Saturday afternoon, the people who had been up all night were exhausted—and played that way. That gave me a tremendous advantage when I sat down: I was rested and refreshed, playing against opponents who hadn't slept for 30 hours or more. I learned that time management played a critical role in poker success. It is a lesson I have never forgotten.

After I had been in New York for a year I had pretty much given up chess and was focused on poker. I remember reading two books that really connected with me. One, by Amarillo Slim, was a 'tall tales' book describing the antics of colorful old-timers like Puggy Pearson, Sailor Roberts, and "Texas Dolly" Brunson. From that book I learned about the World Series of Poker and the big games in Texas. It was my first awareness of poker as a profession and I started dreaming of going to the

WSOP. With the lack of skill and money at my disposal at that time, I knew the idea of reaching such a tournament was a long shot, but Slim's book allowed me to dream about making a living playing poker. The second book that changed the way I viewed the game was David Sklansky's text on Hold'em poker. It was a thin little book, not very fancy, but it made me realize that the game involved tremendous strategy and skill. I vividly remember one of his eye-opening concepts: raising the bet on the flop with a flush draw in limit poker—if you get there you get more money, and if you don't get there you get a free card on fourth street. It made me think about the game and how to use different strategies to extract more money from my opponents.

I continued to play in bigger games as my skills increased. I joined a weekly $5–$10 game up on 57th Street. At one point my bankroll had grown to $8,000. That's when I heard from another player that '... they had started playing poker at the Mayfair Club...' which was a world-renowned bridge and backgammon club. I decided to give it a try. It had been two and a half years since my arrival in New York and I felt I was up to the challenge.

The game was $50–$100 with a buy-in of $1,000–$2,000. With my bankroll of $8,000 I was risking a huge portion my savings, and my sanity—and as it turned out, for good reason. I was broke within three weeks. It wasn't the first time I had gone broke, but I had never lost this kind of money. I didn't lose fifteen bucks, I lost thousands of dollars. Fortunately, I had friends with money, and they backed me in the next game. With renewed vigor and maximum focus I won money in that game and I've never looked back.

One thing I took away from the Mayfair Club experience was the difference between being 'broke' and being 'poker broke.' If you've established yourself as a good player and earned a reputation of being honest and trustworthy, you'll always be in the action, because there will always be someone willing to back you. If you have little skill or little credibility in your poker circle, you are truly broke—no one is going to back you.

HOWARD LEDERER

The Mayfair Club is where I learned the skills that have made me the poker player I am today. In fact, it was at the Mayfair Club where I got my true start as a real poker professional. It was where I came of age in this business. The learning environment there was quite unique. The Mayfair Club was home to world championship level bridge, backgammon, and gin players who were learning poker along with me. All of these individuals were world class at their game, and they brought intellectual rigor, intensity, logic, and discipline to the game. They each brought a unique perspective to the table, looking for the counter intuitive play that could lead to success—tactics I had never been exposed to before. And, best of all, the people I played with shared their ideas and insights, discussing and comparing notes on how best to play the game.

♣ ♥♠♦

If you have little skill or little credibility in your poker circle
you are truly broke – no one is going to back you.

♣ ♥♠♦

The Mayfair Club was a tremendous learning environment for honing one's playing skills, a virtual graduate program for poker excellence. "Class" was in session every day. The poker game would start around 4:00 p.m.—timed to coincide with the closing of the stock market, because the game was filled with Wall Street professionals. The games would last until midnight or later. Afterward, a small group of us would retire to the local bar and spend several hours over drinks discussing the night's play. There'd be a lot of banter – "Hey, what did you have that hand?" "Why did you play it the way you did? I might have played it this way," or "I would have played it that way." There was a lot of idea exchange as well. What was particularly interesting is that even though poker is a singular pursuit at the table, five or six of us turned it into a group-learning experience. All of us got better by sharing our poker insights and ideas. We developed a sense of camaraderie around this common interest. We realized that we can compete as individuals at the table, but also can share our ideas later as a group and become better players in the process. We were like a rising tide for boats: the group was rising on the tide together. Of course,

not every player at the Mayfair Club participated in these post-game analyses. There were five or six people out of thirty or so regulars who formed this core group. I don't think it's an accident that many members of that core group went on to enjoy very successful poker careers: people like Jay Heimowitz, Mickey Appleman, Dan Harrington, Erik Seidel, Jason Lester, Steve Zolotow, and Noli Francisco.

Some people credit the Mayfair Club with hosting the greatest home poker game ever played. Whether that's true is open to conjecture, but one thing is certain: without the Mayfair Club experience I would never have developed the skills necessary to become a professional poker player, at least not in the high-stakes sense. When you're playing in $1–$3 and $2–$4 games you're basically playing with casual players who are looking to have fun. The guys at the Mayfair were not that kind of people. I would strongly suggest to the reader that if you want to get really good at poker, find a group of friends who are really enthusiastic about the game, who are pursuing it seriously, and encourage post-game discussions like the ones we had. I have no doubt you'll become a better player for your efforts.

♣ ♥ ♠ ♦

But by the early nineties I felt I had finally outgrown New York in terms of poker. For the next level, I'd have to go to Vegas.

♣ ♥ ♠ ♦

I played at the Mayfair Club for almost a decade and, except for a few forays to Nevada, that was the epicenter of my poker world. But by the early nineties I felt I had finally outgrown New York in terms of poker. The biggest game in town was $150–$300, and I knew if I wanted to elevate my play to the next level I'd have to go to Vegas, where the toughest games were played by the most highly skilled competitors. I moved there in 1993 and began a whole new round of post-Mayfair poker education. It turned out that Vegas, like the Mayfair Club, was a great learning environment. Competing against guys like Chip Reese and Doyle Brunson made me a better poker player. Once again I was reminded that the only place you really learn how to play poker is at the table, playing against people who are better than you. Fortunately, in most poker games there are also opponents who are weaker than you. You can still make money by beating those people and having enough left over to pay "tuition" to your superior opponents.

♣ ♥♠ ♦

Once again I was reminded that the only place to really learn how to play poker is at the table, playing against people who are better than you.

♣ ♥♠ ♦

At this writing I have been playing poker for 25 years. Some people ask me, "During all that time, was there ever a moment when you knew you had what it took to be a successful professional?" The answer is yes, and that moment was at the final table of the WSOP in 1987. It involved a particular hand I played against the chip leader, Johnny Chan, who at that time was probably the best overall poker player in the world. I had a wired pair of threes and opened the pot on the button. He called and the flop landed J-9-2. He checked and so did I. The turn was a 4 and he bet. I felt I had the best hand, but I knew that if I contested the pot I might face a bet for all my chips on fifth street. I gave the board a long look, for about a minute, and then I timidly called. The river card was another 4, pairing the board, which was a great card for my hand. But if Johnny had a 4, he already had me beat. Thus, if my hand was good on fourth street, it was still good at the river. Johnny moved me all in, and I called instantly, winning the pot and doubling up. At the time there were five guys at the final table, but even after that hand, I still ended up finishing in fifth place. The hand didn't gain me anything monetarily. It did however, instill a sense of confidence in me—that I could play with anybody.

Of course, one hand does not make a poker career, but if there was

ever a hand that gave me the confidence to say, "hey, I've got what it takes to be one of the best players," that hand was it. It was not just making the play against Johnny Chan, it was making it at the final table in the main event, plus the willingness to look bad if I was wrong. I stuck to my guns and did what I thought was right, and didn't let the crowd or the moment cause me to lose my nerve.

Looking back on my life, I have no regrets about choosing poker as my career. It's provided me with a good living, and it has taught me valuable lessons about

♣ ♥ ♠ ♦

myself and about life. I've learned that becoming a good poker player requires you to be brutally honest and objective about yourself. You must understand your weaknesses and work to improve them. I believe you have to develop a comfortable relationship with yourself; you have to learn to like yourself if you want to win at the poker table; otherwise, you'll find subtle ways to self-destruct at the table. You also have to develop a comfortable relationship with money. That isn't easy. A lot of people out there have a dysfunctional relationship with money. I certainly didn't grow up with much wealth. You have to learn to deal with money issues if you want to play poker professionally, and those issues have nothing to do with the technical aspects of getting better at the game. But they have everything to do with managing who you are and developing yourself as a person. You also have to train yourself to stay focused on the big picture: you don't win every day at poker, and it takes a certain amount of emotional maturity to accept the ups and downs of the game.

How would I like to be remembered as a poker player? I hope people would see me as a tough opponent, a gentleman at the table, someone who loved poker and was a student of the game. I'd also like to be

HOWARD LEDERER

thought of as a poker educator, someone who brought the game to a lot of people and helped them improve their play. Of course, I'd also like to leave a legacy of victories: in the WSOP, the WPT, and the big cash games as well. And, finally, I'd like to be remembered as an honorable and trustworthy player. To anyone contemplating a poker career I would say: it is absolutely critical that you establish yourself as a person with integrity. If you achieve this, you'll feel better about yourself, you'll have friends who appreciate you, and, as a person who can be trusted, you will be in a better position to get financial backing should you need it. Always consider this: if someone runs a business and goes bankrupt, they can open up a new business under a different name and start over; but in poker, your name is all you have, so if you sully that name, you've got to deal with the consequences of that indiscretion for the rest of your life. ♣

CHAPTER FOUR

Visit Howard at HowardLederer.com and at Full Tilt Poker (www.fulltiltpoker.net). Howard and his wife, Suzie, support the Las Vegas Boys and Girls Club (www.bgclv.org), an organization dedicated to improving each child's life by implementing self-esteem, courage, and positive values.

HOWARD LEDERER

CHAPTER ✦ FIVE

PHIL HELLMUTH JR.

PHIL HELLMUTH JR.

If the World Series of Poker had baseball's equivalent of an all-star lineup, Phil Hellmuth Jr., winner of a record-setting eleven gold bracelets, would be batting clean-up. Phil was inducted into the Poker Hall of Fame in 2007. In addition to his dominating performance in the WSOP, Phil has cashed for over $10 million and holds numerous titles in poker tournaments throughout the world, including the 2005 National Heads-Up Poker Championship.

A success beyond the tables as well, Hellmuth has written a New York Times best-selling poker book, "Play Poker Like the Pros," and has been involved in developing/starring in several television shows. In recent years, he has put together numerous merchandising deals, including his own "Poker Brat" line of clothing and has had his name and/or photo reproduced on a wide variety of commercial products (in June 2008 he appeared on 12 million "Milwaukee's Best" beer cans). Phil has become "poker's face", as recognizable to card enthusiasts as Tiger Woods is to golf fans.

Although he is sometimes referred to as the "Poker Brat" for his colorful tantrums at the tables, he is a highly spiritual person deeply devoted to his wife and two sons. When Phil was asked to name his favorite celebrity, he replied: "Any celebrity who keeps family #1."

I'm a firm believer in the power of positive thinking. Johann Goethe, the renowned German man of letters, once wrote about starting a new venture, "Once you take the first step forward, all manner of great things will fall into your path and speed you along your way." Truer words have seldom been spoken, and I have seen them reflected in my own life. I was raised by parents who taught me that I had the power to shape my own future and that great things could happen to me if I devoted my energies to sustaining a sound personal philosophy and focusing on worthy goals.

When I was growing up, my mom posted a notebook card on the bathroom mirror with three profound thoughts "You are what you think," "You become what you think," and "What you think becomes reality." These inspirational notes were the first things I'd see when I brushed my teeth every morning.

I was born and raised in Madison, Wisconsin, a college town over 1,700 miles from the casinos of Nevada. My parents would never, even remotely, have dreamed I would become a professional poker player. Why would they? My mom is a sculptor. My dad is a Dean at the University of Wisconsin, a highly respected, even prestigious position that did not lend itself to an association with something so crude as gambling. As the oldest of five children, it fell upon me to set examples for my brother and three sisters. It was fully expected that I would go to college, get a degree, and pursue a career in an academic or professional field such as law or medicine. As disappointing as it would be for my parents to hear later, such choices were "not in the cards."

I was 12 when I first played poker. My friends and I played cards in the neighborhood, using the red, white, and blue plastic chips one could purchase from the local dime store. During my early teen years I spent summer vacations at my grandfather's summer home on a lake in northern Wisconsin, and I'd play poker there too, with other youngsters from the area. Once in a while an adult would join the game, but primarily it was just a bunch of kids playing cards to have fun, make a few dollars, and kill time—nothing serious.

CHAPTER five

But in these formative years, I would occasionally experience visions that seemed to me a foreshadowing of my future and my success. One of those times, when I was 15 or 16, I was playing poker with my friends. It was a Friday night and the game was pretty casual. "Take It to the Limit" by the Eagles was playing in the background, and the song made me pause and reflect. I remember thinking, even at that time, that it would be me betting to the limit.

♣ ♥♠ ♦

Her name was Rose Gladden and she was fairly well-known for her purported ability to see angels. She started reading the palms of the people who were with me but nothing particularly enlightening was being said. When she got to me, she took my hands and suddenly her face began turning blue. It was a bit scary but felt very real.

♣ ♥♠ ♦

My life began changing after I entered the University of Wisconsin. I never really embraced my studies, but I did find poker games and began to play frequently. Several semesters into college I began playing regularly in a $5 Texas Hold' Em game at the Memorial Union. (The Union had made national headlines in 1968 when a group of students took serious exception to the recruiting efforts of a company that made napalm for the Vietnam War.) The game being played there attracted a strange mix of players, from cab drivers and students to professors and doctors. Because the university frowned upon gambling on campus, we played with Austrian coins, which were sufficient to convince the authorities that we weren't playing for 'real money.' Cashing in, however, did present some challenges.

I had mixed success in the Union game until my tenth week. That week, I was the big winner, taking home $300. Up to that point I had never had much extra cash. My parents were not wealthy—particularly with five children to support—and I had to help cover my college living expenses by finding work. The job I found was in the primate laboratory on campus. Every morning from 7:00 a.m. to 11:00 a.m. I would clean out the monkey cages, an onerous job that I do not recommend for those with

delicate sensibilities.

Primates have disgusting habits, such as slinging their own feces about. Part of my job involved using a high-pressure hose to blast away the chunks of hardened monkey feces that had been thrown against the walls the night before. After I won the $300 playing poker I took my next gamble, a few days later. I looked at the walls encrusted with monkey feces and then looked at my fresh stack of poker winnings and made the easy decision. I left the job at the primate laboratory to pursue poker. I loved poker, the hours were more attractive, the money was better, and the air was definitely fresher.

♣ ♥♠♦

The psychologist asked what plans I had. I told him that I was convinced that I would do incredible things with my life. His response was not what I expected. His response startled me, but really pissed off my mother.

♣ ♥♠♦

It was around this time that I first met Tuli Haromy. He held a Ph.D in biochemistry from the University of Nevada, Las Vegas, and he was a genius. At the age of 18 he had been paid $25 an hour (a lot of money in those days) to help the university troubleshoot their computer system. When I met Tuli, he was already 32 years old, with a wide variety of life experiences under his belt, and I was a college junior living hand to mouth. Despite our differences in age and experience, we became best friends. Our common bond was a love of poker. He loved the mathematical aspects of the game, and he was a solid player in his own right. He taught me a lot about the game.

Tuli was also a great money manager and a hard-nosed, no-bullshit businessman. I learned about his frank business nature firsthand. Sometime after I left my primates job to play poker, I hit a dry spell and went broke. Tuli loaned me $100, but took my driver's license as collateral. It wasn't personal to Tuli—it was business, and it was a lesson I learned the hard way. That would be the first and last time I would be unable to support myself playing poker.

CHAPTER ⬥ FIVE

I didn't have enough money to play poker—or even to pay the rent—and I needed my driver's license back. I decided to drop out of school and get a job, so I went to work at a local farm. Farming is extremely hard, back-breaking work. I would have to drive my motorcycle to the farm at 7:00 a.m. in freezing cold weather, tend the fields for 8 or 9 hours

♣ ♥ ♠ ♦

a day, tasseling corn and tilling soil. It was a humbling experience, and it took me three months to slowly rebuild my bankroll and pay Tuli what I owed him. I did however, have enough left over to stake myself at the poker tables again.

The decisions I was making created serious issues with my family, especially with my father. My dad wasn't happy that I had dropped out of school. He was even less happy with the other decisions I was making, mostly concerning poker. During that time, he and I were at odds a great deal—all the time, really. We'd often argue loudly, and neither of us would back down. There were times my dad and I would yell so much at the dinner table that my mom would pick up her plate and just leave the room. Once, my parents took our whole family to see a psychologist, presumably to allow us all to get our feelings out on the table and to develop better relationships. The whole family went, but I knew it was really for my benefit.

We all sat around in this group, each taking turns talking to this guy about our feelings toward each other. The psychologist, at one point, looked to me and asked what plans I had in life. I told him I was convinced that I would do incredible things with my life.

His response was not what I expected. He told me that on the basis of

what he saw, there was nothing to support those kinds of aspirations, and that I was basically setting myself up for failure. His response startled me, but really pissed off my mother. She jumped up and said, "Who do you think you are? Don't tell my son that he can never be anything special!"

That was the end of that: one trip to the psychologist—done. Good for Mom.

♣ ♥♠♦

"A donkey is someone who carries money on his back all the way to Vegas and is nice enough to drop it off for us." Although I was thrilled at the opportunity to play in Las Vegas, I didn't want to make a "jackass" of myself in the process.

♣ ♥♠♦

I did return to school, mostly to appease my parents, but I did not stop playing poker. One of the players in the Student Union game, a prominent psychiatrist, had a weekly Wednesday night $100 buy-in game at his house. I started playing, and quickly realized that this new 'doctors game' involved serious money and my success in this game fueled a serious boost to my self-confidence. I think I was the only guy in the game without a string of initials like Ph.D. or M.D. after my name, and yet I was crushing this game and the players in it! Having a Ph.D., or an M.D., as much as I respect that, doesn't mean that you have a better shot at reading people well, or that you have a solid understanding of game theory. The minimum buy-in was $100. Several players would purchase $500 or $1,000 in chips. A person could lose or win several hundred dollars in a single evening's play. One glorious evening in the "doctors game" I won $2,700. It was the greatest amount of cash anyone had ever won at that game.

Encouraged by my success at the poker tables, I dropped out of college, this time for good, in my fourth year, and began playing poker full-time. In addition to those Wednesday night sessions, Tuli and I began hosting games ourselves. Soon, I had built my bankroll up to $20,000. I had also just turned 21, and was anxious to put my poker skills to the ultimate test—playing against the best in Las Vegas. I was curious to find out just

how good a poker player I really was. I could beat the home-town games, but could a home-town champion beat the Vegas professionals?

Vegas had a term for young hopefuls like me. We were called 'donkeys.' Puggy Pearson, a colorful, cigar-smoking fixture in the poker world, had coined the term and defined it this way: "A donkey is someone who

carries money on his back all the way to Vegas and is nice enough to drop it off for us." Although I was thrilled at the opportunity to play in Las Vegas, I didn't want to make a jackass of myself in the process.

My first trip to Vegas was a memorable one. On New Year's Eve in 1985 I walked into the Dunes poker room—ready to play $20–$40 stud eight or better for the first time in a casino setting—and was directed to an empty seat next to Telly Savalas! I thought to myself: "Holy cow, that's Kojak in the tuxedo on my right." It was a little intimidating, but he

♣ ♥ ♠ ♦

turned out to be a really likeable guy. A few hands into the game, he leaned over to me and whispered, "You and me, kid, we're the fish here." And he was right.

I played a long time before I allowed Telly's prediction to come true, but eventually I lost my entire bankroll, $3,000 in traveler's checks. The experience was disappointing, shocking, humiliating and enlightening— all in one. In Madison I had never quit a game. I was the kid who had no other place to be. If there was an all-night session, it was always one of the other guys who had to leave the table and go back to his family or job. I would just play on, and why not? There was nothing else but poker in my life at the time, so there was no reason to leave the game.

But in Las Vegas the game never broke up. Fresh players rotated

in, around the clock. The poker games just kept on keeping on—and so did I. I once played for 50 hours straight, more than two days without stopping—no sleep, little food, and only a few restroom breaks. It was all for naught, however. In the end I lost every dollar. Penniless, broken, and exhausted, I made the walk of shame to my room, which had now been empty for two nights. I collapsed on the bed, falling into a deep sleep before my head hit the pillow. Six or seven hours later, I was rudely awakened by a loud banging on my door. It was hotel security. I had completely forgotten that I was supposed to spend the night before with Tuli at his home in Vegas. Tuli who had been unable to wake me by phone and was worried, had enlisted the aid of hotel security to bang on the door and, if necessary, break into my room to make sure I was still alive.

♣ ♥♠♦

I played for 50 hours straight, more than two days without stopping - no sleep, little food and only a few restroom breaks. It was all for naught, however. In the end I lost every dollar. Penniless, broken and exhausted, I made the walk of shame to my room, which had now been empty for two nights.

♣ ♥♠♦

I went back to Madison, beaten but not broken. I vowed to return, and did just that—nine times in nine months. I flew back and forth from Madison to Nevada, steadily losing the $20,000 I had so carefully saved. It became a recurring nightmare, but it wasn't a dream. I'd hit Vegas, lose my money, go back to Madison, win enough to stake my next trip, head back to Vegas, and lose the money, all over again. But the process served a purpose. Even as I continued to lose, I was gaining more and more confidence in my ability to beat the Vegas poker tables. I could see that the pros were all human too, and prone to making mistakes. I was positioning myself to take advantage of that knowledge and become a consistent winner. I needed to take my game to the next level. But could I? It was a pivotal time in my life. At that moment I experienced a couple of epiphanies that would forever reinforce the decision to make poker my profession for life.

CHAPTER   FIVE

The first epiphany came to me in the form of a vision, an image from a dream that recurred now and then, even when I was awake. In the vision, I'm sitting at a poker table winning most of the hands, crushing the opposition, with towers of chips in front of me. I'm wearing a brown robe, the kind a monk would wear, with its hood over my head. At first, I didn't understand what the image represented, only that it gave me a profound sense of confidence in my abilities.

Looking back at the vision now, I believe the robe and hood represented the need for me to develop discipline and self-control at the table. Just imagine a poker player who is as devoted to his game as a monk is to his faith. Discipline and self-control are factors that define a winning player, and factors I continue to struggle with even today.

♣ ♥ ♠ ♦

It became a reoccurring nightmare, only it wasn't a dream.
I'd hit Vegas, lose my money, go back to Madison, win enough to
stake my next trip, head back to Vegas and lose it all over again.
But the process served a purpose.

♣ ♥ ♠ ♦

The second epiphany was the result of a real-life event that happened about six months after my first trip to Vegas. At the time, I was struggling with heavy losses and wondering if the life of a professional poker player was really what I wanted. I was back in Madison at the time, heading to a poker game with two friends. The game was small stakes compared to the games I'd been playing in Vegas, but necessary if I was to rebuild my bankroll. I was feeling sorry for myself, going from high-stakes Vegas poker to a potentially boring $3–$6 hometown game when one of my friends suggested we skip the session and play some pool at a local bar. It was 11:00a.m., and it was early in the spring. There was still snow on the ground, and it was cold outside. I decided to go along, if for no other reason than to avoid playing the game that I had little heart for.

The bar we ended up in was a dive. It was dark, shabby, and the few patrons inside were already feeling the impact of the cheap beer, whiskey, or whatever other mood-altering chemical they happened

to be consuming. My friends ordered beers, reached for cigarettes, and proceeded to a lone pool table in a corner of the bar, where they began to drink, smoke, laugh, tell bullshit stories, and gamble on a game of 8-ball.

♣ ♥ ♠ ♦

As I stood there, idly watching them, it suddenly occurred to me with great clarity how out of place I felt in that bar. I remember asking myself, "What am I doing here? I don't smoke and I don't drink much, yet here I am in a bar, drinking at noon. I don't enjoy going to bars. This is not for me. This is not my path." The experience hit me like a cold bucket of water sloshed in my face. I walked to the back door, opened it wide, and was blinded by the bright sunlight reflecting off the ice and melting snow. It reminded me of the cleansing white light people are said to see in near-death experiences; it flooded my senses. I suddenly had this overwhelming desire to get the hell out of there, and fast. I knew that I couldn't drive my own car, so I made my apologies to the guys and took a taxi home.

When I got home, I went directly to my desk, pulled out my journal and wrote, "OK, this is it. If you're going to play poker for a living, then you're going to be the best." I then wrote down a list of life goals. Word for word, they were:

1. Win the "Big One" at the WSOP
2. Meet and marry a wonderful woman
3. Write a New York Times bestselling book
4. Buy a beautiful house
5. Buy a nice car

CHAPTER   FIVE

6. Win tons of big poker tournaments

I was still pretty much a kid, but from that moment on, I was committed to the goals I had set for myself. No matter how many years it took, I was ready to pursue them with steadfast purpose. Never in my wildest dreams did I ever imagine that I would achieve all these goals before my 25th birthday.

It was on my tenth trip to Las Vegas that I finally broke into the "win" column. Instead of feeling elated by my victory, I felt a sense of panic. It was as if I had become used to losing, as if winning was something new and a bit scary. I remember calling my mom and asking her what she made of the panic attack. She said, "It's your winning: handling success is a tough thing to do, too." I had never thought of it that way. My mother had always shared a great deal of wisdom with me. It took a lot of winning in Vegas before I could feel comfortable walking away on the plus side of the ledger.

♣ ♥♠♦

On more than one occasion I would lose all my poker profits before I made it out of the casino. Craps was particularly harmful for me. Poker players have a term for individuals who win at cards and then squander away their profits at games they can't beat: leak.

♣ ♥♠♦

One of the problems I faced when I did start winning at poker was to avoid losing what I had won by playing the craps table or the other casino games. I'd take the money I had just won in Hold'em and plunk it down at the baccarat or craps table. And just like that, poof, it was gone. On more than one occasion I would lose all my poker profits even before I made it out of the casino. Craps was particularly destructive for me. Poker players have a term for winning at cards and then squandering away the profits at games they can't beat: 'leaking.' I was taking a serious leak at the craps table, pissing away my hard-earned dollars at a game where the casino always held the "nuts."

I had fallen victim to behaviors that are all too common among younger players who suddenly start winning a lot of money: taking too many chances, playing too recklessly, making foolish bets, and ignoring

the most basic precepts of good money management. But in one sense, my leak there was a blessing. I started to develop a gag reflex at the sight of a craps table. I had lost so much of my winnings in that fruitless pursuit that I knew I had to make a change. I finally wised up and quit playing the casino games pretty much altogether. It got to a point where even seeing a dice game made me almost physically ill. It's an emotional reaction I gratefully embrace to this day.

Craps wasn't the only problem I had to overcome in my struggle to become a successful poker player. There was also the relationship issue with my father, who is a respected professional in the academic community. You can imagine how he felt about my decision to quit college and become a gambler. He was woefully disappointed, and he let me know about it in no uncertain terms, and at every available opportunity. He thought education was everything, and wanted me to stay in school and set an example for my younger siblings.

Beyond this seemingly insurmountable disagreement, my father is a mellow, easygoing man. But he was so strongly opposed to the direction I was taking my life that it placed a tremendous strain on our relationship, impacting my whole family. I learned how to handle his disappointment as best I could. I was living in my own apartment at the time, but frequently went to my folks' for dinner. When my father started to lecture me about playing poker, I'd leave. I'd tell him, "All right, Dad, if you want to argue with me about playing poker, I'm leaving and I'm not coming back for a month." Sure enough, he'd hassle me about it and I'd walk out the door. Once, I didn't come back for a month and a half. When I did return, we'd go through the same routine again—and again. It got old. We'd have this argument every time we'd see each other. He'd start; I'd argue back for a while; then I'd leave. This went on for a couple of years, until I began winning tournaments and making serious money.

I think my dad finally eased up about my poker career in August 1988, after my great run in the Bicycle Club Casino in L.A. He began to see how focused I was. More important, he saw me developing as a professional. And perhaps most important of all, he began to see the

potential of it all. I finished second to Erik Seidel in the preliminary event at the 1988 Diamond Jim Brady tournament and cashed for $68,000. The next day I entered the main event, and won it all for $145,000, defeating the top three tournament players in the world at the final table: Johnny Chan, Jack Keller, and T. J. Cloutier. I had a nice bankroll packed away.

♣ ♥♠ ♦

I wanted to take my father on a trip too, so I asked him where he'd like to go. I suspected he'd choose a place like Australia or New Zealand, somewhere he had wanted to go in the past. His answer, however, was totally unexpected – even mind-boggling.

♣ ♥♠ ♦

As excited as I was to be able to have money to buy things for myself, one of my first priorities was to share my success with my family. I thought back to something that my mom had told me. She was a very progressive person; she had studied philosophy and was very much a new age thinker. She told me once that she saw me as a tree, strong and sturdy with deep roots. A tree with broad branches extending over the members of my family, providing them with shelter and protection. I embraced that analogy. It offered me a great sense of responsibility.

I gave my brother and one of my sister's about $10,000 a piece for law school. And I helped another sister all the way through college. I began taking my brothers and sisters on vacations. I took my mom down to the Florida Keys to swim with the dolphins and study Shamanism. I wanted to take my father on a trip, too, so I asked him where he'd like to go. I asked him to choose a place like Australia or New Zealand. His answer was totally unexpected—even mind-boggling.

"I'd like to see you play in the 1989 World Series of Poker," he said. To say that I was unprepared for that response would be an understatement. I was nearly speechless. Typically, I perform better when my family is watching me play in tournaments, but the idea of the man who had for so long questioned my career choice watching over my shoulder during a tournament just didn't compute. For a minute I went on mini-tilt as I considered what he was asking. Certainly, I wanted my father to be there,

PHIL   hELLMUTH JR.

— 71 —

but I needed him to understand a few things. I told him if he went to the WSOP, he'd be bored. He shrugged that off. I told him I'd be busy playing and wouldn't have time to spend with him. That didn't deter him either. I told him that for the entire tournament he would have to stay completely out of my line of sight while I played. He still wanted to go. Finally, I told him that I would let him think about it for a while and revisit the idea later.

Eight weeks went by and he was still thumbs up on the idea. I told him I would come back home for Christmas and chat about it again. He was still determined to go. I was prepared for this answer, and I had a reply of my own ready. I told him, "If I win it, then I'm going to buy you a new car." As it turned out, of course, I did win the main event. Having my father there when I won was incredible!

In fact, one of the most memorable moments of my life was when I won the last hand. I threw my hands up in the air and within seconds I was scanning the room for my dad. I spotted him running toward me through the crowd and the security guards trying to stop him, because there was $1 million in cash on the table. It was a bit of a circus. I waved him through the barriers, and all I could think about was reaching him and giving him a great big hug. His embrace was much more than a hearty congratulatory hug. It was as if he were saying, "Son, I was wrong about you. This poker thing is pretty damn cool and you are incredible at it!" I still think of my dad afterward, as he was being interviewed by the press, and I could tell that he really was the proud father. Priceless!

Once I won that main event, I decided to open my life up and loosen up a bit. I had been so completely focused on achieving my goals that I wasn't reaping any of the rewards. After winning the main event I thought it was time to realize some of the material goals I had set for myself such as buying a car and a home.

I bought a brand new Cadillac — one of my goals. I was still living in a student apartment on the campus of the University of Wisconsin. It was a nice place, gorgeous really, but I knew virtually no one else in the

building. A few weeks later, I had been playing all night and was coming home. I was heading to my apartment and a beautiful woman appeared around the corner—BOOM! I was instantly smitten. She had an empty clothes basket in her hands, and had obviously just left the building's laundry room. We walked toward each other and our eyes met. All I could do was say, "Hi." She smiled and returned the greeting and moved on.

♣♥♠♦

I knew she would have to come back for her clothes, and my apartment was just on the other side of the laundry room, so I quickly ran into my place, washed my face, brushed my teeth and hair, slapped on a little deodorant and casually lingered in the hall, staking out the laundry room and locking myself out of my apartment in the process. I called my sister Molly, who had a spare key, to come let me back into my apartment. Meanwhile, I waited, and waited. When Molly arrived, I told her what had happened, and added, "This would be a great story, if I ever marry this girl."

It seemed like I waited for hours. I felt a little like a nerd sitting out there just waiting, but finally she appeared. I was nervous, but I was determined to chat with her. She was friendly and we talked a while. Her name was Kathy. I finally mustered up the nerve to ask her out. It was a Tuesday and I asked to see her that evening. "I'm busy," she said.

"Well, what about tomorrow night," I replied.

"Sorry, busy then too," came the reply.

"Thursday?" I was beginning to get worried.

"No."

I was deflated. She was obviously not interested. I mean, who in

the hell is busy every night in the middle of the week? I told her it was nice seeing her, and turned to make a quick getaway and avoid further humiliation, when I heard her say, "I could go out Friday."

♣ ♥♠ ♦

Looking back on my poker career, I realized that the issues I had with dice and the relationship with my dad were giant roadblocks to my professional success – and I had hurdled them both. Yet, there was one final, personal demon I needed to conquer.

♣ ♥♠ ♦

Things started out a bit shaky. I picked Kathy up in my new Cadillac and immediately I could see a puzzled look. I knew what she was thinking, "Who is 24 years old, living in a student building and driving a car like this?" When I told her, that I was a poker player, during the date, it nearly ended our relationship before it began. I could just see her wheels spinning as she was thinking, "He's probably on drugs, out every night all night long, sleeps until noon... "

But things picked up, and Kathy became my wife—another goal achieved—and we remain happily married to this day.

Looking back on my poker career, I realized that the issues I'd had with dice and the relationship with my dad were giant roadblocks to my professional success, but I had hurdled them both. Yet there was one final, personal demon I needed to conquer—my lack of self-esteem.

Those of you who follow my career may be shocked to learn that I have esteem issues. You see me merely as the "Poker Brat," an over-emotional, outspoken player who often gets carried away when things aren't going well. But things are not always as they seem. It's true that I get very emotional and defensive when I lose. When someone plays a hand poorly against me and wins, I take it personally. In my mind, people are not seeing a bad beat—they are thinking that I've been outplayed. I feel compelled to defend my competence, a response that never turns out well.

Why the low self-esteem? Looking back, I see many contributing factors: I always had bad grades as a student, something a father who is

a dean at a university can hold over your head. (My siblings all did very well in school.) I knew my grades were a disappointment to my dad, and I felt unworthy. I didn't have many friends in high school or college. What I did have was poor grades and serious acne, and a bad case of warts! My self-esteem was low for decades. In time, my emotional outbursts led to the birth of the "Poker Brat" — the poker player who constantly has to prove himself.

The Poker Brat is a character I'm not proud to play, and I'm working to shed the image from my persona. Emotional outbursts make for good television, but they don't improve my play, and they certainly don't endear me to the fans. I conjure up the image of the brown-hooded monk, and I'm reminded that he would have the control to eliminate such outbursts. I hope to do the same. Fortunately, the Poker Brat doesn't exist away from the poker table, when I'm with family or friends.

With the exception of a few setbacks along the way, life as a poker player has been good to me. My journey from poker amateur to professional was achieved quickly (less than four years elapsed between the time I started playing poker in college and my WSOP championship victory in 1989), and largely devoid of the personal demons that seem to haunt some of today's greatest players. I'm still happily married, have a wonderful family, and enjoy good health, and I'm engaged in an occupation I'm still passionate about. I doubt that anyone can ask for more in life.

Would I recommend poker as a good career path for others? It depends on the person asking the question. If one of my sons were to ask about becoming a poker professional, I'd tell him, "It's a hard way to make an easy living, and it requires discipline and the right mental attitude." I believe, first and foremost, that top professional poker players must be tenacious: they must be driven to succeed, and must be willing to learn and work hard at their craft. They must be dedicated to poker, and passionate about it. There will be bad times, and they must persevere through them.

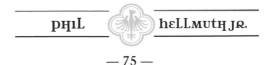

PHIL hELLMUTH JR.

Good money management is also critical to achieving poker success. In fact, it's as important as any playing strategy. When players don't learn proper money management, they'll be more likely to blow both their bankroll and their chance to stay in the action. All poker players, no matter how good they are, will experience losing streaks—I have witnessed more than a few professionals become addicted to alcohol or drugs because they couldn't manage their money or deal with their losses. Great poker players need to practice skillful money management and stay away from drugs, alcohol, and other temptations that can brutally impact their game and their well-being.

I'd also tell the would-be poker professional to behave as ethically and honestly as possible. Poker players have a long memory, and if they see that someone is involved in something improper, they will remember it forever.

Finally, I'd recommend that anyone who wants to become a professional should develop the ability to read the body language and facial expressions of their opponents at the table. In fact, this ability might be the single most important thing separating tournament champions from also-rans. If you're good at reading people, you'll win a lot of money. If you're not, you won't. It's that simple. It doesn't matter how good your math skills are, you've got to read people well to win.

Poker is, in the final analysis, a game that reveals much about ourselves and our opponents: our hopes, our fears, how we deal with adversity, and the ways in which we handle success. Someone once asked me how I wanted to be remembered as a poker player. It would be this way: as someone with sound ethics and integrity, as a man who never cheated at the game, as a fierce competitor who never gave up, who gave his all and left everything on the table. And, perhaps, as the greatest poker player who ever lived! ♠

CHAPTER five

You can learn more about Phil at PhilHellmuth.com, play poker with him at UltimateBet.net, and visit his store at www.PokerBrat.com, where you can find his full line of Poker Brat Clothing Company clothes and hats, Phil's House Publishing books, DVD's, and downloadable tutorials.

Phil's book *Play Poker Like the Pros* was a New York Times bestseller, and his cell phone game *Phil Hellmuth's Texas Hold'em* with Oasys Mobile has over 1 million U.S. users. His four-hour poker course, *White Belt to Black Belt*, is available at iAmplify.com, and his autobiography, *Poker Brat*, will be released in May 2010.

Phil is on the Advisory Board of The TASER Foundation for Fallen Officers (www.taserfoundation.org), a non-profit organization with the mission to honor the service and sacrifice of local, state/provincial, and federal law enforcement officers in the United States and Canada lost in the line of duty by providing financial support to their families.

PHIL   hELLMUTH JR.

CHAPTER ✤ SIX

CHAU GIANG

Although he has won three WSOP bracelets, Chau Giang is not as recognized as many others in high-stakes poker, like Phil Hellmuth, Phil Ivey, or Daniel Negreanu. But his reputation as a big-time cash player earns him the same level of respect as his more famous colleagues, particularly from inside the poker community.

Giang's relative anonymity among the general fan base is explained by his resistance to playing on the tournament circuit, and his general ambivalence toward celebrity status. He prefers to play online and in the "Big Game" at the Bellagio, instead of traveling from tournament to tournament. A committed family man, Giang sticks to tournaments close to home, so he can be near his wife and young family, who live with him in Las Vegas.

Away from poker, Giang is a humble and gentle soul who enjoys talking about his children. As a cash-game player, he has ridden winning streaks to astronomical levels, but he also has suffered crushing setbacks in casino play that would have broken the spirit of most. Giang is a survivor, and his harrowing journey from Vietnam to the United States is a true rags-to-riches story.

The war had been over for two years. The Communists had attained their goal, defeating the Saigon regime. As I prepared to get onto the boat headed for America in 1977, I glanced back at my homeland, Vietnam, believing it to be for the last time. It had taken me a long time to save up the seven ounces of gold for currency to pay for my passage on the boat, but I was now getting ready for the journey, under cover of darkness. (You were not allowed to leave Vietnam without permission, and permission was never granted, at least not to the United States.)

♣ ♥ ♠ ♦

Just about the time I thought I was home free I saw the North Vietnamese authorities arrive. There would be no trip to the United States that day. And for the crime of trying to leave my country illegally, I would spend my next five months in a Vietnamese prison.

♣ ♥ ♠ ♦

A friend in America had told me of the freedoms and privileges that were afforded to people there. I wanted this for myself, even if it meant making the trip alone, with almost no money. I believed if I worked hard, I could live the American dream myself. But just about the time I thought I was home free, I saw the North Vietnamese authorities arrive. There would be no trip to the United States that day. And for the crime of trying to leave my country illegally, I would spend my next five months in a Vietnamese prison. The gold was gone, too, and I knew that when I got out of jail, I'd have to start all over.

I was born in Vietnam in 1955. As a teenager I loved to gamble, and in those days, gambling was quite common. One of the games I played was No-Limit Five-Card Stud with a stripped deck. The game is similar to the Stud game played in America, but with the cards 2-7 removed from the deck.

I also played a lot of Chinese Poker. In this game, each player is dealt a 13-card hand from a standard 52-card deck. Thus, no more than four players can play at a time. The player then divides his cards into three poker hands, called "settings." Two of the settings contain five cards each,

called "back" and "middle" settings, and one, the "front" setting , contains three cards. The back setting must be the highest ranking hand, and the front must contain the lowest-ranking hand. (In this game, straights and flushes do not count in the three-card hand.) The cards are then arranged in order of setting in front of the player. After all the players have set their hands, each player announces in turn whether or not he is playing his hand.

My father worked as a builder in Saigon, and my mother sold noodles on the street. I was one of three kids, and like most kids we often played poker right on the bustling street corner.

Poker was played everywhere on the streets of Vietnam, and I played a lot of poker growing up, though the games were quite different from those played in the States. I also gambled a great deal on sports like soccer. When I was unsuccessful in that first attempt to reach the United States, I had no idea what I'd do when I arrived, but I wasn't thinking it would be poker.

♣ ♥ ♠ ♦

The jail time did nothing to dampen my spirit. I was still determined to make it to the west. When I was released from jail I went right back to work, saving everything to earn enough for the trip. Eventually, I earned another seven ounces of gold, and this time I got out of Vietnam, though my journey to the United States was far from easy and far from over.

The boat did not travel directly to America. Our first stop was to be Thailand, several days away, but our boat met with misfortune before our arrival. We were boarded and robbed five times by people whom Americans would call "pirates," although these raiders had guns instead of eye patches and swords. Not enough that we were robbed of all our money, our boat was robbed of all its food and water. I don't remember

how long that voyage took, but it seemed as if we were sailing many days with no food or water—a miserable experience.

When we reached Thailand, my fortunes would not greatly improve. I had no money and no assets of any kind. I also had no family or friends in Thailand and, more important, no sponsor in the United States. Accordingly, I was placed in a refugee camp, where I stayed for four months while the authorities sought a sponsor for me.

♣ ♥♠ ♦

Our boat met with misfortune before our arrival. We were boarded and robbed five times by people who Americans would call "Pirates," although these raiders had guns instead of eye patches and swords.

♣ ♥♠ ♦

Eventually, I did find someone willing to sponsor me in America, but I had yet another obligation to fulfill; I was transferred from a refugee camp in Thailand to another refugee camp, this time in the Philippines, for the purpose of learning the English language and something about American culture. I would be there for another four months, and after all that study, English was still very much a foreign language.

Finally, I was off to the United States. My sponsor lived in Colorado Springs. When I stepped off the plane, I had a total of ten dollars in my pocket. I met my sponsor but still did not understand a word he said. All I knew was "OK." No matter what he said to me, I responded, "OK, OK." It was 5 degrees below zero in Denver, and there was snow everywhere. Just imagine how a poor refugee from hot, muggy Vietnam would react to a Denver winter.

I had no job, no money or skills, and couldn't speak the language. I lived with my sponsor for two months and applied for welfare. My first job, in 1980, was at a Kentucky Fried Chicken establishment. I worked there for six months, at $3.35 per hour, but communicating was a struggle. Fortunately, I found a Chinese restaurant nearby. I spoke both Vietnamese and Chinese, and a job there seemed natural.

One of the waitresses at the Chinese restaurant was also a dealer at a

poker club. She asked me one day, "Do you play poker?" I said, "Of course I do," and before I knew it I was losing all my money playing 7-Card Stud, Hold'em, Omaha, and other games I couldn't spell or pronounce.

Later, I met a man in the restaurant who offered me a job in Florida. The job paid more and the weather was more to my liking, so I moved. Even though I made more money there, my experience playing poker was no better. I made more money, but I lost it all. After about a year, I decided to move back to Colorado, and I began working at a different Chinese restaurant.

♣ ♥♠ ♦

I had no job, no money or skills and couldn't speak the language. I lived with my sponsor for two months and applied for welfare initially.

♣ ♥♠ ♦

This time, my fortunes began to change. After about six months I started to win, and began winning regularly enough that I decided to take the plunge; I quit my job and began playing poker full time. It was about 1983 that I decided to become a professional poker player, and I've never looked back.

Two years later, my confidence and bankroll were strong enough for me to feel comfortable moving to Las Vegas. I played at the Golden Nugget, $20–$40 Limit Hold'em. In my first year I made about $100,000. I then started to play for higher limits, first $50–$100, then $100–$200, and then still higher.

I didn't play a poker tournament until 1990, when I entered the World Series of Poker. Prior to this I had concentrated my efforts on cash game poker. I didn't win for three years, but in 1993 I won my first bracelet, in the $1,500 No-Limit Ace-to-Five Draw Tournament. I also won a Limit Hold'em Tournament at the Four Queens Casino. The second win came just two months after the first.

As you can imagine, I was riding high. I said to myself, "Alright, tournaments are fun! I can make more money!" I began a tournament tour—Las Vegas and California. Before I knew it, I had made over a

million dollars. I couldn't believe it. I was now a millionaire. I was living the American dream.

I decided that it was time for me to test the limits of my game, and I began playing in the biggest games I could find, with the best players in the world. With a million-dollar bankroll, I believed I could take on the likes of Chip Reese, Doyle Brunson, Bobby Baldwin, and Lyle Berman. These were games that started with $4,000–$8,000 limits. Later, we'd kick it up to $8,000–$16,000 limits.

♣ ♥♠ ♦

Before I knew it, I had made over a million dollars. I couldn't believe it. I was now a millionaire. I was living the American dream.

♣ ♥♠ ♦

I turned that $1 million into $20 million in what seemed like a snap of the fingers. It had actually taken about two years, but it went by so fast it didn't seem that long. It was an incredible run. Brunson's son, Todd, even bought into 25% of my action at one time, and he earned a tidy $2.5 million from my efforts.

The stakes I was now playing for kept me away from tournaments for a while. I felt I could make more money in these high-stakes games. The money came so quickly. Even today, I don't play a lot of tournaments. Of course, I will still play the Main Event and some of the bigger tournaments in Nevada and California, but I want to stay near my family, who live with me here in Las Vegas.

To an outsider looking in, you'd think things were going really well for me. I was a refugee from Vietnam living the American dream, making huge amounts of money—over $20 million. What could be better than that?

Unfortunately, *winning* $20 million in Las Vegas and *keeping* $20 million in Las Vegas are two different things. I was good at the large cash card games, no doubt. But those games didn't happen every day, or even every week. Lower-stakes games now bored me. They didn't hold my attention, or generate the thrill of the high-stakes game. So I

sought new avenues for excitement, and unfortunately those avenues were in the casino games, where the house is heavily favored to win.

I began to play craps and baccarat. The experience was a disaster. I lost everything. Everything! I lost all $20 million. What could I do at that point? I had to go back to playing small limits again, but this time I stuck exclusively with poker. No more casino games. I started winning again, slowly at first, with small limits. Before I knew it, I was back up to $200–400 limit games,

♣ ♥ ♠ ♦

and then higher limits once I rebuilt my bankroll. It took a while, but I did it.

♣ ♥ ♠ ♦

The other lesson I learned was that I am a poker player, and I need to stick to what I know how to do—poker. I need to resist the games I cannot beat—the casino games.

♣ ♥ ♠ ♦

I learned some extremely valuable lessons. Winning that kind of money can put you on top of the world, and make you believe you are invincible, but losing it all is a strong possibility, and the humbling experience can have a greater impact than the thrill of winning. I had also lost about $3 million in the stock market over the past few years, so I decided that was not for me either.

The other lesson I learned was that I am a poker player, and I need to stick to what I know how to do—poker. I need to resist the games I cannot beat—the casino games. Still, after almost 30 years of playing poker, I get a thrill every time I play. It's in my blood. There are days when I still play around the clock, and I love playing poker more than any other activity. I love it here in Las Vegas, too. I brought my family here with me, and I get

to spend time with them and put the kids to bed almost every night.

Poker has also opened some fun opportunities for me. One of the more interesting ones was playing a small part in the movie "Lucky You," with Eric Bana, Drew Barrymore, and Robert Duvall. The way that came about was interesting: during one of our large cash games, movie director Curtis Hanson was sitting with Doyle Brunson, watching him play. As the game went on, Curtis began telling tell us about this poker movie he was making, and he hoped to have some real poker stars be part of it. I asked him right away, "Hey, I'd like to be in the movie. It would be fun." He said, "Don't worry, Chau, you are already on my list."

♣ ♥ ♠ ♦

The movie is about the world of high-stakes poker. Eric Bana plays Huck Cheever, a player who goes all out, all the time. Huck sets out to win the main event of the 2003 World Series of Poker, and finds that his biggest opponent, personally and professionally, is his father, L. C. Cheever, played by Robert Duvall. Huck's dad, it seems, was a poker legend who had abandoned Huck's mother years earlier. Huck learns that to win in the games of life and poker, he must try to play cards the way he has been living his life, and to live his life the way he has been playing cards. I played the role of one of the poker players, and had a good scene with a speaking part. I still have the check I earned from that movie.

Online poker began to interest me, too, and playing electronically keeps me challenged. I play on Full-Tilt under the handle "La Key U." (The name is a spelling-variation tribute to the movie "Lucky You.") In 2008, I made more than $5 million online alone. One of the things I love

about online poker is the variety of games available there. I'm pretty good at just about all the games, and I love mixing it up. In the big cash games at the Bellagio, you're playing high-stakes No-Limit Hold'Em, and that's it. Online, you can play 7-Card Stud, Omaha Hi-Lo, Pot-Limit, No-Limit, Tournament, Sit & Go, and more; playing the different games helps to keep the mind sharp.

♣ ♥♠♦

Unfortunately, <u>winning</u> $20 million in Las Vegas and <u>keeping</u> $20 million in Las Vegas are two very different things. I was good at the large cash card games, no doubt. But those games didn't happen every day or even every week.

♣ ♥♠♦

I have a foundational belief about poker: that it's a skill game having elements of luck and not a luck game having elements of skill. I believe this very strongly, and I believe it's one of the reasons I play well. Yes, someone with pocket deuces can beat another person holding pocket aces, but not very often. Reading your opponent is very important, and it's a big part of how I play my game. I play hands I know I can win, and I'm not afraid to throw down a big hand when I know it's a loser. I think that's really important. A lot of players out there want to hang onto their pocket aces when, after the flop, they know the odds are that their opponent has a flush or a straight. I get to know my opponents well. I will sense that one of them has A-A or A-K, because I know how he bets those hands, and knowing it makes it easy for me to give up A-Q or Q-Q in those situations.

This is not to say that there is not some luck involved. Once during the World Series of Poker my opponent called "all-in" and I called, putting all my chips at risk. I had K-K and he had A-A. I was already in big trouble, but it got worse when the flop came... 7-2-A. My opponent had three aces, and I was all but drawing dead. I got up from the table, shook my opponent's hand, said my goodbyes, and left. I had walked all the way to the parking lot before a guy caught up to me and informed me that I had just hit K-K on the turn and the river to win the pot. So, certainly,

CHAU GIANG

♣ ♥ ♠ ♦

luck is a factor, but over the course of time a skilled player will always win over a lucky player.

My son is almost 13 years old and he wants to play poker, but he's too young to make that decision. I told him there's plenty of time for that in the future. Right now I want him to go to school and enjoy his youth. If he still wants to become a professional poker player after college, I'll be happy to teach him. He's a smart boy and a good student, and I want him to have opportunities to choose whatever path he wishes.

I have now developed somewhat of a name for myself because I'm a winning poker player. My sister, who still lives in Vietnam, tells me that I'm famous back home. People here recognize me from ESPN and the WPT. The fame means little to me, however. I don't seek fame. I seek games I can win. Whether I win $20 million or lose $20 million, I'm still the same person inside, and celebrity status does not change things.

♣ ♥ ♠ ♦

I have a foundational belief about poker; that it's a skill game that has elements of luck and not a luck game with elements of skill.

♣ ♥ ♠ ♦

I see a lot of players who gain their reputation more from talking and creating good theater for TV, rather than from how well they play. This is not my style, though it does not bother me when I'm at the table.

I think of myself as a lucky man. My wife and I have a wonderful family. Fifteen years ago, while I was here in the States, a good friend of mine told

 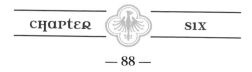

me of a lovely woman back in Vietnam. She made the introduction, and I flew to Vietnam to meet her. We hit it off very well, and I flew back to meet her again. Fortunately for me, she agreed to marry me and move to the States. We have been together ever since. We have a thirteen-year-old son and two daughters, eleven and eight. I have a sister in Vietnam still, married with two children. I try to stay in touch, and I offer my support whenever I can.

♣ ♥♠ ♦

My opponent had three aces and I was all but drawing dead. I got up from the table, shook my opponent's hand, said my goodbyes and left. I had made it all the way to the parking lot before a guy caught up to me and informed me I had just hit K-K on the turn and the river to win the pot.

♣ ♥♠ ♦

My biggest moment came in 2004, when I won my third bracelet in the $2,000 Pot-Limit Omaha Tournament. There was $187,920 in first-place money, and the event was televised. The money, however, was not my motivation for winning that particular tournament, nor was the prestige or the bracelet. Although I had shied away from celebrity status, my children had wanted to see me play on television. That was my motivation. I remember my son saying, "Dad, you're a big poker player like all these other guys. How come you aren't on television?"

So I played my heart out in that tournament, not for the money or for the bracelet or the fame, but so my children could see me winning on television. The feeling I had, knowing that my family was watching, made it seem more as if I had won $10 million.

Over the next few years I hope that poker fans in America will get to know me better. I'm still learning English, and conversations are becoming more and more comfortable. I tend to worry that people won't understand me. When the television cameras are on, I tend to be less talkative than many others, because I still do not feel comfortable speaking English in front of cameras. But when some people do recognize me and ask me for

autographs, it makes me very proud.

I'm 53 years old now, but I never see myself retiring from poker. I love it too much. If I'm still healthy when I'm 80, I think I'll still be playing poker. I don't care if I'm broke or worth more than $100 million, I'll still be playing. ♦

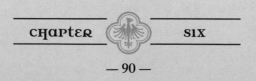

You can visit Chau at ChauGiangPoker.com and play
poker with him at Full Tilt (www.fulltiltpoker.net)

CHAPTER ✤ SEVEN

Annie Duke

Annie Duke is one of poker's enduring superstars. A mixed-game standout in the world's highest cash games, Annie is also an author, poker instructor, and frequent guest on radio and television shows worldwide.

In 2004, she won her first WSOP bracelet in the $2,000 Omaha eight-or-better event. Later that year, she added a first-place finish in the Tournament of Champions, winning the $2 million event, beating Phil Hellmuth heads up. She recently released her autobiography, *Annie Duke: How I Raised, Folded, Bluffed, Flirted, Cursed and Won Millions at the World Series of Poker.*

Annie is a mother of four and the sister of Howard Lederer. She has degrees in psychology and English from Columbia University, but decided to pass over an academic career for poker, at the suggestion of her brother, whom she later knocked out of her very first tournament appearance.

As of 2008, Annie holds the women's record for most money finishes at the WSOP. She refuses to play in women's only tournaments, claiming that poker is one of the few sports where men and women can compete on equal footing. Duke has won over $3.5 million in tournament play as of 2008.

I was 16 years old when I left home to spend a semester in New York City working with autistic kids at Belleview Hospital. I did it as part of my high school's independent studies program. During my spare time I'd go downtown to visit my brother, Howard Lederer (page 46), at the Bar Point club where he played in a daily poker game. It was small stakes—$1–$3, $3–$6—and they'd play weird things like Jacob's Ladder and Criss Cross. I'd sit there for hours and watch him play. Everybody in the club treated me like I was their little sister. And that's how I was introduced to the game of poker.

♣ ♥ ♠ ♦

My brother was one of the big losers in the game at the time. He was an 18-year-old kid, and he was paying for his poker 'education' at the table. It wasn't like today, where someone can learn the game on the internet for free. There were no academies to attend, or DVD's to study, and there were very few instructional poker books to read. Back then, you were basically on your own: you had to try to figure things out for yourself. I would watch my brother go broke and have to sleep in the back of the Bar Point and sweep up after the game to make money. But he was a fast learner. By the time I returned to New York to attend Columbia University he was beating the Bar Point tables and wanting to move up to the $50–$100 game at the Mayfair Club. To get the necessary bankroll, he formed a conglomerate and sold off pieces of himself to relatives and friends. I think I had about 2 percent of him.

During my years at Columbia I was very busy and didn't really get a

chance to watch Howard play. But I remember that every month he'd send me around $400, my dividend for backing him when he needed a bankroll. By the time I graduated, Howard had become a very successful player living in a Manhattan penthouse. Even so, I never entertained the idea of becoming a poker player myself – not then, anyway. Perhaps it was because my initial exposure to the game had made me see it as a 'backroom club' kind of activity, not very appealing. In addition, my dad was a teacher and I knew my parents would be much happier if I continued my education. Given my success as an undergraduate, staying in school seemed like a safe choice. I decided to pursue a doctorate at the University of Pennsylvania, which had one of the best programs in my field, cognitive psychology, which is the branch of psychology that studies such mental processes as how people think, perceive, remember, and learn.

♣ ♥♠ ♦

I didn't want to lose. I was worried about the money
but more worried about disappointing my brother.

♣ ♥♠ ♦

What was perhaps a defining moment in my life occurred while I was in graduate school. My brother invited me to come visit him in Las Vegas, where he was playing in the World Series of Poker. I was 21 or 22 the first time he flew me out. When I arrived, he took me to dinner at Hugo's Wine Cellar in the Four Queens Casino. I remember being impressed by how fancy the place was. Of course, back then I saw Chili's as upscale. I was living on a graduate student's income—$13,000 a year. The few times I could afford eating out, it was at a place called Salad Alley, where a meal cost $3.00. So I thought it was really extravagant for my big brother to put me up at the Golden Nugget and take me to a fine restaurant. The trip was a great break from my studies. I spent a few hours at the blackjack tables, but most of the time I watched Howard play poker.

The following year he flew me out to Vegas again. We were sitting in Binion's coffee house, discussing plans over dinner, when Howard asked, "Why not try playing some poker this trip instead of just watching it?"

annie   duke

I told him I didn't think I could play at that level, but he didn't blink. "You've watched me play a lot. Don't worry. You'll do great." He took a napkin off the table, wrote down a list of starting hands I was allowed to play, and sent me off to try $1–$3 limit Hold'em at the Fremont. The strategy kept me on a short leash. Basically, I was permitted to play A-J or better in unpaired hands and two sixes or better if I had a pair. I took the napkin and headed for the casino. I still had misgivings, but I went anyway. I had grown up in a card-playing family—I was my dad's bridge partner by the time I was 14—so the idea of playing poker wasn't that scary, but actually betting money on the game against opponents with more experience than I was unnerving. I didn't want to lose. I was worried about the money, but more worried about disappointing my brother.

♣ ♥♠♦

We were sitting in Binion's Coffee House,
discussing plans over dinner, when Howard asked, 'Why not try
playing some poker this trip instead of just watching it?'

♣ ♥♠♦

Fortunately, I never had to find out. The first time I sat in the game I got very lucky and won around $300, which was a whole lot of money to me. I played several more times after that and came out ahead for the trip. I recall talking with Howard about my play: asking him questions about what I should and shouldn't have done. I could tell he was pleased with my interest in the game. The invitation to Vegas became an annual occurrence. Howard would fly me out and I'd play in limit cash games while he was playing in tournaments. When he'd make a final table I'd go and sweat him, and when he had free time we'd go to dinner and talk about poker.

I only played poker when I was in Vegas. During the rest of the year I focused on my studies, like a normal student. But each time I came out for the WSOP it became more difficult to leave and return to the University. I was really torn about my future. On one hand, I wanted to stay in Vegas and play more poker; on the other, I felt an obligation to

continue my education and not 'let down' everyone who had supported me during graduate school.

Things came to a head during my fifth year at Penn. I had recently gotten married, and was working hard to finish up my Ph.D. At the same I was applying to various universities for my first teaching position. My first job interview was at NYU, a top-tier school and a tremendous career opportunity for a new hire. Part of the interview involved a 'doc talk,' where I had to speak about my research interests to the faculty. The night before the presentation I had such panic about it that I made myself physically ill. I began throwing up and couldn't stop. It wasn't so much because I was nervous about the interview as it was that the interview itself forced me to consider spending the rest of my life in academics. It was not what I wanted, but I wouldn't let myself acknowledge it. I kept thinking about all the people who had invested in me— my mentors

♣♥♠♦

at school, my parents, even the federal government, which had given me a fellowship. That last part may sound a bit unusual, but that fellowship would have gone to someone else who needed it, and here I was thinking about throwing it away. I was freaking out over the prospect of taking a job I didn't want!

I ended up not going in for the interview. I went back to Philadelphia, dehydrated from vomiting and ended up in the hospital. I wasn't able to keep anything down for two weeks. It was essentially the equivalent of a nervous breakdown. I became so wrought with anxiety that I couldn't

function. It was horrible. When I finally got out of the hospital, I knew I needed a break. I called all the schools where I had scheduled interviews and canceled them. I put my studies on hold for a year and moved to Montana with my husband. I needed some time for recuperation and self-reflection. I needed to sort out my life.

♣ ♥ ♠ ♦

Each day when I finished playing I'd drive home, call my brother, and ask him questions about hands that had caused me difficulty at the table.

♣ ♥ ♠ ♦

Not long after our arrival in Montana, my brother invited my husband and me down to Vegas. We went, and we had a good time. I had moved up to $4–$8 limit Hold'em and did really well. During the trip, I spoke with Howard about my situation. I told him I didn't know what I was going to do for money now that I had left grad school—and that I was a little panicked. He told me poker was legal in Montana and suggested I play there, because he believed I had talent for the game. Up to that point I had never thought about playing poker for a living, but I decided to give it a try. Howard gave me a $2,400 bankroll to get me started.

I went back to Montana and began playing at a place called the Crystal Lounge. It was in Billings, about a 40-minute drive from our home. At the time, pots were capped at $300, so the games didn't go larger than $10–$20. The Crystal Lounge dealt two regular limit Hold'em games, a $3–$6 with no check-raise and a $10–$20 where check-raising was allowed.

The first month I won $2,800 playing five days a week, five to six hours a session. Interestingly, I didn't play later in the evenings when the drunks would sit in and the game would get really good—good in the sense that people were willing to gamble with anything. That's because six people would each stick 50 bucks in before the flop, which ceased to be poker as far as I was concerned. Instead, I played in the afternoon and early evening before the drunks came in, with a bunch of old guys who

CHAPTER SEVEN

were playing on disability checks and their Social Security checks. Because they were playing with limited funds they weren't gambling as much, so I could run over them. I never had to bump up against the $300 cap on the pot, and that suited me better. It sounds kind of ruthless to take money off players betting their retirement money, but it was their choice to gamble that way.

Each day when I finished playing I'd drive home, call my brother, and ask him questions about hands that had caused me difficulty at the table. Over time, my play got better, and so did my questions. Howard described it

♣ ♥ ♠ ♦

this way: initially, he could do other things while I was asking questions—read the newspaper or watch TV, but before long he could tell I was evolving as a player, because he had to put his stuff down and pay full attention to what I was asking.

At the end of a year I had made $30,000 at the tables, a lot more than the $13,000 I was earning as a graduate student and better than the $25,000 starting salary I would have made as a new assistant professor. Even so, I wanted to complete my Ph.D. I flew to Pennsylvania, spent two months finishing my thesis research, and returned to Montana to write the dissertation. It never got done. I was too busy playing poker to do any writing.

With the approach of the 1994 World Series of Poker, Howard called and suggested I return to Vegas and play in the opening event.

annie ✦ duke

It was $1,500 limit Hold'em, and it attracted the biggest field of players of any event. I flew in and started playing satellites, winning several of

them. I used my satellite winnings to buy into the $1,500 tourney. There were approximately 600 players and I finished, I think, fourteenth. I won $13,000. One of my brother's friends, Steve Zolotow, was at a table with me for a good part of the tournament and reported back to Howard that he thought I was very good, and talented at the game.

I decided to sign up for the next limit Hold'em event, which was a $2,500 buy-in. While I waited for the tournament to begin I played in more satellites, winning about half the ones I

♣ ♥ ♠ ♦

entered. There were not a lot of women playing back then, and I think it gave me a distinct advantage at the tables. I made it to the final table in the $2,500 tournament and cashed $35,000, in spite of a really bad beat. I still remember the hand: I had 10-10 off-suit against K-9 suited, clubs. The guy raised, I re-raised, he called, and the board came three small cards, one of them a club. I bet and he called. The turn and the river were clubs, including the ace, and the guy showed the nut flush. The hand cost me two-thirds of my stack, but I still came in the money.

After my win in the $2,500 event, my brother told me I should enter the main event. I hadn't really played no-limit Hold'em—my only exposure to the game had been through the satellites—so I wasn't too sure that that was a good idea. "Well," he said, "Go play in some super satellites and see if you can win your way into the main event."

I followed Howard's advice, and won a seat in my first super satellite. Then I went out and played another super satellite and won another seat.

So I ended up with quite a bit of money going into the main event. I decided to play in one no-limit Hold'em preliminary event, to get a feeling for the game and practice for the 'Big One.' I got knocked out pretty early, and it was an expensive bit of training.

In the main event I drew a seat at Howard's starting table. So here I was in my first WSOP final event and I'm playing against my brother. About halfway into Day One I opened a pot for $800 with aces, and my brother moved in on me for $6,000. I called, he had A-K, and I ended up knocking him out of the tournament.

♣ ♥ ♠ ♦

In the main event I drew a seat at Howard's starting table. So here I was in my first WSOP final event and I'm playing against my brother.

♣ ♥ ♠ ♦

I promptly burst into tears—I was really upset. I'm not a cheater, and I would never soft-play my brother. My brother and I have always played hard against each other. Still, I thought he would be mad at me. I knew this main event was very important to him—he had been trying to win it for a decade—and here I was, knocking him out in my first appearance. Of course, he wasn't angry with me, and I pulled myself together enough to finish the first day as one of the chip leaders. I stayed in contention right to the end of the second day, when I raised on the button with two kings and the big blind moved in on me. I quickly called for most of my chips and he turned over A-3. The door card was an ace, knocking me down to around $30,000. A few hands later I limped in with a pair of sevens against Doyle Brunson's A-J and busted out. I came in like twenty-third in the main event and won $21,000. Altogether—cashing in three of four events and winning multiple satellites—I ended up returning to Montana with $70,000.

I didn't stay long. My brother called and said I should move to Las Vegas, because he believed I could be one of the greatest players ever. I recall laughing at him. Howard always had a much greater vision

for me than I had for myself. I wanted to go to Vegas, and Howard's encouragement sealed the deal. My husband and I rented a U-Haul and planned the move so I would arrive in time to play the 1995 WSOP. I didn't feel good on the trip. It turned out that I was pregnant with our first child. I hesitated to tell my brother. He had put so much time and effort into helping me develop as a player. I didn't want him to think my pregnancy was a sign that I lacked commitment to the game. It turned out that he didn't think that at all. When I broke the news, he was very happy about the whole thing. I do remember him telling me, "Annie, don't mother other people's kids at the table. You still need to be cutthroat and take their money."

♣ ♥ ♠ ♦

Howard always had a much greater vision for me than
I had for myself.

♣ ♥ ♠ ♦

I gave birth to my first child, Maude, six weeks before the start of the World Series. My husband brought her to the Horseshoe once the tournament began. I cashed in the first four events I played, nursing my baby during breaks in the action.

♣ ♥ ♠ ♦

In the years after the 1995 World Series I worked on developing my skills in cash games. I started playing $50–$100 limit Hold'em and then branched out to other games like stud and razz. (When I started playing stud, I dropped down to a $5–$10 table while I learned the game. Everyone thought I had gone broke!) Most of the big games in the poker room were mixed games, so I worked at becoming a mixed-game specialist. As I got better, I played for higher stakes and was fortunate enough to avoid the wild bankroll swings that

many new players experience.

There was one occasion, however, where my table losses almost drove me to quit the game. It was in 2002. I was expecting my fourth child, and made the mistake of playing in the last trimester of my pregnancy. I had no business being at the tables: I was tired and emotionally spent. I ended up losing a quarter of a million dollars, and it really shook me up. Here I was, the main breadwinner for our family, with three kids to care for and a fourth on the way, and I was on this massive losing bender. It made me question if I should be playing at all. I took four months off and really thought

♣ ♥ ♠ ♦

about what I wanted to do. I decided to return to the game, but at lower stakes. I stepped back to a level that was appropriate to the amount of money I had left. I went from $1,000–$2,000 to $80–$160 Omaha 8 or better. In a few months I had won all the money back again.

♣ ♥ ♠ ♦

Here I was, the main breadwinner for our family, with three kids to care for and a fourth on the way and I was on this massive losing bender.

♣ ♥ ♠ ♦

Very few poker players are willing to make a step-down the way I did, to get their game back on track. Unfortunately, they get their egos wrapped up in the level they're accustomed to play at—they don't back off—and then end up going broke because of it. Anyone who plays poker long enough is going to experience losing streaks. Avoiding tilt and financial ruin during these downturns is crucial. Playing at smaller stakes is one way to rebuild bankrolls—and self-confidence—at the same time.

annie duke

Looking back at the events of 2002, I realize that even when financial losses made me consider giving up poker, I never lost my love for the game. Being raised in a card-playing family goes a long way toward explaining my feelings. When I was able to support myself for a year on my table winnings in Montana, it was a turning point in my life. I realized I could do something I was passionate about—playing poker—for a living. That's when I decided to pursue a career at the tables. I've never regretted that decision to this day, even when the chips were down. ♥

You can visit Annie at www.AnnieDuke.com and play poker with her at UltimateBet.net. Annie supports and is a founder of Ante Up For Africa (www.anteupforafrica.org), a non-profit that raises money and awareness for Africans in need. She is also a board member of Decision Education Foundation (www.decisioneducation.org), which improves the lives of young people by empowering them with effective decision-making skills.

annie duke

CHAPTER ✦ EIGHT

scotty nguyen

Scotty Nguyen is one of the most dynamic and accomplished poker players in the game. His tournament earnings exceed $10 million, and he is considered by many to be one of the greatest poker tournament mixed-game players in the world. His colorful personality and flamboyant style have made him popular with many fans and highly controversial with others.

His achievements include the WSOP Main Event championship in 1998, where he won a million dollars. That was his second WSOP bracelet; he won the $2,000 Omaha 8 or Better event the year before. Since 1998 he's added three more: the $2,500 Pot-Limit Omaha, the $5,000 Omaha Hi-Lo Split Eight or Better, and most recently the $50,000 H.O.R.S.E World Championship. In total he has five bracelets and 36 WSOP cashes, and he currently sits in the fifth spot on the WSOP all-time money list.

Scotty also won a WPT Main Event Championship in 2006 at the Gold Strike World Poker Open, cashing in for $969,421. The win put Scotty into a league of his own as the only player ever to win the live MTT Triple Crown, winning the WSOP Main Event, the WSOP $50,000 H.O.R.S.E. event, and, a WPT Championship.

I was born in Nha Trang, Vietnam, a coastal city and capital of the Khánh Hòa province, on the south-central coastline. The city is well known for its beautiful beaches, and attracts large numbers of tourists and affluent travelers. During the time of my early youth, however, Nha Trang was deeply engaged in the ugliness of the Vietnam War. I have seen atrocities firsthand that no child should ever have to witness.

♣ ♥ ♠ ♦

As a youth I would be exposed to horrible things just walking to school and back. One schoolmate was blown to bits playing soccer in an area that turned out to be a minefield. At night, we would hear bombs going off; the next day you'd see a pile of rubble sitting where a neighbor's house used to be. I saw dead bodies piled in semi trucks like garbage. At times, there were people in the trucks who were mortally wounded but not yet dead. I saw so many atrocities as a youth that I actually grew numb to it.

I was the oldest of thirteen children in my household. Eight of the children were my brothers and sisters. The other five were cousins who had been adopted by my mother and father when my aunt was unable to bear the hardships of the time and committed suicide. My mother was a special woman. She provided a safe, comfortable home for us. We weren't rich, but she made sure we were all fed and clothed, and went to school. And as it turns out, my mother was actually the one who got me interested in poker.

I played poker on the streets in town as a seven or eight-year-old. Poker was played on every street corner. We played a form of blackjack and a form of five-card stud with one card down and four cards up. It was a no-limit game. My mother actually played cards for money. I would sit

behind her and watch. Occasionally, she'd leave the table and hand me her cards and have me play them for her. My dad, though, hated poker with a passion. If he caught me playing, he'd bring me home and beat me with a rubber hose. He'd beat me so hard that my skin would bleed and bits of my flesh would stick to the hose.

In Vietnam, the father of the household had complete and total rule over the people living in it. What the father said was gospel—no questions asked. It was common to see a man beat his wife to the point of unconsciousness right on the street in broad daylight. Bystanders could do nothing but watch. My mother received her fair share of this abusive treatment at the hands of my father. I can't tell you how many times I would cry for her. After she would be beaten, my dad would leave, and all the kids would gather around her, comfort her, and cry with her. I sometimes still cry today when I think of it.

♣ ♥ ♠ ♦

I'd go over the wall into the American soldiers' camp and buy cigarettes, gum, candy, gas, and other supplies and resell them in my town.

♣ ♥ ♠ ♦

As the oldest of the thirteen children, I was expected to accept responsibilities and provide for the family. I was needed to bring in money. My father was a mechanic, but didn't earn much, and I began hustling to earn money for the family. I'd go over the wall into the American soldiers' camp and buy cigarettes, gum, candy, gas, and other supplies and resell them in town. Typically, I'd pay them five bucks for as much as I could carry, and resell the items in town for fifteen or twenty dollars. I was so small that American soldiers thought I was cute; they loved me. They would call to me, "Hey Scotty, what does your town need? I have stuff to sell. How much do you need?" At eleven years old I became the primary breadwinner for my family. My mother didn't have to work, and my brothers and sisters could continue to go to school. This was the time when I developed my overwhelming sense of responsibility for my family—something that remains a big part of my life today.

I hustled for three years until I was 14 years old and drafted into the army. This may come as a shock to some Americans, but 14-year-olds were commonly drafted into service in Vietnam. And it was horrifying how many young teenagers were drafted and never saw home again. We saw many young men in our town sent off to fight and never return. One of my brothers was right behind me in age, and my mother was concerned that both of us would meet that same fate.

My mother was determined that this would not happen to us. She sold everything she owned so that the two of us could escape Vietnam. And when you get the opportunity to escape, you have no idea where you will land. Some people would land in Thailand, Singapore, or the Philippines. My brother and I landed in Taiwan, where we remained in a refugee camp for two years. We were two of the younger boys in camp, and the American government found us sponsors in the United States.

♣ ♥ ♠ ♦

I knew that I could have gotten into serious trouble for what I was about to do, but I decided to take the risk: I approached the woman and told her about the situation.

♣ ♥ ♠ ♦

My brother and I were separated. He ended up in Orange County, California, a year earlier than a sponsor was found for me. My sponsor lived in the Chicago area, and that is how I made it to the States, along with three other Vietnamese boys who I had never met before. I'd never seen snow before I arrived in Chicago. It was so pretty, but soon I learned how bitterly cold the winters were there.

As it turned out, my sponsor was not such a good person. He wasn't sponsoring us to relieve our oppression in Vietnam. He wanted us for cheap farm labor; we worked every day, all day, from 6:00 a.m. in the morning until evening. He fed us and gave us clothes to wear, but we weren't allowed to go to school, and he certainly didn't pay us for our backbreaking work. The farm we lived on was a mile from the next house, and even if we found someone to complain to about the way we were treated, we couldn't speak a single word of English.

CHAPTER EIGHT

One day, my sponsor held a party at his house, and enlisted us as servants for the party. At a certain point, I overheard one of his guests, a woman, speaking Vietnamese. I knew that I could have gotten into serious trouble for what I was about to do, but I decided to take the risk: I approached the woman and told her about our situation. She was horrified, and told us to remain quiet until she could speak to her husband.

♣ ♥ ♠ ♦

As it turned out, her husband was an American doctor with connections. Within a short time, we were sent to new sponsors. I was sent to Orange County where I was reunited with my brother.

The difference between my sponsors in Illinois and the ones in Orange County was like night and day. To this day, I still call my California sponsors Mom and Dad. I called their four children my brothers and sisters. They were wonderful, generous people, and they treated me just like one of their own kids. I now had my own room; I went to school and they gave me money to go to the movies and hang out with friends.

In my senior year of high school, I found out that my family in Vietnam needed help. My younger brother called me and told me how bad things were for the family. I knew it was time for me to quit school, get out on my own, and work so I could send money back home. I dropped out of school before I graduated, got a job, and lived in an apartment with six of my friends.

I found out quickly that I had no usable skills for anything but the most entry-level jobs, and barely made enough money to survive, much less send money home to my family. As a Vietnamese refugee, I found that employers could get away with paying us well below minimum wage.

scotty nguyen

I sometimes worked for a dollar or two per hour. I admit that even though times were rough, I did little to improve things for myself. I resorted to stealing things like clothes and shoes. It was petty theft; nothing big. If I got caught, they'd slap my wrist and send me out the door and tell me never to come back. I could have spent my money much more practically, but instead I spent it on beer, cigarettes, and women. Even though I had little, I was having a good time, while my family was suffering back home. And that weighed on me.

After a while, I thought to myself, "What am I doing? My mother sold everything she owned to get me safe passage out of Vietnam so I could live a better life, and *this* is what I do." I knew I had to make a change—a monumental change. I spoke to my friends about it and told them, "We have to move to where the opportunities are."

Back home in Vietnam, there were two American cities that everyone knew, two cities that represented prosperity and success. Those two were Las Vegas and Hollywood. I told my Vietnamese friends we needed to move to one of those cities and start a new life and find our own success. My choice was Vegas. There were six of us who agreed to go. Some of my friends wanted to go to Hollywood instead. In order to choose, we each anonymously wrote down the name of our preferred town and stuck it in a bowl. The vote was 4-2 and off to Las Vegas we went.

♣ ♥ ♠ ♦

By this time I had heard enough English to understand what they were saying, and I could speak a little. So I approached one of the busboys and said, 'Do you think I could get a job here?

♣ ♥ ♠ ♦

Keep in mind that I wasn't thinking of poker at this time. I had now been in America for over five years and had never even touched a card. We pooled our money; all together, we had about $1,500 to get our new life started. It wasn't much, but we were used to not having much. None of us was even 21 yet, but we were fearless. We hopped in the car and headed for Las Vegas. We made it only as far as the California/Nevada border

before we hit a serious setback, one that would send everyone but me back home.

Whiskey Pete's is before right on the state line and functions as a pit stop, a gas station or your first opportunity to gamble, depending on which choice you wanted to make. Guess which choice we made, baby? We walked into Whiskey Pete's and our mouths were open and our eyes were as big as saucers. The slot machines were lined up all silvery and sparkly, and we could hear the musical sounds they made

♣ ♥ ♠ ♦

when the people would pull the handles—and of course the sounds of the coins spilling out when there was a payoff.

All four of us started feeding the one-armed bandits. Quarter after quarter fed the beast. I'm not sure how long we were there before security asked for our IDs, but they threw us out of the building when they found we were under age. It turned out that we didn't get thrown out soon enough. I had just six dollars left in my pocket. Between the six of us, we had only forty dollars left. Las Vegas was only a half an hour away; it was night time and we could see the lights. But with only forty dollars left it might as well have been halfway around the world.

With our tails between our legs, we turned the car around and headed home. Twenty minutes into the trip home, I made them stop the car. I told them, "Look, we're already here. Vegas is our dream! Let's not go home without at least seeing it. We have enough money for gas there and back. We can even buy some food. Let's at least go see Las Vegas and then we'll go home."

We arrived in Vegas and I was instantly smitten. There were

scotty ⬥ nguyen

beautiful, half-naked women running all over the place, and they were all waving and smiling at us. We had no idea they were hookers. We were young and naïve. We just thought they were very friendly. After we drove around a bit, we saw a sign advertising a very cheap buffet, and by then we were hungry. The buffet was at the Holiday Inn Casino, which is Harrah's today.

The place was packed. The buffet was only $1.89 per person for all you could eat. While we were eating, I noticed two busboys cleaning the tables. One of them was complaining that they were short-handed. By this time I had heard enough English to understand what they were saying, and I could speak a little. So I approached one of the busboys and said, "Do you think I could get a job here?"

The busboy pointed to a small woman passing by. "That's the boss. You can go ask her." So that is exactly what I did. She listened to me for just a few seconds, and she asked me to follow her into the office. "If I hire you, when would you be able to start?" I said, "How about right now?"

She looked at me and laughed, "Sorry, no blue jeans or tennis shoes. You have to have black slacks and black shoes. I'll provide the uniform top. You start at 4:00 p.m. tomorrow." I was elated and scared at the same time. I had just gotten a job, but I had no black pants, no black shoes, and no place to stay. All I had was a lot of enthusiasm and six dollars, minus the $1.89 for the buffet.

I told my friends that I had just got a job. They told me I was crazy and pleaded with me to go back with them. But my mind was made up. I told them, "You guys go home. I'm staying." I had given the busboy a two-dollar tip for pointing out the boss. I found out later that this was as much as he would make that entire day in tips. That left me with about two dollars. It was at this job would acquire the name, "Scotty". The manager said I was to go by "Scotty" because nobody would be able to say the name "Thuan".

That restaurant had one Vietnamese busboy; he was the same age and, more important, the same *size* as me. I went to him with my story:

my friends were gone. I just got a job, but all I had was two dollars. I had no place to stay and needed black pants and black shoes. If he could help me out, I would pay him what I could when I got my check. I felt a bond with him instantly. He said to me, "Wait for me until my shift is over. You can come and stay with me until you're on your feet. I'll help you." His name was Son, and we have been good friends ever since. I'll never forget what he did for me that day.

That night we walked to his two-bedroom apartment where I found a total of nine guys living with him. Each person had a small section of space reserved to sit and sleep. The longer you lived there the nicer spot in the apartment you got. Off to the side was a filthy old couch, ragged and nearly broken in half. That was my place to sleep. The next day I started my new job in black pants and shoes borrowed from Son.

♣ ♥ ♠ ♦

I won $1,000 to $2,000 over the next few days, chasing this one guy from one table to the next, obsessively playing against him until he was busted.

♣ ♥ ♠ ♦

I was a busboy for six months. Every day, I'd walk past the poker tables when I went to work, and when I left for the bus to go home. I got promoted to bussing the tables in the area where the employees ate lunch, and got to know the poker dealers and pit bosses pretty well. They all liked me.

I approached the boss, "I'm almost 21," I said, "Do you think I could be a poker dealer for you?" He told me that his best friend owned a poker dealer school and I could learn the ropes there. Although I could not afford to go on my own, he offered to front me the money for the program; I could pay him back when I became a poker dealer. So every day, until I became a dealer myself, I went to poker dealer's school in the morning and started my shift at 4:30 p.m.

Soon after my 21st birthday, I became a Texas Hold'em dealer at the Holiday Inn Casino. I dealt cards night in and night out. As I watched

scotty nguyen

- 115 -

the players bet, bluff, fold, and raise, I started thinking to myself, "These guys are playing badly. I can beat them all. " I really wanted to *play* the game, not just deal the game. I began saving money a little at a time, intending to build a bankroll. I already lived humbly, but with my new mission I lived even more frugally. I slowly accumulated money, waiting patiently for an opportunity to play for myself.

♣ ♥ ♠ ♦

The actual start of my poker career, however, did not come about as a result of a thoughtful, carefully considered decision; my career actually began as a strong message to a very large jerk. I was dealing cards as always. I was part of a poker dealer's circuit run by Doug Dalton. For a while I dealt cards in Lake Tahoe. One day a guy appeared at my table and began to taunt me. He played at my table night after night. He'd verbally abuse me; he'd cuss me and make racial slurs about my Vietnamese background. I tried ignoring him for several days but he wouldn't stop. One night I finally reached my limit; I was furious. I stood up and tossed the entire deck of cards at him. "I tell you what: you deal," I said, "Tomorrow night I will be here as a customer and play alongside you. And when I do, I will bust your ass!" I made good on my promise. I quit my job and walked out.

The next day I was back as a player as promised, waiting for the guy to show up. He finally arrived and, also as promised, I played at his table until he was busted. I won $1,000 to $2,000 over the next few days, chasing this one guy from one table to the next, obsessively playing against him until he was busted. To this day, I don't know if I would ever have become a professional poker player if it weren't for this one asshole pissing me off. I'm sure I would have played the game at some point, but

with this guy, I was on a mission. I didn't want to just beat him; I wanted to break him. If I had never got upset with this guy I might still be a poker dealer today.

In a way, I owe this guy some thanks. I never knew his name, but indirectly he played a part in the success I have enjoyed.

I spent some more time playing cards at Lake Tahoe, and came back to Las Vegas with about $15,000 in my bankroll. When I got back, I heard about a tournament at Bob Stupak's Vegas World Casino. Up to that point, I had never played in a tournament, but I read about it with interest. There was going to be a $1,000 Pot-Limit Omaha tournament, with re-buys. There were a couple of good reasons not play it: not only had I never played in a tournament, I had never played Omaha either. I had been building confidence and winning regularly, though, so I thought I'd try. I began navigating my way through the tournament. I think I re-bought four times, but I continued to knock people out. Before I knew it, I was at the final table and heads up with poker legend, Seymour Liebowitz. "Scotty, he said," you want to chop it? I had no idea what he was talking about. He said, "We split the prize money 50/50 right now and just play one hand for the trophy."

I said, "How much do we split if we chop it?"

"$85,000," he said.

I said, "What? You mean . . . each?" I didn't believe him. He repeated it. It was true. So I said, "Let's chop it, baby!" I took that money, moved to cash games, and got on a hot streak. Everyone wanted to play me. I played games I had never heard of before and won. And I didn't stop at just card games. I was winning $30-40,000 a night in craps. I was hot and I was cocky. In eleven days I made $700,000.

I continued to win, building my bankroll to well over $1 million. At 23 years of age I had made more money than most people make in a lifetime. I was staying in rooms that cost over $3,000 a night, and this was in 1985. At times I had single bets on the table that were more money than most people made in a year.

scotty nguyen

Three months later, I had lost it all.

I lost everything shooting craps. I lost $1 million in just four hours at Caesar's Palace. It was a humbling experience.

I swallowed my pride and went back to work. I called my boss back at the Holiday Inn Casino, which had changed to Harrah's, and asked for my old job back as a poker dealer. I went from tipping people $400 to $500 per night to making $60 to $80 a night and working for one and two-dollar tips. I had learned my lesson, and I started saving my money again.

♣ ♥ ♠ ♦

For two months I dealt cards. My last paycheck was $270. I took that and left my job as a dealer for the last time. I started my comeback with small-stakes games, $1-$2, $2-$4 blinds, and worked my way back up. I went places where people didn't know me. I had it all and lost it all. I learned the value of protecting my money, and would never look back again.

There would be other times when I would struggle and have to borrow money from my poker friends. But I always paid my debts, and no one ever had to chase me down for their money. If I borrowed money from someone and couldn't pay them back right away, I'd go over to their house with what I had, give it to them, and promise that I'd be back – and I would.

My defining moment in poker came on May 11, 1998. This was both the greatest and most tragic day of my life. Nothing else has been close. That was the day I won the World Series of Poker Main Event. It was a $1,000,000 payout, and to win it I had to navigate the largest field in

history up to that time. It was huge. This is when the whole world became aware of Scotty Nguyen.

When it came down to heads up play, I faced Kevin McBride. I had J-9. McBride raised before the flop. I called. The flop came 9-9-8, and I now held a set of 9s. I checked. He bet $120,000. I just called. On the turn came another 8. I checked again. He bet $240,000. I made him wait as I considered my next move. After a bit, I just called. The river came and it was another 8. So the board had a full house, 8s over 9s, but my 9 gave me a better full house, 9s over 8s.

I checked McBride's chip stack. He had $470,000 left in chips. I stood up and yelled, "All in." McBride was carefully considering my bet, and that's when I delivered the line that's become famous in the poker world. "Kevin," I said, "If you call, it's gonna be all over, baby!"

♣ ♥ ♠ ♦

I know there are a lot of very good poker players out there who say this, but one day I'd like to be remembered as the best ever in the game.

♣ ♥ ♠ ♦

McBride called. I raised my hands. It was over. I had won. For the moment, I was the happiest man alive. Just a few hours later, however, what started out as the proudest night of my life turned into the MOST horrifying nightmare I could imagine. I had called home to share the news with my family in Vietnam. Dung, my younger brother, answered the phone and I told him all about it. He was ecstatic. He was so proud of me. He drove all over town, sharing the news and celebrating my victory with friends. On the way home, however, he was hit by a truck and killed. There is not a day that goes by that I don't wish that I'd never won that tournament. If I had not won the tournament, Dung would be alive today. For that reason, I will never wear my 1998 WSOP bracelet. Now, eleven years later, I still cry for my brother every time I think of it.

The tragedy strongly reinforced the importance of family to me, and I sometimes lie awake in bed worrying that something else will happen and I will not be able to provide for my family.

scotty nguyen

♣ ♥ ♠ ♦

I met my wife Julie about four years ago. My meeting her was a stroke of sheer luck. The Bellagio had given me four tickets to the fights; they were ringside seats, where it's common for the observers to get blood and sweat from the fighters on their clothes. I was really excited to go. On the day of the fight, however, I discovered that my tickets had disappeared. When I tried to get more tickets, all I could find were nosebleed seats that a friend of mine had. But I took them.

During the fights, I left my seat and stood in line for a drink. After a bit, I felt a tap on my shoulder. When I turned around I saw this gorgeous woman asking me, "Aren't you one of those famous poker players?" I was instantly smitten by her beauty and told her, "Yes I am, baby." She told me she was in Vegas on vacation from Oklahoma and had a friend back home who would love to have my autograph. I gladly provided it, and chatted with her briefly; her name was Julie, and she was in the real estate business. I asked her out for a drink. She said no; she didn't drink. I asked her to meet me at the Fontana Bar after the fight; again she said no. I asked for her number, and she gave me her business card.

I went back to my seat and sat down, disappointed. After a few minutes I turned around and there she was, sitting right behind me. I tried calling her during the fight, but she wouldn't answer. She was focused on the fights.

Later, when she got back to her hotel, she showed her friend my autograph, which was not very legible. When her friend asked which poker player she met, she said she didn't know my name, but knew that I was a famous Asian player. Her friend said, "Oh my goodness, you met *Johnny Chan!*"

CHAPTER EIGHT

So my future wife went back home to the Midwest thinking I was Johnny Chan. I started blowing up her phone with calls and messages, but she would never answer. Julie finally saw me playing on television and realized that I wasn't Johnny Chan, but she still wasn't taking my phone calls. It turns out that she had googled me and thought that I was still married; the truth was that I was already divorced.

I persisted with my calls to her. I left frequent messages. I told her, "I'll fill up your voice mail every day until you answer." One day, when I had been feeling

♣ ♥ ♠ ♦

particularly low, I called her again. She must have guessed by the tone of my voice that I was sad, because she finally answered. I had been calling her for 90 days. Once I convinced her that I was actually divorced, the door opened for us to build a relationship. I'm so lucky that she agreed to marry me and so proud to be building my family with her.

♣ ♥ ♠ ♦

To this day, my mother continues to work hard to provide for other people, and I'm proud to help her. Three times a year I provide personal financial support to 6,000 families in Vietnam.

♣ ♥ ♠ ♦

As long as I can move, breathe and play cards, none of my family will ever have to worry about whether they can put a roof over their head, food on the table, or clothes on their back. I realize that I've gone beyond what would normally be expected, in terms of financial support. Part of the reason I feel so confident about this is the overwhelming sense of responsibility I feel for my family, and for the people of my homeland; another part of it is my desire to give my mother a sense of peace, knowing that her children will always be comfortable and safe. My mother worked harder than any woman I have ever met, and I would do anything for her.

To this day, my mother continues to work hard to provide for other people, and I'm proud to help her. Three times a year I provide personal financial support to 6,000 families in Vietnam. The average family size in Vietnam is five, and it gives me a tremendous sense of peace and honor knowing that I can help feed up to 30,000 people several times a year. People in this country don't understand how others continue to suffer in Vietnam, and how little it takes to help. I do it on my own, with my own money. I never ask for a dime from anyone else. This is something I do for myself and something I do for my mother. She travels to Vietnam ahead of time and determines how the money can best be put to use, and makes sure that it helps as many people as possible.

As for hobbies, I love to cook. Most people are surprised to hear that. My favorite meal to prepare is a Kobe beef dish that I make for my wife. I call it my "Get out of jail free" dish. Whenever I do something that upsets her, I come home and there is a fresh cut of Kobe beef in the kitchen waiting for me. This is my cue; if I want to make up with Julie, I had better make her that dinner. When I make that dish, there is no sharing, either. She eats it all. I also love to prepare pork chops and chicken. When I make pork chops, no fork or knife is needed. I cook most of the nights I'm home. It's a small price to pay for peace in the house. I also love tending to my garden.

I have many good years of poker left in me. I'm proud to have accomplished what I have, but I know there are many other chapters yet to be written. I know there are a lot of very good poker players out there who say this, but one day I'd like to be remembered as the best ever in the game. I'm not sure I could play my best if I didn't have that goal in mind. If I were to place a bet on who history will remember as the all-time greatest, I'd place that bet on myself and go all in. And all I'd say to anyone about it is, "If you call, it's gonna be all over, baby!" ♥

CHAPTER EIGHT

You can visit Scotty at ThePrinceOfPoker.net. Scotty's favorite charity is very personal and rewarding: many times a year, he works with his mother in targeting and providing substantial financial assistance to Vietnamese villages and families in need.

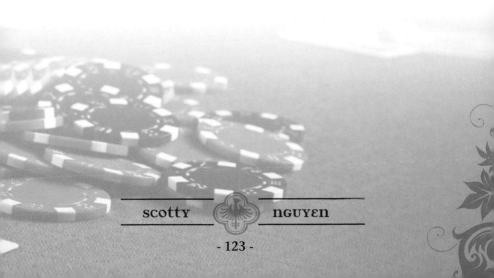

scotty nguyen

CHAPTER  NINE

Layne Flack

Layne Flack is one of the most talented, colorful, and successful young stars in contemporary poker. He is one of the few poker professionals to hold both WPT and WSOP titles, and he has amassed six WSOP bracelets and over $4 million in tournament winnings.

Layne's style is quick and assertive. He plays fearlessly, and has no problem putting his chips into the pot. He frequently shifts gears, so that his opponent never knows what kind of cards he's playing, and one of Layne's biggest strengths is his ability to outplay opponents after the flop. He also has an amazing ability to read his opponents. When Layne Flack is at the top of his game, he's one of the most feared players in poker.

Winning two major tournament titles in a row (which he has now done twice) has earned him the nickname of "Back to Back Flack." With his continuing success on the tournament circuit, it looks like poker professionals will be working hard at "catching Flack" for a long time to come.

My story is probably not one that will ever serve as a roadmap for future generations. Even though I've enjoyed a huge amount of success in life, there is no one out there who would ever hear my story and say to themselves, "I want to follow his path to success." There was a period in my life when I'd win tens of thousands of dollars one week, lose everything in a matter of hours, and sleep in my car for days on end. For me, life was incredibly fast, filled with incredible temptations, euphoric highs, and cataclysmic lows. Some days I'd party all night with famous people and beautiful women, and other days the effects of drug abuse left me not caring whether I lived or died.

♣ ♥ ♠ ♦

Some days I'd party all night with famous people and beautiful women, and other days the effects of drug abuse left me not caring whether I lived or died.

♣ ♥ ♠ ♦

This chapter has a happy ending, however. Through personal perseverance, self-determination, and help from family and very good friends, I've managed to overcome very serious self-destructive behavior and regain control of my life, growing professionally in the process. With six WSOP bracelets and one WPT title, the best news is that there are many chapters left for my life's story. That story begins in Rapid City, South Dakota in 1969. Imagine a five-year-old boy walking around all day with a deck of cards in his hands. That was me as a child. Cards were my way to connect with people. It didn't matter where I went, I would always try to find someone who was willing to play cards. I did that so much that some of my friends and family got sick of seeing me, with the deck always at the ready in my back pocket. By the time I was seven I had learned to play poker, hearts, gin, spades, canasta, pinochle, and cribbage.

I lived in Rapid City only for a year. Our family then moved to Montana, and we lived there through my sophomore year in high school before we moved back to South Dakota, where I went to college.

I started playing cards with my dad when I was four. My brothers and sisters didn't want to learn the games, which was fine with me. I could

play one on one with my dad on those very rare occasions when he was actually home. It was difficult growing up without my dad around very much. He was a young father who had four children by the age of 26, trying to grind out a living for his family, working six and sometimes seven days a week. Even when he was home, getting his attention was a difficult thing for me to do, but I always tried. In little league baseball, other kids would do something neat and look up to share the moment with their dad. My dad never got to come to my games. When I did get some time with him, card playing allowed us to share a common bond.

♣ ♥ ♠ ♦

I had a deuce in the hole and a deuce on 4th-street. My opponent had two eights showing on the board. He bet and I called. I called. I saw his eights on the board. All I could manage to do was call?

♣ ♥ ♠ ♦

I credit much of my competitive spirit to my attempts to bond with my dad. He was so busy, and gone so much, that I felt I always had to do something extraordinary to get his attention—to make him slow down long enough to take notice. So I always pushed myself to be better and better, thinking it would earn me more time with him. On one occasion when I was 12, we were in a bowling alley, my dad sitting in the bar with his friends. I'd bowl five strikes in a row, but when I'd run up and tell him about it, he'd barely turn around. So I'd run back down and bowl a sixth strike, then a seventh. I'd try anything to get his attention.

As often as I played cards in my youth, I hardly ever played for money. I would join a few kids in dice games for nickels and dimes every so often, but the family games and the poker I played during my high school years were for fun, not cash.

My first real experience playing poker for money occurred after I graduated from high school and moved to Montana. In Montana, it seems like there's a casino on every corner, with slot machines lined up like infantry, all locked and loaded. I landed a job as a busboy in an establishment that included a restaurant and bar with a casino. Within six months I became the night manager. The owners decided to put in a card room and I was all for that, wanting to get involved immediately. I told them, "I'll do a study on how we can make this work." The "study" involved me going to one of the casinos down the street and playing in a $1–$3 stud game, just to get a feel for how the business was handled.

It was the first time I had played poker for money. I was extremely nervous, and it showed. At first, my objective was not to look like a complete rookie, out of place and uncomfortable. I also had to ask probing questions that a normal player wouldn't ask, because I was trying to learn about the business and not just the game. I had to understand how the games were played if I ever wanted to open a card room.

♣ ♥ ♠ ♦

Needless to say, this first experience was humbling. I played horribly. In one game of five-card stud, I had a deuce in the hole and a deuce on fourth street (the final card dealt in stud). My opponent had two eights showing on the board. He bet and I called. I *called*. I saw his eights on the board. All I could manage to do was call? The guy said "Son, why would you call? You should have raised or folded. " I knew he was right, but just said, "I was thinking of bluffing, but I just didn't go through with it." It was obvious that I wasn't ready for the WSOP.

After a time, however, I *was* ready to play poker from the other side of the table. I hung out at the card room for a while, played and studied the

game. I realized I could make money conducting my own card games. I found a place where a guy had recently quit running a card room. It was perfect for me. I leased the room and restarted the game. I was a good dealer. You could deal any game in the world as long as the pot didn't go over $300. I got to know the clientele, and dealt the games they liked to play most. It was a good transition job between high school and college, and I kept dealing until I started my freshman year at the University of South Dakota.

I must admit that I did not take to college well. I paid my way through the first two years playing poker, making money in card games with two roommates during the fall and spring semesters. I also scored additional funds during summer breaks by dealing poker in Deadwood and playing in local tournaments, winning several. Back on the school front, my grades were horrible. This was no big surprise—I never went to class. I didn't see the need to. I thought to myself, "I'm going to school for business management and that's what I was doing before I came to school in the first place. Which is really better: business experience or a university education?" I opted for experience, and decided that playing and dealing poker beat studying and sitting in the classroom.

When I decided to quit college I had been seeing a girl who was training to become a poker dealer in Deadwood. Angie landed a job dealing at tournaments at the Peppermill Casino and we left for Nevada together. She dealt the tourney and I bought in. As to side games in that trip, the stakes were the biggest of any game I had ever played in, a $20–$40 limit. We stayed in Reno after the tournament ended. I started playing in other small tournaments and cash games around town, doing pretty well. My bankroll stayed around $2,000 to $3,000 even though I could have gone broke at any time. But even at this early stage of my poker career, I wasn't afraid to put my money in the center of the table. In one particularly good month I won $10,000.

We stayed in Reno for about a year. We had our daughter Halie in 1995, so we decided to move back to Montana, near family. I opened another

card room and began dealing poker again. I did this for about three years, until our relationship ended. Angie took our daughter and left. It was tough to give Halie up, but I knew it was the best thing for her. With little left to keep me in Montana, I decided to try my hand at tournament poker in Las Vegas. I had my eye on the $1,500 no-limit Hold'em event at the Hall of Fame Poker Classic.

♣ ♥ ♠ ♦

My parents made me think I was just a kid from a ranch in Montana that would be chewed up and spit out in the big city. 'You couldn't go there and buy a job,' was the way they phrased it.

♣ ♥ ♠ ♦

Moving to Vegas was a big deal for me. For years I had talked to my parents about moving there, and they had done everything possible to discourage me. Here I was running my own card rooms in Montana, but my parents made me think I was just a kid from a ranch in Montana who would be chewed up and spit out in the big city. "You couldn't go there and buy a job," was the way they phrased it. "What are you thinking about, kid?" Well, at least I wasn't left wondering how they felt.

I went anyway. "What the hell," I told myself, "it's a vacation." I didn't really intend to stay. I just wanted a shot at a tournament. I got together with a few buddies and made the trip. I had a couple of thousand dollars saved up; in Montana that was a *lot* of money. So there I was, and I tried to win enough money playing satellite games to buy my way into the $1,500 tournament. That didn't work. Then I tried my hand at $20–$40 cash games, hoping to grind out my entry fee. That fizzled, too. I went broke and wired home for an additional $1,000. Third time proved to be the charm: I entered another satellite, won, and went on to capture the $68,000 first prize in the no-limit Hold'em tournament. And it didn't end there. After winning that prize I jumped into a $300–$600 Omaha hi-low game, which included the likes of Sam Grizzle, Johnny Chan, and Dave "Devilfish" Ulliott, and won an additional $26,000.

I thought, "They could put bars all around Las Vegas now, because I am never leaving." After a taste of the big money and fast life of Las Vegas there

CHAPTER   NINE

was no way you could get me back on the ranch. I did make a quick trip back to Montana to pay off some old debts, help out a few friends financially, and get my belongings together. Then, five months later, I packed the car and headed to my new home. It was Vegas or bust!

Actually, it was Vegas *and* bust. Initially, I arrived back in the city and things got off to a terrific beginning. I made three final tournament tables in four months, including a $64,000 first-place finish in the $500 no-limit Hold'em Carnival of Poker and a $133,000 payout for finishing second in the WSOP $2,000 no-limit

♣♥♠♦

Hold'em event. Making money was not my problem.

My problem was dealing with the temptations in Las Vegas—the dark side of the town. I was just a kid from South Dakota. I didn't know how to handle myself around drugs, booze, women, celebrities, and lots of cash. I was completely unprepared to deal with the 'anything goes' lifestyle. I hung out in a tight circle of people who played hard—parties, alcohol, nightclubs, women, drugs. There were many times I found myself flat broke. People around me were into all manner of things that you didn't see too often in Montana. Drugs, for example. I liked and respected a number of these people, and I started doing drugs with them. It was casual at first, but soon it began to escalate, and before too long the drug use got really out of hand. Drugs were a demon that nearly ruined me.

I ended up sleeping in fleabag motels on many occasions, and those were on good nights. Other nights, I got kicked out of parking garages for sleeping in my car when I couldn't afford even the cheap motels. One time,

LAYNE FLACK

before a big tournament, I had to have my brother wire me $40 just so I could eat.

I'd win money in poker tournaments and then blow it on casino games. Some of the things that happened to me would be comical if they weren't so tragic. Like the time at the Luxor; I dropped my last $10,000 playing baccarat. To play baccarat or any game, frankly, it makes a fair amount of sense to have at least a basic understanding of the game. I didn't. I just made bets on 'banker' or 'player' and waited to see what happened. I lost my money—that's what happened.

♣ ♥ ♠ ♦

I liked and respected a number of these people, and I started doing drugs with them. It was casual at first, but soon it began to escalate, and before too long, the drug use got really out of hand.

♣ ♥ ♠ ♦

It was a long time before I was able to handle Vegas, with its myriad temptations. It's still a challenge. I don't think people realize what a danger Vegas can present to the naïve or weak-willed person. When a new player asks me what it's like in Vegas, I tell them: "When you move to Las Vegas, you will immediately be greeted by the sharks. The sharks will put a fence around the city while you sleep. You won't want to get out, but even if you did, you couldn't. You'll be a dolphin in an ocean of sharks. When you arrive in Vegas you will see all the sharks and want to be like them. You'll want to be one of the well-dressed predators who strut around the casino, flashing their gold watches and diamond rings. And I don't mean that the sharks are just the poker dealers and pit bosses; the women who come to town can be sharks, too. They are different kinds of sharks, but sharks nonetheless. They know how to get you to want what they have—and you *will* want it. You will think that risking everything is bold and adventurous, and that most people won't have the balls to do it, but you will. And then you'll end up paying a steep price for your cockiness."

Vegas has lessons to teach you, but the price of that education is steep. One Christmas vacation I lost $200,000 just betting sports. You have to find ways to protect yourself; you have to learn who you are, and then you

have to use that information to your advantage. Once you know who you are—with all your faults and bad habits, your weaknesses and strengths, then will you be in a position to protect yourself and learn how to move forward with your life.

When it came to surviving Las Vegas, I did one thing right: I never made enemies. I had grown up in Montana, where we learned the importance of building relationships and showing respect to others. When you do that, they almost always reciprocate. Maybe not right then, but it's like money in the bank. And when you build relationships, you have friends when you need them most. This philosophy made a real difference in my game, and my life.

One incident involved Johnny Chan. He was a player I looked up to, someone with the kind of career I longed to have for myself. One time, after winning a tournament, I got involved in a side game and lost almost everything I had won. It was a huge amount of money, and I was devastated. That's when Johnny came up to me and said, "Don't worry about it, kid. It's happened to me too. Get some sleep and I'll stake you in tomorrow's no-limit tournament." The fact that a player I respected so much had enough faith to back me with his own money was a tremendous ego boost. True to his word, Johnny staked me in the tournament—*and I won it!* We ended up splitting the winnings. I was happy to do it.

♣ ♥ ♠ ♦

Johnny Chan has given me a great deal of support and guidance in the world of poker. Two other people within the world of poker have helped me deal with extremely difficult circumstances outside of poker. Daniel

LAYNE fLACK

Negreanu is one of them. He came to my aid in a major way in 2004.

I was enjoying good success at the tables in 2002 and 2003, but the lifestyle I was living was rapidly catching up with me. In 2004, things really started to go downhill. I was living in a one-bedroom apartment with my girlfriend, Paulette. I couldn't pay the rent. I wasn't eating. The drug use had nearly consumed me. Paulette called my family on several occasions. She'd say, "You need to come out here. He's in serious trouble." But every time my family called, I would convince them that Paulette was just trying to get attention. It was all an act on my part. I was in horrible shape. I didn't care if I lived or died. Thankfully, Paulette had the presence of mind and the fortitude to call my brother and convince him that I needed help.

♣ ♥ ♠ ♦

And I don't just mean that the sharks are just the poker dealers and pit bosses; the women that come to town can be sharks, too. They are different kinds of sharks but sharks nonetheless.

♣ ♥ ♠ ♦

Neither Paulette nor my brother had money, but they knew that I was close with Daniel, and that I had helped Daniel out years before. My brother called him on my behalf and said, "Daniel, Layne is in really bad shape. I love my brother more than anything. He needs real help. I'm afraid we're going to lose him." Daniel stopped him on the spot "I'm here," he said. "What do you need?"

That night Paulette came to me and said, "Layne, you're in a really bad way. If I get you into rehab, will you go?" I was at the end, rock bottom. I knew this might be my last chance, so I said, "Yes, I will. But where will we come up with that kind of money?"

"Your brother has already spoken to Daniel," she said. "He's taken care of everything." I was speechless. Daniel had paid $60,000 out of his own pocket to get me into drug rehabilitation. It was an act of kindness that I'll never forget. I have no idea what might have happened to me if he had not been there.

The rehabilitation was a huge help, but it did not solve my problem.

CHAPTER NINE

It only put a bandage on it. Fortunately, I managed to stay off drugs long enough to win my fifth bracelet in 2004, but soon after that the dark side of the Vegas lifestyle sucked me back in, and I found myself right back where I had started. The slip also cost me my relationship with Paulette, who could no longer deal with my self-destructive behavior.

♣♥♠♦

'Daniel, Layne is in really bad shape. I love my brother more than anything. He needs real help. I am afraid we are going to lose him.'
Daniel stopped him on the spot, 'I'm here,' he said, 'What do you need?'

♣♥♠♦

Fortunately, another good friend, who saw what I was going through, knew I'd benefit from meeting Fast Eddie Felson. Eddie is the greatest pool hustler who ever lived, and the inspiration behind the main characters in the movies "The Color of Money" and "The Hustler." He's over seventy years old now and lives in downtown Vegas. Eddie is a very wise man. He has seen the best and the worst of what Vegas has to offer, and understands how to counsel people. He became my life coach. I believed in him and he, in turn, taught me to believe in myself.

The first time I met Eddie, I was nearly despondent. I was virtually in tears and scared to death, but Eddie reassured me. "Look kid, I understand what you are going through. You need to trust me. Everything's going to be alright." And he was right. My association with Eddie was one of the best things that has ever happened to me. He coached me on dealing with drugs, women, and all the other things that make up the darker side of Las Vegas. For a solid year, I went to work on myself, and Eddie was a big part of it. I cleansed myself of drugs, avoided the nightlife, and recharged my batteries. I turned away from the people who had led me down that destructive path. It was a very difficult thing to do, but I did it and I have never looked back.

I had won five bracelets in five years when I moved to Vegas. I was basically drug-free while winning the first three bracelets. While winning the fourth bracelet, I was in the early stages of my drug use, but had not

Layne   fLack

yet started to spiral out of control. The fifth bracelet came in 2004 after Daniel's friendship enabled me to go through rehabilitation. I had not yet slipped back. But after I won that fifth bracelet, my drug use became a serious problem again and my play suffered. It wasn't until I had kicked the drugs for good and overhauled my lifestyle that I was able to finally win that sixth bracelet, in 2008.

♣ ♥ ♠ ♦

I managed to stay off drugs long enough to win my fifth bracelet in 2004, but soon after the dark side of the Vegas lifestyle sucked me back in and I found myself right back where I had started.

♣ ♥ ♠ ♦

I believe the reason I've won so consistently at poker has been my ability to read people and to play fearlessly. My willingness to risk everything is a byproduct of the times when I had nothing. I'll put all my money in against an opponent at any time, and my opponents know it. As long as they know that, they won't be as likely to come back at me. If I go broke, well, my attitude is, "I'll see you again tomorrow." I believe I have a sixth sense when it comes to cards. I also have a good memory, and I never forget a hand or who I played it with. Boredom and discipline are my two greatest enemies. As long as I play focused, and with a lot of heart, I believe I can leave the table a winner.

Because I've encountered so many personal setbacks in my life, some people ask me if poker was a wise career choice. I always answer "Yes." Poker has taught me a lot about myself and about life in general. Even though some of the lessons have been painful, I'm a better person because of them. Poker is something I love to play. It's my passion. The game has also allowed me the opportunity to make some great friends, and to experience some great moments.

For example, without poker I would never have had the opportunity to be friends with a guy like Jerry Buss. I met the owner of the Los Angeles Lakers through Johnny Chan. One day I was playing with him in a $600–$1,200 game when he was short on cash, so I lent him $80,000.

Jerry and I played heads up for a WPT title a few years back. The room

CHAPTER ✦ NINE

was really chilly, and Jerry was kind enough to give me his Los Angeles Lakers championship jacket from the 2001–02 season. All the players had signed the jacket, and there was a special conference championship patch on it. He didn't just lend it to me, he gave it to me to keep. I think he regrets his decision, though. He told me that every time he gets on the plane with his team, they watch the rerun of our WPT event and see me beat him. He tells me I'm the kid he made famous. That's the kind of guy Jerry is—a real gentleman.

As for poker providing me with great memories, none will beat the time I brought my daughter, Halie, to watch me compete in the 2004 Ultimate Bet Poker Classic in Aruba. It was right after I had got out of rehab, and I had arranged for her to make the trip to the island. It was going to be the first time she had ever seen me play, and we were both really excited about it. Unfortunately, when we arrived at the tournament, we were told she couldn't watch me play, because the tables were inside the casino and children weren't allowed there. The only way she would be able to see me compete was if I made it to the final table, because that was the only segment of the tournament that would be played outside the casino. That meant I would have to beat 786 out of 792 players if I wanted to have Halie see me play. Every day I fought and fought. I played with all the energy and skill I could muster. I had promised Halie she could see me play, and I didn't want to disappoint her.

I ended up making it to the final table and getting the chance to play in front of my daughter. Before the final competition began, one of the reporters asked me to do an interview and I said, "Can my daughter do

Layne Flack

it with me?" The reporter said no, and I started to walk away. I guess he changed his mind, because the next thing I knew Halie and I were being interviewed together.

I remember being asked, "Layne how do you feel? We know you just came out of rehab."

I answered, "I feel as if I'm back." My daughter added, "I thought it was *back to back*, dad!"

After the interview, Halie sat right behind the tournament table and watched me play. I got to heads-up, and we got it all in for $7 million. I had two nines against two deuces. A deuce hit the turn and I ended up with a second-place finish. I'll never forget playing harder than I ever had in my life, knowing that I had to make the final table so I could keep my promise to Halie.

I'm at a good place in life now. I recently picked up my sixth bracelet in 2008, winning $577,725 in the $1,500 pot-limit Omaha tournament. I'm engaged in business ventures, and other exciting opportunities keep coming my way. Poker will always be a major part of my life, and I will always play the game full speed ahead. Fifty years from now, my tombstone will probably read, "He brought light to a room and fear to the table." ♦

CHAPTER   NINE

You can visit Layne at LayneFlack.com. Layne supports the Shriners Hospitals for Children, which is an international system of 22 hospitals dedicated to improving the lives of children by providing specialty pediatric care, innovative research and outstanding teaching programs. Learn more about them at www.ShrinersHQ.org.

LAYNE ⚜ FLACK

CHAPTER ✤ TEN

CHRIS FERGUSON

CHRIS FERGUSON

Chris "Jesus" Ferguson is one of the most respected poker players in the world today. His tournament successes are legendary - five WSOP titles (including the Main Event championship in 2000), the NBC National Heads-up Poker Championship in 2008, three WSOP Circuit Championship Titles and over $7.5 million dollars in winnings.

Using a mathematical and analytical approach, Chris refined his game playing live opponents on the internet years before the onset of the online poker revolution.

His trademarked long hair, beard and cowboy hat make him one of the most recognizable faces in the game. One of poker's true gentlemen, Ferguson's pleasant disposition and quiet demeanor conceals a killer instinct that separates his opponents from their chips with methodical efficiency. When not playing tournaments, Chris can often be found online at Full Tilt Poker, a site whose software he helped to develop.

Most fans who follow poker closely know him simply as 'Jesus.' This has been Chris Ferguson's nickname for most of his adult life, "When you look at me it's not hard to figure out why," Chris said, "I don't think any one person gave me that nickname - it just happened." As he would later find, that nickname is fairly common. Clean-cut men in business suits often stop him on the street and say, 'Hey Chris, I used to have long hair and a beard and people called me Jesus, too.'

♣ ♥ ♠ ♦

Chris played games his entire life. Growing up in Pacific Palisades his childhood was a happy one. His school and social lives were pleasant and free of the emotional scars that seem to have hardened many people in the game today. His family was pretty close and spent a lot of time playing games together. Poker was just one of the many games his parents taught him when he was little. Today, Chris doesn't recall exactly when he started playing poker, but he will tell you it was for money, "I was in the fourth grade playing with friends from school. We'd find time between classes and sneak away to have our poker games, mostly five-card draw with a lot of wild cards," Chris recalled. "I remember losing $.35 in one pot and feeling really bad about it." Triple queens lost to a flush and his lunch money was history.

By the time Chris got to high school he was playing with a group of schoolmates on a regular basis. Each weekend the game was played at a different friend's house. Stakes were increased to a $.50 limit and

CHAPTER   ten

a variety of different games were played. Basically, if you could invent a game, Chris and his friends would play it. "It was dealer's choice and we'd go around the table playing these crazy games," Chris reflected, "The sessions lasted until 2:00 or 3:00 AM and twenty bucks was a big win or loss at the time. All during my high school years I played poker for the fun of it." Winning money was nice, but it was the love of the game, and the challenge it presented that held his interest. From the very beginning Chris Ferguson was looking for an edge, and that edge usually involved a clear understanding of the odds and mathematical probabilities of the game.

Chris continued to play while he was in college. Part of the time he played poker on the internet on an IRC channel, an early version of an online poker room where no money was involved – just bragging rights. He also took the occasional trip to Las Vegas where he'd play in low-limit ($1-$4) stud games. "I found that if I played like a rock—waiting to play only premium hands—I could make about $4 an hour," Ferguson said, "I played for the challenge—to see if I could make a living at poker—and if you believe $4 per hour is a living, then I guess I was successful."

♣ ♥ ♠ ♦

From the very beginning I was looking for an edge, and that edge usually involved a clear understanding of the odds and mathematical probabilities of the game.

♣ ♥ ♠ ♦

It was around the beginning of 1994 that Chris' attitude changed toward poker. He decided to take it more seriously and began an earnest effort to master the game. It was between 1994 and 2000 that Chris came into his own as a poker player. He focused on developing his poker skills from a mathematical standpoint using game theory and computer modeling to reveal tactics for playing poker more successfully. "I would run computer simulations for thousands of poker hands and betting sequences to determine optimal strategies for table play," Chris said, and he could do it, too. He holds a Ph.D

CHRIS ♦ FERGUSON

in computer science so using computers to help understand the best mathematical way to play was a very natural way for him to master the game.

♣ ♥ ♠ ♦

There are a lot of people out there that will tell you they enjoy playing poker but there aren't many who will tell you they enjoy dissecting and analyzing poker the way I do.

♣ ♥ ♠ ♦

Many people will tell you they enjoy playing poker but there aren't many who will tell you they enjoy dissecting and analyzing poker the way Chris Ferguson does. Many poker players use a mentor or teacher to bring them along. That wasn't the case with Chris, a self-taught player. In his case, he was his own mentor. He'd analyze thousands of hands and develop his own poker strategies. Still, Chris believes most players would benefit from a friend that also really enjoys playing. "I'd recommend every player get themselves a poker buddy, a person that shares their passion for the game," Chris said, "I never had one myself, but I wish I did. Think about what you can learn by just sitting down with a buddy and discussing each hand, how it developed, what happened and what might have been."

At the same time Ferguson was developing his mathematical approach to poker he was putting it to the test by playing in tournaments in Las Vegas and throughout California. "In 1994 and 1995 I had not played in many big games, but I had built a great deal of mathematical models. Mathematical analysis showed me more than odds; it showed me how I should play in certain situations," Chris said, "a lot of players had an idea about their odds to win when they were dealt a certain set of cards, but not many players were taking that analysis to the next level."

Chris noticed that many of the top poker pros in the world weren't playing the game the way that they should. "I had developed computer models and knew exactly how to play in certain situations." He realized that even the best players in the world were making

critical mistakes in these situations. Even the big money-makers had a lot of room for improvement, it seemed. When Chris discussed his ideas with some of the top players they failed to understand how powerful those ideas were and stuck to their old ways. "It was amazing to see some people disagree with me," Chris said, "even when I could mathematically prove I was right. This showed me that even the really good players did not understand certain situations as well as I did even though I was a beginner at the time."

♣ ♥ ♠ ♦

Unless I could afford to play in the higher stakes cash games, and I couldn't, I wasn't going to find highly-skilled players to compete against.

♣ ♥ ♠ ♦

When asked why he chose to play in tournaments rather than cash games to perfect his poker skills, the answer might surprise you; "Back in the 1990s my main goal was to learn to play poker at the very highest level, and I discovered that—with my limited bankroll—the best way to accomplish that goal was to compete in tournaments rather than cash games," Chris said, "That's because, unless I could afford to play in the higher-stakes cash games, and I couldn't, I wasn't going to find highly-skilled players to compete against."

Chris found that the people playing the lower-stakes games weren't out to win big money, they were there to have a good time. He realized some of these people weren't playing good poker: they were calling too many hands, seeing too many flops, going for too many miracle draws. He knew he wasn't going to improve his skills playing in these games. Tournaments, on the other hand, were a different matter entirely. What Chris discovered about tournaments—even the lower-limit ones— was that the players were all business. "Tournament players weren't there to throw their money away gambling—they were actually trying to win," Chris said, "And they took it hard when they lost. Those were the people I wanted to play against."

Chris decided to put serious effort into learning the game in

the mid-90s. He realized that the best was to make substantial improvements to his game was to face professionals who were already playing at the highest level. Those players were not playing in low-stakes cash games. "The big time players were playing in high-stakes cash games and in tournaments," Chris observed. "At this time, I couldn't afford to play the high-stakes games, but I could afford the lower buy-in tournaments. In those days, you could find a lot of really great players in tournaments with relatively low buy-ins."

♣ ♥ ♠ ♦

I wanted to find the toughest game with the best players, so I could learn the most. This might not be the most cost-effective way to get a poker education and I'm not sure I'd recommend it to others but it worked for me.

♣ ♥ ♠ ♦

So Chris made a choice to go up against the best players he could find in tournament play. "In those days, they didn't have very many large buy-in tournaments. There may have been two $10,000 tournaments and a few $5,000 tournaments a year, but nothing like today. In today's poker environment, you'll find a lot of players that won't play in smaller tournaments, but back in the mid-90s there wasn't the large number of tournaments like there is today. Consequently, you'd find great players playing in a lot of smaller tournaments. That's where I wanted to play."

By doing so Chris was able to take his game to a new level by playing against established pros like T.J. Cloutier, Men the Master and Phil Hellmuth. "I know that many poker pundits say a poker player's dream is finding a weak game, one where opponents are literally giving you their money." Chris said, "But that isn't the way I felt at all and that's not the kind of game I wanted to play back when I was learning poker." Just like everything else, Chris' approach was logical; he found a way to get the best education from the best players in the game while investing the least amount of money.

The year 2000 was when Chris' poker career took off. Up to that

point he'd spent half his life at UCLA; five years as an undergraduate and 13 as a graduate student. In 1999 Chris received his Ph.D in Computer Science. "At the time I was planning to pursue a career in the stock market," Chris reflected, "I intended to use my computer analyst skills on the financial community." And in fact, he did just that for a while, becoming a day trader. Ironically, the job ended up jumped-starting Chris' poker career. The money he earned as a day trader was used to pay entry fees for his early tournaments. It worked out well; a year later Chris won the Main Event at the WSOP.

♣ ♥ ♠ ♦

It wasn't all that long ago that even the best online players were lightly regarded in the poker community. In fact, there was a time that when a player was referred to as 'an online player' it was code for 'this guy sucks.'

♣ ♥ ♠ ♦

A lot of people in Chris' life - friends, teachers and parents - were shocked that he spent years earning a Computer Science degree and then chose to play poker full time. "To be perfectly honest, I was a little surprised myself and slow to admit it at first," Chris said. Even with the WSOP victory Chris was not prepared to call himself a professional poker player – not yet. For Chris, the game was still a hobby, a challenge, a subject worthy of study but not a career. It wasn't until a couple of years after he won the Main Event that he accepted poker as his profession. "A friend introduced me to someone else as a professional poker player and I started to deny it," Chris recalled, "Suddenly, I had an epiphany: I am a professional poker player." Chris accepted it at that moment. Although he intends to pursue other career paths in his lifetime, Chris contends that poker will always be a part of his life.

In addition to the live events, Chris also enjoys playing online at FullTiltPoker.com. It wasn't all that long ago that even the best online players were lightly regarded in the poker community. "In fact, there was a time that when a player was referred to as 'an online player'

CHRIS ● fERGUSON

it was code for 'this guy sucks,'" he said. That's all changed. Online poker has undergone an amazing evolution and Chris Ferguson is one of its first success stories. He was playing online as far back as 1989, long before all the special effects, colorful graphics and funny avatars. On the computer screen was simple text-based numbers and it wasn't as interactive as today's online games. What it did do, however, was allow Chris to learn a great deal about no-limit Texas Hold'em. Back in 1989, no-limit games had not yet gained popularity. If you were lucky you might find one or two no-limit games around. The online experience Chris gained and brought to the tables in live games gave him quite an advantage over many other players.

♣ ♥ ♠ ♦

Think about it this way; math never lies – <u>ever.</u> If you have an ace in the hole and two more come on the flop, you know there is one left out there somewhere, but only one. Tells, on the other hand, lie all the time.

♣ ♥ ♠ ♦

While a great deal of the poker community turned its nose up at the young upstarts emerging from cyberspace, Chris knew that the young guns would make their mark, "I had a great deal of respect for the online superstars from day one," Chris said, "because that's how I started out with the IRC Poker Channel."

Chris realized from his own experiences that some of these internet players were seeing way more hands than their live tournament counterparts, "I could play 300 hands of no-limit Hold'em in an hour. That's 300 different learning experiences in an hour. If both the live player and internet player learn the same amount of information per hand, the internet player learns more than five times faster than the live poker player. Think about it this way," Chris said, "a 22-year old internet player playing multiple tables has the ability to see more hands in a few years than Doyle Brunson has seen playing live poker in his lifetime."

CHAPTER ten

While a number of players believe that the cards themselves don't matter nearly as much as the ability to read their opponents, Chris believes that a fundamental understanding of poker is paramount to success. "Some live players use 'tells' as a crutch," Chris says, "It's more important for players to understand how to play their cards at a fundamental level as opposed to playing their cards based on 'tells.'"

"Think about it this way; math never lies – ever," said Chris, who points out if a player has an ace in the hole and two more come on the flop, you know there is one left out there somewhere, but only one. Tells, on the other hand, lie all the time. Players frequently hide or create false tells. They want to deceive you. They can't deceive the math. Chris has advice to newer players; first learn the math. This is one reason why the online players are often so strong.

"When a lot of players say math is not that important in poker they are simply referring to recognizing the odds that one pair of cards will beat another pair of cards. I agree - it's not that important," Chris says. "Game Theory is a subset of mathematics, however. It can be used to show you exactly how you should play your hand and that is of paramount importance. People who say that math isn't important don't know the right math."

It is common for people to want to draw comparisons between Chris and players that may have dropped out of school to play poker. They may ask, 'How can some of these players compete with Ferguson's degree in computer science when they didn't graduate college, or

♣ ♥ ♠ ♦

in some cases high school?' "I always tell them the same thing," said Chris, "These top players are extremely intelligent, whether they went to school or not. They could not attain a championship level of play if they weren't really smart. One of the things I learned in 18 years of study is that going to school may make you educated but it won't necessarily make you smart. Players who are able to play at the highest levels without a lot of formal education make up for it by being smarter in other ways."

Chris learned a valuable lesson when he challenged himself to turn $0 into $10,000 on Full Tilt. "This challenge taught me a number of things about poker," Chris said, "like the importance of bankroll management and the necessity of moving down in limits after a string of losses. It's very hard for people to discipline themselves to moving down in limits when they start to lose, but that's exactly what they need to do to save their bankroll."

A lot of players, Chris feels, play it exactly the opposite and pay a steep price. "Whether it's pride or ego or something else," Chris continued, "a lot of players actually play higher after heavy losses, trying to make the money back quickly. For most people, that simply doesn't work."

"On this $0-$10,000 Challenge," Chris added, "I was never allowed to buy-in for more than 5% of my bankroll." By using this strategy, Chris was able to win money beyond the $10,000 plateau and continued to build his bankroll. Even today you can check out his progress and learn more about the $0-$10,000 Challenge at

CHAPTER ten

ChrisFerguson.com. "The way it was set up, the system forced me to play for lower limits when I lost," Chris said, "If my bankroll was $2,000 I could buy in for a $100, but if my bankroll was only $200, I could only buy in for $10."

♣ ♥ ♠ ♦

After playing fourteen-hour-days at the table with the understanding that just one bad decision can end your tournament life you learn not to sweat the small stuff.

♣ ♥ ♠ ♦

Chris believes one of the greatest things about a poker career is the freedom it affords the player. Players have the freedom to do what they want, when they want. They have no boss. They're relying on themselves.

Away from the tables, Chris has a reputation for being a swing dancer. "It seems every reporter likes to ask me about my West Coast Swing Dancing," Chris says, "I used to dance at least five times a week." Sadly, there is not a very large West Coast Swing Dance community in Las Vegas, so he hasn't danced with any regularity in about five years. "But the minute someone opens up a West Coast Swing Dance club in Vegas," Chris adds, "I am there." Chris started to play golf about a year ago, but hasn't developed a big love for the game yet and says he is still looking for things that interest him.

Because he plays primarily in tournaments travel becomes an issue. With poker tournaments being held all over the world, you would think the travel would be a great benefit. The problem for Chris comes with spending substantial amounts of time in airports, hotels and poker tables. "It usually doesn't leave me any time for site-seeing or enjoying the tourist destinations," says Chris, "The grind of constant travel can really wear me down. That's why I am cutting back on my travel schedule and playing fewer tournaments."

Freedom is not the only benefit Chris enjoys from his poker career. A poker career has also taught him the value of dealing with adversity. "It's amazing what a few years of playing no-limit Hold'em

CHRIS ✦ fERGUSON

tournaments will do to put things in their proper perspective," Chris will say, "After playing fourteen-hour-days at the table with the understanding that just one bad decision can end your tournament life you learn not to sweat the small stuff. After two decades of playing tournament poker I can honestly say that when small things go wrong, I don't worry about it." Chris contends that poker forces players to deal with adversity on a regular basis and when a player can master adversity at the tables, he can master it anywhere. On the other hand, Chris will say, if you can't master adversity at the poker table, you won't be mastering the challenges in life.

♣ ♥ ♠ ♦

Chris contends that poker forces players to deal with adversity on a regular basis and when a player can master adversity at the tables, he can master it anywhere.

♣ ♥ ♠ ♦

Even with the benefits Chris has enjoyed in his poker career, he would still not recommend it as an occupation for everyone. Like any career, Chris believes a person has to do more than just love the game. They really need to consistently demonstrate the skills necessary to play at a high level.

People often ask Chris what makes him successful at the tables. Those who know his background wonder if his poker talent comes from his 'math genes.' It's a good question given his bloodline. Both his parents have Ph.D's in mathematics. "I'm not sure how much heredity plays a role in my tournament victories," said Chris, "My father helped me significantly with my mathematical analysis of poker." However, Chris' poker success goes well beyond his mathematical grasp of the game. In fact, as important as math is Chris is the first one to say that a player can't rely on it alone. "Understanding probability is important," Chris says, "Processing things logically is also important. There are more subtle skills, however, that are critical to a successful player."

CHAPTER ten

A major reason Chris wins at the tables is how hard he is for other people to read. He works hard at eliminating tells or any behaviors that might give away the strength of his hand. Many players know they are playing before a large crowd or a television audience and it impacts the way they play the game. For Chris, when he is at that final table, it doesn't matter whether he is on television or a small audience – he is totally focused on the game. At the same time, Chris is excellent at reading other players, particularly when they are trying to bluff. His legendary calm demeanor is a huge asset as well. Many players—even top professionals—will get very upset when things go wrong and end up on tilt. Chris Ferguson, however, always plays under control.

♣♥♠♦

Understanding probability is important. Processing things logically is also important. There are more subtle skills, however, that are critical to a successful player.

♣♥♠♦

Since he is primarily a tournament player he sometimes feels he is an outsider in the poker world. Many of the top players have developed friendships playing in cash games. They sit all night at a table with the same group of people. Chris doesn't play live cash games - only tournaments.

"At the table itself, I'm usually pretty quiet and reserved. I'm always focused on the hand in play," Chris says, "it certainly doesn't mean that I don't enjoy the game or appreciate its entertainment value." Chris actually enjoys playing with the colorful personalities and the trash-talkers. That surprises a lot of people but to Chris, it makes the game entertaining and fun. "The only thing that does upset me is sitting at a table with people that are rude to each other," he said, "There is no place in poker for that."

Beneath the calm exterior Chris Ferguson is a fiercely competitive player. He never gives up. He plays his best in every hand: short-

CHRIS FERGUSON

stacked or super-stacked, it makes no difference. At no time in the tournament will he ever throw in the towel! Often players who become short-stacked just mentally surrender, but not Chris, "As long as I've got a chip and a chair I'll be competing with all the energy left in my body," Chris promises. "Different things drive different people to success. For me there is a great sense of accomplishment in being very good at something that I like so much." ♠

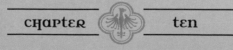

CHAPTER ten

You can visit Chris at ChrisFerguson.com and play poker with him at Full Tilt (www.fulltiltpoker.net). Chris supports Save the Children (www.savethechildren.org), the leading, independent organization creating lasting change for children in need in the United States and around the world.

CHRIS ✦ FERGUSON

CHAPTER ⟡ ELEVEN

ALLEN CUNNINGHAM

ALLEN CUNNINGHAM

Allen Cunningham is, by anyone's standard, one of the most successful poker players to play the game. Playing professionally since he was 18 years old, Cunningham already has 39 career tournament money finishes and five WSOP bracelets, and he's still shy of his 32nd birthday. In 2005 he was named the WSOP Player of the Year. A calm, analytical and friendly player, the California native was recognized in 2006 by his peers as the Best All-Around Player under 35.

After his impressive fourth-place finish in the 2006 WSOP, which netted him over $3.5 million in prize money, Cunningham put together an impressive string of victories. In 2007 he won the $300,000 Mega Match on "Poker after Dark" and the $325,000 Vegas Open Championship main event and then, in May 2008, he won nearly $500,000 in the WSOP Circuit Event at Caesar's Palace. His live tournament winnings exceed $10 million, with no end in sight. "Clever Piggy," as he is known on-line at Full-Tilt Poker, lives in Las Vegas with his girlfriend and fellow poker player, Melissa Hayden, and their dog, Muffin.

♣♥♠♦

I was born in Southern California in 1977. We lived on a military base there until my father was transferred to Germany, where we remained until I was four. When people ask me what I remember about Germany, all I can say is, "Snow." By the time I started elementary school we were back in Orange County, and just before I started the fourth grade we moved to Bloomington, California, just down the road from Riverside. The circle was complete. We would remain there until I graduated from high school. My high school experience was fairly typical and pretty uneventful. I had friends, but I wasn't one of the cool kids. There weren't many students there who excelled academically, and in some ways it seemed as if there was peer pressure for students to strive for mediocrity. I was not a great student, but was in some honors classes and received decent grades. I played some sports; I was on the track team and earned a brown belt in karate.

I learned poker through a series of games that my family played for funny money. We played cards a lot. It was dealer's choice, and we each would call weird games with made-up rules. It was fun. I was around 12 at the time and really looked forward to playing these games with my family. I was already pretty good at them and won with regularity. It sparked something in me, and by the time I was 15 I was already wondering what Las Vegas would be like.

The first time I played for money was in my senior year of high school. I attended German camp with other students in my class. German camp

was just a student club. We all went places together and spoke German to each other. While we were there, a few of the guys started a poker game for a $5.00 buy-in, five-card draw with wild cards. One of the guys knocked me out and I lost my five bucks. If that guy is still around today, he is probably saying to his friends, "Ich habe Allen Cunningham in Poker geschlagen." Then I started college at UCLA, planning to be an engineering major, although I was never sure that was the best thing for me. But I was good in math, and thought I'd get a good job with an engineering degree. Who knows? If I had never played poker, I might be in a cubicle somewhere saving money to start a business.

♣ ♥ ♠ ♦

I think it's fair to say that at this point I started to develop a compulsion about playing. I recognized that gambling could be a serious obsession but, like so many, I still kept going back… and going back… and going back.

♣ ♥ ♠ ♦

The summer after my freshman year at UCLA I started to play poker once a week with my friends at an Indian casino. I had put together a small bankroll from my job delivering pizza. Yes, I delivered pizza, complete with the funny-looking hat and the geeky shirt. We played some Texas Hold'em, but mostly seven-card stud. I still wasn't very good, but I did notice that to win you had to be considerably better than your opponents, because the rake—the share that the house takes—was so high. You had to completely dominate your opponents to really win any money.

Even though I was losing money overall, I began to notice patterns in how people were betting and playing. My mind was always working to develop new strategies. A lot of this early experimentation failed to bear fruit. I would win some, but then I'd lose again, and overall I lost more than I won. But I didn't give up.

In my second year of college, I continued to make the drive nearly every week to play poker in the casinos. I think it's fair to say that at this point I started to develop a compulsion about playing. I recognized that gambling could become a serious obsession, but like so many others I kept going back and back and back. I didn't have much money, so when I'd lose

$100 I would sit and obsess about the loss until my parents sent me some money for college expenses. Some of that money went toward some very skimpy meals. The rest found its way back to the poker tables.

I never really had a poker mentor. No one took me under their wing or gave me advice. I did almost all of it on my own, through trial and error. I do remember trying to imitate the mannerisms of a few regulars that I thought were good players. I'd copy the way they tossed in their chips, tilted their heads, or stared someone down. But for the most part, I developed my own strategies—both good and bad.

My parents were peripherally aware that I was playing, but they really had no idea how focused I had become, and how unfocused in class. I began screwing up in school, but still continued to play each week. There were several times when I seriously questioned myself—what I was doing? Every time I lost, I replayed the whole scenario in my head while driving back to school. I reflected on what I had done wrong and what I would do next. But the following weekend, I'd be off to the casino and, more often than not, losing money again. I felt awful about it, but that didn't stop me stop playing.

On one of those soul-searching drives, I zoned out behind the wheel of my car. I ended up running a red light and rear-ending a little old lady in the car in front of me. I felt horrible as I watched this poor, elderly woman stumble out of her car. Someone nearby called the police. Although the woman wasn't physically hurt, it was obvious that she was a little shaken, and she started dramatizing the event to anyone who would listen. Everyone around was looking at me as if I were some degenerate, bullying a frail little woman who was probably delivering cookies to the nearby orphanage, for all I knew. And as if the situation wasn't humiliating enough, when the officer asked me what had happened, I began to describe the accident in an animated fashion, pointing out the positions of the cars, the directions we were heading, and that sort of thing. Near the end of my diatribe, I turned to point out some inconsequential fact and ended up stabbing the poor woman in the eye with my finger.

CHAPTER ELEVEN

This was not one of my better days. Fortunately, the woman lived and even kept her eyesight—well, as far as I know, anyway. And I had survived a very embarrassing situation. But that brief lapse of concentration did not deter me from my quest to learn more and more about poker. In fact, it taught me a lot about the important role that concentration plays at the table, and how even a momentary lapse could derail me. I also learned that I should stay away from little old ladies.

About that time, I began reading poker books and trying to refine

my game through playing small buy-in tournaments. Doyle Brunson's Super/System comes to mind. During spring break of my sophomore year of college I went to one tournament, with enough money for the buy-in but not enough money for a re-buy. In those tournaments it was very difficult to win without the opportunity to re-buy, so I knew I was taking a risk. Miraculously, I became a ten-to-one overall chip leader, including the players who had re-bought. I found myself at the final table and won $150.

♣♥♠♦

I took that money and I won another $200–$300 playing $6–$12 cash games, and then later scored another $200 on top of that. Soon, I won an additional $500, and found myself holding a $1,000 bankroll. That was more money than I had ever won previously. As I look back on it, this was the period that began my winning momentum.

What I discovered was that there was indeed a great cure for the depression and obsession brought on by habitual losing. That cure was *winning*. A healthy dose of winning is the perfect prescription for many

gambling problems. When I was losing I had this burning need to get back out there and play again at all costs. When you gamble and lose and continue to go back, it feels like an unhealthy obsession. When you finally win, it feels as if dedication and hard work are finally paying off. It's funny how that works. Certainly once I began winning, the burning need to play all the time faded, and I was able to sit back and relax.

I dropped out of school before the final quarter of my second year and started playing every day, mostly $6–$12 or $10–$20 Hold'em. I started winning regularly, building confidence and a bankroll along the way.

♣ ♥ ♠ ♦

On one of those soul-searching drives, I zoned out behind the wheel of my car. I ended up running a red light and rear-ended a little old lady in the car in front of me. I felt horrible as I watched this poor, elderly woman stumble out of the car.

♣ ♥ ♠ ♦

My parents knew that I had dropped out of school before the final quarter. They had invested a lot of money in my education, and they worried that I was throwing all that away for poker, a game no one in my family believed to be a real career. At this point, my parents assumed that I would go back to school the following year. I let them think this was true because, frankly, I wasn't ready to abandon ship and become a professional player—at least not yet.

My next stop was some of the L.A. casinos for higher stakes. The first time I went in I didn't realize you had to be 21 to play. I was 18 at the time and sat down at a table. Another player asked me how old I was. I lied and said I was 20. Apparently, I was a lousy liar. The player informed me that I needed to be 21 to play legally. Had anyone else asked me about my age—they didn't— I would have heeded the advice of my new friend: "21" would have been my response.

Soon I was playing $20–$40 and $40–$80 tables, and I built a $20,000 bankroll pretty quickly. At this point I was feeling the groove. At a casino called Lake Elsinore, I won a $5,000 tournament. It was my first big win,

and I was still only 20. Though I had won, I recognized that I was still pretty raw, even though I had dominated the rest of that field. I knew that playing in Las Vegas would give me the experience I needed to take my game to another level, and my birthday was just around the corner.

Sure enough, on my 21st birthday I showed up at the Four Queens Casino and played the Poker Classic. I didn't do well. It was a good experience, though, and I was now playing in the big leagues, alongside the likes of Erik Seidel, Steve Ridell, and others I had read about in *Card Player*. Soon after that, things started to take off for me. By the time I was 22 years old I was a fixture in the smaller Las Vegas tournaments. At 23, I won Best All-Around Player at The Bicycle Club. Then I won five major tournaments and came in second, to Howard Lederer, in the $5,000 buy-in Omaha eight or better event at the WSOP. I was caught up in a whirlwind of success.

♣ ♥ ♠ ♦

Next was Mike Sexton's Tournament of Champions where I made the finals. As I walked into the casino that day, I had an epiphany. Mike Sexton announced to the audience, "Here's Allen Cunningham, a rising star on the poker circuit." I think it was at that moment that I realized I had indeed arrived. After I won my first bracelet in 2002 I began to have a small change of heart. This was still prior to the national poker boom, and I began to wonder about my future. I decided to go to Santa Monica Community College to build enough credits to transfer back to UCLA. I thought I would go back to get my degree, and I cut my poker playing back to part time. When I was just one class short of what I needed to earn my way back into UCLA, the poker boom hit the nation with full force. Chris Moneymaker won the WSOP, and the WPT was picking up steam too. Poker had hit the big time. Grand-scale tournaments began popping up everywhere, and there was big money to be made.

This time I dropped out of school for good, and got back into poker full-time, just as it was beginning to explode. So the time back in school didn't pan out the way I had envisioned, but there was one major benefit to my game. The time away from the tables had allowed me to recharge my batteries, and I came back pretty refreshed.

♣ ♥ ♠ ♦

As I said earlier, gambling had become somewhat of a compulsion for me. What I discovered was that there was indeed a great cure for the depression and obsession caused by losing.

♣ ♥ ♠ ♦

When I returned, I expanded my horizons a little outside Las Vegas, playing tournaments in Atlantic City and in Tunica, Mississippi. I also played in a heads-up tournament in Vienna, Austria, with my friend Daniel Negreanu. In the early days, I had experienced some hazing and learned that the good old boy network—the inner circle of seasoned professionals—wasn't all that excited about another youngster trying to break in. I remember playing in a $1,000 buy-in no-limit tournament sitting at the same table with Phil Hellmuth. I was playing extremely well and running over everyone in the tournament. Phil was being Phil, and berating me for my overly aggressive play. He thought I was a good player but was playing loose, and he was really letting me have it verbally. It was like Phil was saying, "Welcome to the big leagues, kid."

I am best known for my calm demeanor at the tables, even in high-pressure situations. People never see me go on tilt, or even show any reaction at all. Many of the players in the poker community love to talk smack to each other, or try to get under their opponents' skin by raising their voices, trying to make them feel small for the way they had played a hand. The truth is that this type of behavior doesn't impact most of the professional players.

CHAPTER ELEVEN

Along the way, I developed relationships with other really good players, like Daniel and John Juanda, and we would all talk things through and try to help each other—when we weren't playing against each other, that is. All players have their own styles. Daniel is famous for his scary ability to read players well enough to guess what cards they are holding. Others really lean heavily on the probabilities.

I was voted by my peers as the best player under 35 years old, an honor I'm really proud to have. I think the way I carry myself, and the calm demeanor I have at the tables, were a big reasons for that honor. Prior to poker being played on television, there was much less grandstanding, challenging, or ill-tempered behavior at the tables. Some of that negative behavior is for the benefit of the cameras. ESPN edits the shows, and the louder and more colorful players get air time.

For me, it was a conscious decision to become a calm, collected poker machine, and I think it has served me well. I'm disciplined enough not to react to the more animated players on the circuit. Privately, however, I admit that it does get under my skin at times. Usually, it's the nervous chatterboxes sitting next to me, rambling nonsense, who bug me.

At home, it's a different story. When I play on-line and there is no one to hear me, I sometimes yell at the avatar on the screen. The other thing I do that will surprise many people—I celebrate big wins. If I score a big win online, I hoot and holler and act a little silly. More recently, I have been trying to do less yelling when I play badly and more celebrating when I play well—accentuating the positive. I never allow myself to show emotion in a live game, though. At one time a very good poker play named Bobby Hoff told me that it was difficult to beat a player if you can't get under his skin. That's something I've always remembered.

I'm going to try my celebration strategy with my golf game, to see if that translates well. So every time I hit a good shot I plan to skip down the fairway, flailing and yelling in celebratory fashion. I think it might help. It will certainly get some reaction.

For me, even though I have read a great deal and studied the game

aLLen cunningham

seriously, I rely heavily on my intuition. I do some analyzing at the table, but I take each individual situation on its merits and use my experience and intuition to guide me into my play.

I'm at a different stage now—no longer obsessed with playing all the time. I'm perfectly happy and at ease when I'm not at the tables these days. In fact, it takes some of the bigger, more important tournaments to really get me excited about playing. I also find myself substituting a

♣ ♥ ♠ ♦

lot of the live cash-game activity with online play these days. In fact, between tournaments I rarely go to the casinos at all anymore.

I started playing online from the onset of the internet poker revolution, when places like Planet Poker and Paradise started. When Full Tilt Poker opened, I really ramped up my online activity. I am currently a member of Team Full Tilt. I have become so comfortable playing on-line that I actually feel as if I'm better online in cash games than I am in live games. As far as tournaments go, I still really enjoy the live games best.

One of the best ways to win money playing on-line is to play multiple tables at once. I realized early on, however, that I had to develop a strategy that would work in those situations—a strategy that involved bets, raises, re-raises, and folds based exclusively on the cards, and not always on the patterns of behavior of each of the six to eight players at each of several tables.

Of course, paying attention to the play at a single table is always the

CHAPTER ⚜ ELEVEN

best strategy. Tells are different on-line than in live games, but they are still there. Even if you can't look your opponent in the face, you can still watch for who is playing tight or loose, who frequently bluffs or rarely bluffs, who always raises or rarely raises, etc.

I feel very good about my position in life. I can play if I want to, but I have no urge to play every big tournament and I will pass them by if I need to relax for a while. A few months ago, I played a few tournaments in Europe. On the way back home I could very easily have played in two really large tournaments on the East Coast, but chose not to. I enjoy being in a position where I play only when I want to. In that vein, I'll play smaller tournaments here in Las Vegas, because they don't require travel. I usually don't travel for tournaments that have less than a $10,000 buy-in, but here locally, I might play in a $2,000 event.

♣ ♥ ♠ ♦

Many of the players in the poker community love to talk smack to each other or try to get under their opponent's skin by raising their voices, trying to make them feel small for the way they played a hand.

♣ ♥ ♠ ♦

No-limit Hold'em is probably my best game, and I believe I can win every time I sit down to play it. The money is there to win, and you are testing your skills against the biggest names in the game. But there are other games I play well too. One of my favorite games was a $10,000 buy-in super-mixed event. They had all five limit H.O.R.S.E. games, pot-limit Omaha, and no-limit Hold'em. I really enjoy these mixed events. There are a lot of players out there who are skilled at no-limit, but fewer who excel at these others. Badugi I would consider my worst game. It's a draw game. The best players in that game are significantly better than I am at this point, so it's something for me to work on.

Despite my success in poker, it's not a career I would recommend to young people. There are so many people out there chasing fast money, and so many variables to consider. It takes years of play to get a read on just how good you are. New players can lose a lot of money—in some

aLLen ⬥ cunningHam

cases, everything—before they realize that this is never going to be a money-making career for them. It's such a different game to master, and even those who find some early success don't know if it's skill or luck. I have seen players play the game wrong for quite some time but get lucky often enough to win some money. Eventually, it catches up with them.

For those who are thinking about it, I'd recommend playing regularly just as a hobby. Keep your nine-to-five job, and ease into poker alongside what you're already doing. Remember that for every success story, there are literally thousands of people out there who fail and lose their money.

When I'm not playing poker I like video games and golf. I also own a sailboat, and I do a decent amount of traveling. I really enjoy working on my golf game. My girlfriend Melissa is also a poker player, but she doesn't keep a full schedule, and we have plenty of time together.

As for the future, I've made good money with my poker career, and I can see it taking up less and less of my time. I'm open to new opportunities, but I'm not in any hurry to find them. I have time. Poker will always be part of my life. I don't see it ever just going away.

I don't know yet how the poker historians will remember me. Certainly I believe that I will be remembered as one of the players in the game's upper echelon. I firmly believe that, and notwithstanding the success I have enjoyed so far, I believe the biggest milestones and best times are yet to come, but I don't know what they will be. No matter what those milestones may turn out to be, I hope that people will remember me as a good person, and a man who never took things too seriously. ♣

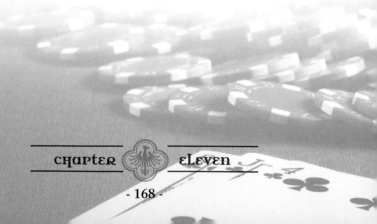

CHAPTER ⬡ ELEVEN

You can play poker with Allen Cunningham at FullTiltPoker.net. Allen supports Opportunity Village (www.opportunityvillage.org), a nonprofit that serves people with intellectual disabilities by providing vocational training, employment and social recreation services that make their lives more productive and interesting. He also supports the Nevada Society for Prevention of Cruelty to Animals (www.nevadaspca.org), as well as the Las Vegas Boys and Girls Club (www.bgclv.org)

aLLen CunninGHam

CHAPTER ✦ TWELVE

CARLOS MORTENSEN

CARLOS MORTENSEN

Carlos Mortensen made poker history in 2007 when he became the first player to win both a World Poker Tour Championship and a World Series of Poker Main Event. He played in his first WSOP in 1999, and was back the following year, finishing at the final table.

His aggressive style and fierce competitive nature paid dividends in 2001 when he returned to the WSOP, this time winning the Main Event to capture the $1,500,000 prize. Mortensen won his second bracelet in 2003, winning the Limit Hold'em event at the 34th Annual World Series of Poker. In 2006 he performed well again, making the final table in three events.

Apart from his success at the WSOP, Carlos is recognized as the most successful player on the World Poker Tour, having won the $25,000 Five-Star WPT Main Event. One of the biggest money winners of all time, Carlos not only is the most recent professional poker player to win the main event at the WSOP, but has continued winning consistently since taking poker's biggest prize.

I was born in Ambato, Ecuador, and grew up on a farm. As a youngster I was a little lazy about studying, and not a great student. Studying didn't interest me so much. Growing up I remember wanting to be a pilot, and I developed a fierce independence very early in life. As early as 12 years old, I was a free spirit and sought adventure on my own. I would sometimes grab my bike and throw it atop a bus and head to one different area or another, riding through the countryside. Sometimes I would be gone for an entire weekend. My penchant for seeking new challenges and my sense of adventure would serve me well later in life, as it did when I moved to Madrid at just 18, becoming a Spanish citizen and seeking a new career. Eventually, all of my family moved to Spain.

♣ ♥ ♠ ♦

Seeking new challenges and my sense of adventure would serve me well later in life.

♣ ♥ ♠ ♦

I lived in Spain for seven or eight years before I learned to play Texas Hold'em. I was about 25, a young man on my own just trying to survive. I had been a bit of a nomad, holding many different jobs at various times. I had a favorite club where I used to play chess. It was there that I would meet Gonzalo Garcia-Pelayo, an extraordinary gambler perhaps best noted for his success in roulette, of all things. He was also known as the man who introduced Hold'em to Spain.

Garcia-Pelayo had an incredible history. In the early 1990s, he observed that certain roulette wheels were not completely random. He noted that small imperfections in the roulette wheels' gears and tiny differences in the sizes of the pockets would cause some numbers to come up more often than others. He meticulously recorded the winning numbers on thousands of spins and conducted a statistical study of the data.

Garcia-Pelayo continuously bet on the numbers that his study indicated came up most often, in the process turning a 5% disadvantage into a 15% advantage over the casinos of Europe. Over a span of a few years, he won more than two million euro's using this system. In effect,

Garcia-Pelayo became "the house", and subsequently started a poker game at the club where I played chess.

I knew little of poker, but that day I had about $100 in my pocket and the stakes were low, so I sat down to play. I remember thinking to myself that the $100 would probably last a few hours. No one in the room other than Garcia-Pelayo knew Texas Hold'em, so all of the players there were really just beginning to learn together, including me. The first day I lost my money, but that day ignited in me a passion for the game.

♣♥♠♦

The night after that first game I couldn't sleep. I kept thinking about the game, wondering how it worked, replaying how I might have played differently the hands that I had lost, or even how I might have won bigger pots on the hands I had won. The evening of reflection paid off. The next day I won $120 or $130. I'm not sure of the exact amount; but the key thing was that I won more money than I had lost the previous day.

The next day I won again, and once again my winnings exceeded those of the day before. I won the next two days as well a total of four days in a row. I still had no idea that there were people who made a living from this game, but I already sensed that I was pretty good at it.

I didn't tell my family that I was playing poker. In Spain, poker was not exactly illegal, but certainly it was frowned upon. The way my family learned that I was playing poker was by seeing me on television. One day I was playing in a house game when it was raided by the police, who recorded the names of all the people who were present. The press heard of the raid and showed up to film the bust for the news. They actually interviewed me. I told them I was a professional poker player, and was going to play in the World Series of Poker in Las Vegas. Three years later I would win there.

♣♥♠♦

I remember looking at Ungar's picture which was taken right after he won $1 million at the 1997 $10,000 No-Limit World Series Championship. Covering his eyes were his trademark sunglasses and fanned all around him was the $1 million in cash. It made quite an impression on me.

♣♥♠♦

One day Garcia-Pelayo brought in the front page of the sports section of a newspaper and posted it on the wall. The page featured an article on Stu Ungar, who had just won the World Series of Poker. Ungar was a fascinating character, widely considered at the time to have been the greatest Texas Hold 'em player of all time. He is the only person to have won the World Series of Poker Main Event three times. He is also the only person to win Amarillo Slim's Super Bowl of Poker three times. I remember looking at Ungar's picture, which was taken right after he won $1 million at the 1997 $10,000 No-Limit World Series Championship. Covering his eyes were his trademark sunglasses, and fanned all around him was the $1 million in cash. It made quite an impression on me.

I found that newspaper page intriguing. In America, gambling was legal in many places, and was certainly not underground. Not only were people making money, but some of them, like Ungar, were making huge amounts of money. Garcia-Pelayo encouraged me to consider poker as a career. He told me he believed that I had good poker skills, and that if I worked hard to develop those skills I too could become a successful professional poker player.

I started my poker career right then and there, playing Limit Texas Hold'em pretty much nonstop from April to October in Garcia-Pelayo's game, with the blinds at $2–$4 and $3–$6. I was pretty much beating everyone in the game, but with so few games to be played, the opportunities for me began to dry up. Garcia-Pelayo's game was the only game in my

area. Worse, it was the same 20 or so players, day in and day out. The house was getting its rake, and there was not much more to be had.

♣♥♠♦

Atlantic City was where I decided I needed to test my skills. The trip would have its difficulties, of course, given I was alone with all my belongings in a single backpack. Oh, and did I mention that I didn't speak English?

♣♥♠♦

I considered two options in October 1997; one was Chiribito. This is a well-known Spanish poker game played with a 28 or 32 card deck (depending on the number of players) containing only the cards seven or eight to the ace, respectively. You are dealt two cards down, as in Hold'em, but you have to use both the hole cards to build your hand. It's a very aggressive game; a straight is considered a so-so hand, and lots of players have good hands. You may have a straight, but the next player may have a flush, and the next one a full house. I had not really played it before, and didn't feel comfortable going up against the professionals who had been making a living for years from Chiribito and other Spanish games. Because I was a Hold'em player, I took my second option and headed to the United States—to Atlantic City!

The United States, I found, was the Mecca for poker, and Hold'em was especially popular

♣♥♠♦

there. Atlantic City was where I decided to test my skills. The trip would have its difficulties, of course, given that I was alone, with all my belongings

in a single backpack. My English, too, was pretty basic, and the trip itself was a challenge. .

When I arrived in New York, first stop at John F. Kennedy Airport, I asked strangers how to get to Atlantic City. I was directed to Manhattan, where I would catch the subway to the bus station. From there, I would take the bus to Atlantic City, famous for its boardwalk, shopping centers, sandy beaches, spectacular view of the Atlantic Ocean, and, of course, gambling.

I had just $2,800 in cash with me when I arrived. I knew I had to live as cheaply as possible in order to sustain my bankroll for my poker stake. The first cold dose of reality that would hit me was how expensive everything is in America. When I started to look around for a place to stay, I found that all the hotels were $150-$250 per night. All I could say when I realized this was, "Uh oh."

♣♥♠♦

Here in Atlantic City, there were many good players at my table and some of them had been playing since before I was born. I was playing way too many hands and before I knew it, I had lost $475... my first day!

♣♥♠♦

My stay was to be 15 days. If I were to spend $200 per night just for the hotel, that alone would total more than three thousand dollars, more than I had with me. I knew I couldn't do that, so I started to walk around the less-attractive areas in Atlantic City and ended up finding a place for around $22 per night. Needless to say, it was not the Ritz-Carlton. I wasn't happy about staying there, but sometimes you have to do what you have to do. And I had made this trip knowing that I was I was headed right back to Spain, where I could resume winning regardless of what happened in the States.

My first game in America was a $2–$4 Limit Hold'em game at the Tropicana. The first thing that struck me was the number of players at the table. In Spain I had played against five other players. Here I was playing against *nine* others. My poker strategy was all based on playing with fewer players, and the difference threw me off my game at first.

CHAPTER twelve

I was also now playing with other "professional" poker players. These guys in Atlantic City were the real deal. In the game I had played in Spain, it was basically Garcia-Pelayo and I who won most of the time. Here in Atlantic City, there were many good players at my table, and some of them had been playing since before I was born. I was playing way too many hands, and before I knew it I had lost $475 . . . on my first day!

I was steamed up pretty good. I went outside and bought a hot dog, which was about all I could afford, and thought about the game—how I was playing and what I needed to do differently. If something good came from that day, it was how much I learned from watching the other professionals. Because I didn't speak English well, there was no conversing with them, but watching how everyone played didn't require translation.

♣ ♥ ♠ ♦

My opponents think I am very aggressive and even crazy at times. I like that image because it gives me an advantage. They don't want to raise my blind because they know I will make a move and force them to make a decision for a lot of chips.

♣ ♥ ♠ ♦

I used what I had learned in the following days, and before I went back home I was playing in the $15-$30 games. I went home with about $10,000. Once again, I began playing Chiribito, which is a no-limit game. In my brief stay in the States, the Hold'em games were mostly *limit* games. I really believe that my experience playing No-Limit Chiribito gave me an advantage when No-Limit Hold'em began to be popular.

In 1997 I made a second trip to America, this time to Las Vegas, for three months. My expenses were much higher this time, but I managed to break even. I really didn't lose, but I didn't come out ahead either. I played primarily at the Mirage, but also at the Horseshoe. I played mostly cash games, everything from $15–$30 to $30–$60, depending on how well my bankroll was holding up at the time.

Returning to Europe, I began to take my game on the road, traveling to play many different games in places like Paris, Vienna, and Amsterdam,

CARLOS MORTENSEN

♣ ♥ ♠ ♦

as well as Spain. I learned a lot by playing a lot, and I played against hugely talented players in Europe. In 1998, when Pot-Limit Omaha games began popping up in Spain, I did well in this very high-stakes game.

My opponents think I'm very aggressive and even crazy at times. I like that image, because it gives me an advantage over other players. They don't want to raise my blind, because they know I'll make a move and force them to make a decision for a lot of chips. They might have the better hand, but they are frequently forced to throw it away.

In my game in Madrid, the poker players there actually took up a collection to stake me in the World Series of Poker. They had confidence in me, enough to stake me for 30% of my action. So I flew to Las Vegas to play in the 1999 Main Event, and I finished in the top half of the field, though I didn't cash. I also brought money for cash games, choosing to play in the Commerce Casino in Los Angeles.

♣ ♥ ♠ ♦

I believe that poker is a people game played with cards, not just a card game played by people. I believe every player has a weakness, situations that make them uneasy. That is when I put them to the test.

♣ ♥ ♠ ♦

In 2000 I started playing more in tournaments. Anywhere a big tournament was being played, you'd find me there. I didn't learn poker by reading books. It was on-the-job training, and that's also how I study poker. I remember every hand and every situation, and then use that information

to help me in new situations. I'm constantly trying to pick up small details other people don't even think about, and I've created my own unique way to play. The strength of my game comes from analyzing the styles of other players, and using their system against them.

♣♥♠♦

Anytime I can bust someone, I do it without hesitation. If I smell weakness, I attack. Either I bust them or they bust me. Sometimes, I am an underdog according to the odds, but if I play, it's an attack.

♣♥♠♦

Anytime I can bust someone, I do it without hesitation. If I smell weakness, I attack. Either I bust them or they bust me. Sometimes, the odds make me an underdog, but if I play, it's an attack. I might be the underdog, but if I have more chips and bust someone on a coin flip, I bust the player and double up. Sometimes I call knowing that I'm an underdog, but believing that I will be able to outplay my opponents. I believe that whatever you really want to do, if you try hard enough you can do it, as long as you never surrender.

I love poker for the freedom it affords me. I don't answer to anyone but myself. When you play poker you risk your own money, and you play the game the way you want to play. You play the tournaments you want, and you pass up the ones you don't want to play.

My nickname is "El Matador", a name people in the United States call me at times. The name references bullfighting, which is a very aggressive sport, and I'm known to be a very aggressive player.

But I don't really enjoy the notoriety of the game. A lot of poker today is theater for television, and that's not me. I don't really seek the fame. If I had my way, I'd probably not play on television at all.

Nor do I really enjoy playing online very much. I don't really trust the hackers, or the technology that keeps track of the stats on all the players. I prefer playing live, where there are no computers to help you. It's just you and your opponent, eye to eye, man to man. That's the way I like to play.

CARLOS MORTENSEN

I didn't really like the introduction of the hole card cam, either. I didn't like the idea of my opponents recording my play and, later, watching every move I made.

Away from poker I love riding motorcycles—my dirt bikes. I love to jump, and I love to take risks. I have friends who ride competitively, and I keep up with them. I also enjoy spending free time with my girlfriend Pastora. We spend a lot of time wakeboarding and surfing and really enjoying the outdoors.

Poker is a hard way to make a living. It's not something I'd recommend for others. Imagine if everybody chose poker as a career. What would happen? I believe that poker is a people game played with cards, not just a card game played by people. I believe every player has a weakness, a situation that makes him or her uneasy. That's when I put them to the test. I'm also hard to read, mixing it up to keep my opponents off balance. One moment I am calculating the odds, and the next time I'm bluffing. Because of my image, I can play many different ways. Over time, everyone over time catches the same number of good and bad cards, but winning in No-Limit is all about bluffing.

I love America, but I do miss the friendliness of Spain. It's a smaller place. People are in the streets, outside, and in bars; they're accessible. In America, people are in their cars. I'm sure I will move back to Spain one day, but for now I'm content to live in Las Vegas and do what I do best, which is playing poker. ♠

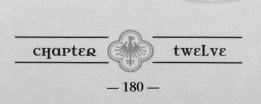

CHAPTER twELVE

Carlos Mortensen, winner of the 2001 WSOP Main Event.

CARLOS MORTENSEN

CHAPTER 🦅 THIRTEEN

ERIK SEIDEL

ERIK SEIDEL

Erik Seidel has established himself as one of the greatest tournament players in poker history. In less than two decades, he has become a final-table fixture: winning eight WSOP bracelets, a WPT title and nearly $10 million dollars in prize money. When he's not battling for another tournament victory, Erik can be found online as a member of Team Full Tilt.

Erik was born in New York and started out as a professional backgammon player, spending eight years on the backgammon tournament circuit before moving on to the stock market. For a time, Seidel traded on Wall Street and played poker on the side, until the market crashed in 1987 and he reassessed his future.

Generally quiet and unassuming, Erik finished second in his first-ever WSOP championship event and made it back to the final table of the championship event in 1999. Erik won his first bracelet in 1994. Thirteen years later he won his eighth career bracelet, tying Johnny Moss for fourth place on the all-time list.

[Interview conducted and chapter written by Phil Hellmuth, Jr.]

Pac-Man was not a good earn for me, but I made money in high school playing pinball and backgammon; poker entered my life at least nine years later. By the time I was in my teens, I was playing backgammon in the Game Room at 75th and Broadway, which was a club just down the street from where I lived, on the Upper West Side of Manhattan. I played backgammon with my high school friends while I went to New Lincoln High School and Baldwin High School. Because I had read Paul Magriel's groundbreaking book *Backgammon*, and because I'd been around real backgammon players, I was the best player in my high school.

My dad worked in a lot of different capacities in the film business. He was a production manager, a producer, an assistant director, and a director, and really he did everything. He worked on the "Soupy Sales" show and was involved with the "Revenge of the Nerds" movies. I lived with my mother and my stepfather, both of them documentary filmmakers. My two brothers, one younger and one older, both played board games with me as we grew up. Upon entering college, I stayed close to home and my backgammon profit center, while I spent one year at Brooklyn College, and half a year at Hunter College. My parents fully supported my decision to play games for a living, and my mother even thought that was great!

My good friend Howard Lederer talks about cutting his teeth playing poker in the Mayfair Club, but before they had poker, the Club was

♣ ♥ ♠ ♦

offering bridge, and then backgammon. By the way, at one point I was happy that Howard had been banned for a year from the poker game at the Club! Back then, we banned all the professional poker players from the Mayfair Club poker game, because we were just a bunch of backgammon and bridge players learning how to play poker for the first time. When the Club finally let some pros into our poker game, Howard was among the first. It was then that Howard and I began to form a close, twenty-year friendship.

One day at the Game Room, I was introduced to Paul Magriel, who was by far the world's best backgammon player, and also the nicest, most generous person. Sometime later he invited me by to play a game with him, and taught me tons of great backgammon tactics and strategy--I think, just because he loved to teach, and because he loved backgammon so much. At that time, Magriel was writing a backgammon column for the *The New York Times* and we would go over some of the games that he wrote about.

♣ ♥ ♠ ♦

> *Back then, we banned all the professional poker players from the Mayfair Club poker game, because we were just a bunch of backgammon and bridge players learning how to play poker for the first time.*

♣ ♥ ♠ ♦

Just meeting Magriel was incredible to me! After all, I had read and reread his book, he was receiving universal praise for being the best backgammon player in the world, and I even watched him on "60 Minutes." I don't know what I would have done had Magriel not entered my life. He was instrumental in my success. When I was 17 years old, Bill Robertie's backgammon column in the *The Boston Globe* praised a move that I had made in a tournament. [*PH note:* Seidel was a backgammon prodigy, but he is too modest to admit it here! Instead, when he is asked about it, he talks about some of the other prodigies that he came up with in the New York backgammon clubs.] To put all this in perspective, there were a couple of guys just two years older than me who were phenomenal

backgammon players, and they were recognized as among the best players in the world: Jason Lester and Roger Low. To me, these guys were the backgammon prodigies. Of course you had Magriel as number one, but he was a few years older.

Although the Mayfair Club is renowned because of all of the great poker players who played there, there was a time when it was the center of the backgammon universe. We had this group of bright games players, and we all hung out together, talked about games, and played together; it was like an incubator for backgammon talent. And Magriel was at the head of it. I mean, he was The Guy at the beginning, and the rest of us learned from him and became better together. When I first played in the Mayfair Club, it was located on 57th Street, between Second and Third. And then it moved to the Gramercy Park Hotel, at 21st and Lexington. Later, when the Club became more about poker, and moved to 25th Street, between Park Avenue and Madison, it was the inspiration for the movie "Rounders."

♣ ♥ ♠ ♦

Later, when the Mqyfair Club became more about poker, and moved to 25th street, between Park Avenue and Madison, it was the inspiration for the movie "Rounders."

♣ ♥ ♠ ♦

Of course, I believe that the Mayfair Club holds an important place in the history of poker. Accomplished poker players like Howard, Mickey Appleman, Noli Francisco, World Champion Dan Harrington, and six-time WSOP winner Jay Heimowitz cut their poker teeth there. The writers of "Rounders," Brian Koppelman and David Levien, played at the Mayfair Club, and used it as a model for their movie.

Before I began my poker career in earnest at age 27, way back in 1988, I had been to Las Vegas many times, because they held backgammon tournaments there, so I was pretty familiar with the city. I don't know how many times I had been there, but I think I was 22 or 23 years old when I went out to play in the first World Amateur Backgammon Championships. In fact, I don't know if I ever played in the amateur event, because by the

time the tournament was launched I was already a professional player.

They also had a pro tournament there, although I never won it. There was betting and side action, though, and I remember drawing poker legend David "Chip" Reese in the first round one year. I thought, "Oh, I'm going to bet on this match because Chip Reese is a poker player and he must be pretty bad." So we bet $1,000. Of course, I thought I was robbing him, but I think he beat me!

♣ ♥ ♠ ♦

During one trip to Las Vegas for a backgammon tournament, I picked up David Sklansky's book on poker. It was actually a $3 pamphlet at that time, not really a book. I read it and I beat the $1–$2 limit Hold'em game that day. This sparked my interest in poker. When I returned to New York, I started playing some no-limit Hold'em poker at the Mayfair Club. Then in October 1987, I lost my job at Paine Webber when the stock market crashed. At the time I was short volatility, which is not a good thing to be when a market crashes. I was completely wiped out, and the guy I worked for, Roger Low, was also wiped out. But for a while there, I was making some good money. I was engaged at the time to Ruah, and I was really without a job and in a panic.

Many of us Wall Street folk thought that the world had fundamentally changed. I had many friends who went belly up, and the amount of pain that people were in at the time was incredible; and I felt that pain to the bone. Add to my desperation the fact that my fiancée, Ruah, was pregnant. I really wondered how I could support a family while living in Manhattan. I felt desperate, but Ruah handled it amazingly well. In fact, she has always had more faith in me than I've had in myself! Whenever

things have been a little rocky, it's been nice to have her full support, her understanding, and her faith that we will somehow be all right.

With no job prospects in Manhattan, and in the midst of a major stock market plunge, I decided to go to the Mayfair Club and play poker more regularly. Things seemed to be going smoothly for me in the poker world, and in early 1988 I won $77,000 over two weeks of play in the no-limit Hold'em game at the Club! And man, that was a huge amount of money to me at the time. Around that time Howard and Dan Harrington, who both had finished at the final table of the 1987 WSOP (World Series of Poker) encouraged me to go to Vegas and to play in the 1988 WSOP. By the way, Howard has always been unbelievably supportive.

♣ ♥ ♠ ♦

With no job prospects in Manhattan, and in the midst of a major stock market plunge, I decided go to the Mayfair Club and play poker more regularly.

♣ ♥ ♠ ♦

One of the strongest memories I have of the beginning of my trip to the WSOP that year, as funny as it may seem, was when I walked into the old Horseshoe Hotel and Casino and saw this drop-dead gorgeous redhead with Thor Hanson. And I thought, "I wonder who that guy is." Of course, Thor has always done well on the female side of the ledger.

I played in nine WSOP one-table satellites at $1,000 a pop and didn't win one. Finally, when I was running out of time, I sold 80% of myself, at par value, to a bunch of friends, including backgammon legends Mike Svobodny and Billy Horan. "Par value" means that they paid 80% of the money ($8,000) for 80% of the action. Normally, though, a player sells, say, 60% of himself for 80% of the money, leaving a 20% "free roll." I wanted the people who were risking money on me to get full value if I did well.

One regret I had was that Howard didn't buy a piece of me, and that really bothered me because, of all of the poker players I knew, I felt he was the one I owed the most to. I did ask him to buy a piece, but I guess he thought I wasn't ready. I also managed to secure a 2% free roll for an

old backgammon friend of mine named Fran Goldfarb, one of the best female backgammon players in the world. Since I hadn't asked my friends for a free percentage for myself, I asked for her.

The 1988 WSOP may well have been the first no-limit Hold'em tournament that I had played in. The first couple of days I was lucky, because I had decent tables, and everyone seemed to play a pretty straightforward game. When I made it to the end of Day Three, it really started to sink in, and at the end of Day Three, with six of us left, I got excited and called Ruah, Billy Horan, and Mike Svobodny.

♣ ♥ ♠ ♦

The next day, Billy and Mike flew out from New York City to sweat me in the tournament's final day.

The final six players at the 1988 WSOP were the reigning World Champion Johnny Chan, poker legends Humberto Brennes, Jim Bechtel, T. J. Cloutier, Ron Graham, and me. I was the least experienced, by a long shot! And I did a lot of things I would never do now. I remember an early confrontation with T. J., where he raised it up on the button with A-10, and I moved all in with pocket fives. T. J. called and my fives held up.

But the hand that was most significant for me, and boosted my confidence the most, came up against Ron Graham. I had been raising pretty aggressively, and I just thought that Ron was going to make a stand at some point, and finally he did. He moved all in for a mountain of chips, and I thought for a long, long time, and I just became convinced that he was bluffing. It just felt like a bluff. Finally, I called him with A-J, and that to me was the big dramatic hand. I mean, I think he had 10-4 off suit or

something. That was the biggest hand, because I took forever, replaying it and replaying it in my mind, and I thought I had a good read on him, but I wasn't sure if it was a real read or a false read. Turned out that I had made a good read, and I won a monster pot.

When it came down to me and Chan heads up, it was a little bit of the "deer in the headlights" kind of thing for me. I was thinking, What the hell am I doing here playing against the best player in the world?! Johnny was already a living legend, and this was my first poker tournament!

♣ ♥ ♠ ♦

When it came to me and Chan heads-up, it was a little bit of the "deer in the headlights" kind of thing for me. I was thinking, "What the hell am I doing here playing against the best player in the world?!"

♣ ♥ ♠ ♦

As far as the last hand goes, I forget what position Chan was in. [PH note: Seidel is talking about one of poker's most famous moments, since memorialized in the movie "Rounders." Seidel had Q-7, and Chan had Jc-9c, and Chan flopped a straight when the board delivered Q-10-8. Seidel checked the flop, Chan bet $40,000, Seidel raised it up, making it $90,000 to go, and Chan, with the best possible hand, just called to set a trap. The next card was a deuce, Seidel checked, and Chan stealthily checked again. The river card was a six, Seidel moved all in, and Chan called and claimed the title.]

I'm a little sick of hearing about this hand! Just when I thought I had heard the last about it, ten years later "Rounder's" comes out! But from my point of view, I still remember the 1988 WSOP as being an amazing four days. And the $280,000 second-place prize gave us a little more financial support, even though I had only 20% of myself. In fact, that $56,000, combined with my side-game winnings, had me pretty pumped up.

One of the nice things about my finish was that so many of my New York friends from the Mayfair had a piece of me. It was great to have their support and to reward it.

I remember that the next year I'm standing in line with my $10,000 to

sign up for the tournament, and Poker Hall of Famer "Puggy" Pearson is in front of me, and he turns around and says to me, "Son, that was the worst play I've ever seen!" I knew Puggy because I had played backgammon with him, and even though his remark was pretty insulting, it was also very funny!

♣ ♥ ♠ ♦

If you look at the disciplined people, you find that they generally hold onto their money. And talented people all too often end up broke.
♣ ♥ ♠ ♦

In the last twenty years I've been fortunate enough to win eight WSOP bracelets and one WPT title. I've been lucky enough to support my two daughters and my wife Ruah playing the game I love.

I would tell younger players today not to gamble beyond their means, and not to get ahead of themselves. Managing your money the right way can make your life so much easier. Managing your money poorly can lead to a lot of unnecessary pain.

I would also tell them that discipline is more important than talent when it comes to being a professional poker player. I mean, think of how many talented people you know who are broke! Then think of how many disciplined people you know who are broke. If you look at the disciplined people, you find that they generally hold onto their money. And talented people all too often end up broke.

I would like to be remembered as someone who loved to play. And I would also

♣ ♥ ♠ ♦

like to be remembered as someone who was always fair and ethical.

I feel so much appreciation for the games world. Backgammon and poker are games that I love to play, games I've learned so much from. For me, these games have been like graduate school. I've learned so much from so many people in this world, not just about how to play these games, but personally, ethically, and socially as well. I have no idea where I would have landed had I not fallen into this career. Every day, I feel fortunate that I get to compete in games that I love. And it even pays the bills. ♠

CHAPTER THIRTEEN

You can play poker with Erik at Full Tilt (www.fulltiltpoker.net). Erik supports the Sophia Academy (www.sophia-academy.org), a learning community in the Greater Providence area for girls from low income families that provides an atmosphere for academic, spiritual, cultural and social growth.

ERIK SEIDEL

CHAPTER 🦅 FOURTEEN

david ulliott

Dave "Devilfish" Ulliott is one of the most fearsome, charismatic and plainspoken characters in poker. In Europe, his name is legendary in poker circles; he has been Europe's top Omaha player twice. The Fish has 33 combined World Poker Tour and World Series of Poker money finishes and is one of the few professionals to ever win both a World Poker Tour title and a World Series of Poker event. His biggest single tournament prize, almost $600,000, came at the Jack Binion World Poker Open on the World Poker Tour. He has also been awarded the "Gambling Personality of the Year" at the U.K. Gambling Awards of 2006, due in part, as he might describe, because he is "one funny bastard."

The Fish has also earned a "Lifetime Achievement Award" in Europe in 2008. In Las Vegas he continued to build his reputation as a world-class poker player. Las Vegas is filled with "characters" in poker. During the interview for this book, Devilfish rummaged through his wallet and came upon a check stub for $1.4 million. He said that he had been walking around with the live check in his wallet for over a year and had just gotten around to depositing it. When he went to the bank, he handed the check to one of the tellers, who was shocked at the condition and age of the un-cashed check. Devilfish said of the teller's reaction, "I'm not sure but I think she may have shat herself."

I would like to dedicate my chapter to my father, Stanley Ulliott, who died in December 2008. He had a tougher life than I. He ran away to join the war at seventeen. He toughened me up. We weren't always close -- but I sure miss him.

* * * * *

I was born in 1954 in Kingston upon Hull, England. It's a rough town, one of the roughest in the country. If you went into a bar in Hull and saw sawdust on the floor, it was probably last night's furniture. I started playing poker at a very early age with my father, mother, and sister, around the kitchen table. As a lad I got a job at G. K. Beaulah's, a place that made shields and trophies. Some of the workers would play poker on their lunch break. I learned a good deal about poker from them. One the guys at Beaulah's, Jack Gardener, was a member of the only casino in town, the Fifty-One Club.

It took some convincing for Jack to agree to help get me into the casino, because I wasn't yet eighteen. I was pretty tall, though, and I had money in my pocket -- the latter was all they really bothered about. I started playing Strip-Deck Stud, with a 32-card deck. I didn't have much money, and what I did have was lost the very first day. It was frustrating but I kept going back, even though the results would get no better. It was a regular thing after a while—losing money, that is. But in this early period of my life, gambling was not the only thing I was doing.

When I was around 17 I met some guys who were very clever villains. Their names were Dave and Fred, and they took me under their wing and taught me what they knew. Eventually, I got better than them. Fred was known to the police as "Stonewall" Fred because of his propensity for singing like a canary to the authorities when the heat was on. For that reason I started to work by myself.

Around the age of 20 I started cracking safes: black outfit, climbing about on the roof, the whole thing. It was all part of my overwhelming desire to get that thrill. I'd steal some money from a safe one night, and blow the whole thing at the track the next day. Once, I lost £5,000 to a

CHAPTER FOURTEEN

bookie and returned that night and robbed his safe. I got my money back and his too, and I lost it all again the next day.

But my luck changed at the casino; I started to beat those games up. I found other big opportunities as well, in private games outside the casino. The only way to find out about these private games was by word of mouth. If people liked you, they told you where to find them. What I found was established games with some pretty rough characters. I played in these private games for many years, from the time I was about 18 until I was about 30 years old. The first game I played was at Mustafa's, down on Louis Street. I started beating that game up pretty quickly.

♣ ♥ ♠ ♦

When I was 19 or 20 years old I was cracking safes. Yes, you read that right I was a safecracker – black outfit, climbing about on the roof, the whole thing. It was all part of my overwhelming desire to get that thrill.

♣ ♥ ♠ ♦

During the time that I played at Mustafa's and other private games, I was still involved in activities more dangerous and illegal than poker. I grew up in an area where it seemed everyone had some scam they were working. No one was safe, not even the criminals. I once knew a guy who was driving about in a truck filled with stolen goods. He stopped off at the bookie to place a bet, and when he came out ten minutes later, his truck had been completely emptied. When he came out the door, he actually saw people running about in all directions with stuff from his truck in their hands. Not long after that, I was with some other seedy characters who removed a panel from the front of a shop door. We climbed through and lifted enough cigarettes to fill our van. We hauled away as much as we could and returned for another load. When we got back, we saw a police car outside the shop. The cops weren't filling out a report, though. They were stealing cigarettes themselves. Eventually, around my 21st birthday, I was caught and did time in Leeds Prison.

But I didn't really learn my lesson. Soon after my release I was back to safecracking and other sorts of activities. Later on, I went back to

prison again, but this time it wasn't for safecracking. I had worked some as a bouncer when I wasn't gambling, and I got into a number of fights. That eventually caught up to me, and I was back in prison for another 18 months.

Prison was no picnic. It was a tough place. I was about 10 stone 6 (that's 146 lbs to you Americans) in those days, but I had lightning-fast fists to go with my lightning-fast temper. Not many guys messed with me. One day I was lifting weights and got teamed up with a spotter who was an absolute lunatic. Just like one of those crazy guys you see in the movies. His was big, mean, and ugly, and he sported a shaved head. I wasn't going to back down from anyone, though. So when he began running his mouth I decided to sort this guy out. I gave him a shot on the side of his head and he fell flat on his face. I was not finished with him; I jumped on him and popped him on the head with a 10-kilo weight. As if that weren't enough, I got up and headed for a bigger weight. It was at that time that the guard grabbed me around the neck and threw me into the showers. To this day I believe that, had the guard not stopped me, I would have hit that guy again with the bigger weight, and who knows, I'd probably still be in prison today.

I've always had a bit of a temper. At another time in my life, before I was in prison, I got into it with a guy in an establishment, managed to get hold of his head, moved him over to the door, and slammed the door on his head about twelve times.

On yet another occasion, a guy took exception to me taking money off him in pool games. He was massive. He punched me and my head slammed backwards into a wall. There were hooks on the wall and one of them sank into my neck. I saw stars and felt sick. I managed to grab him, though. Holding onto the guy, I started to bite on his ear until I was able to shake the cobwebs. Once my head was clear I got on top of the guy and started to punch him. The guy had a head like a block of concrete, though, so I grabbed a tea cup by the bottom and banged the rim of it on his face about twelve times, until I was sure he had got the message. I used to be a bit of a bastard.

CHAPTER FOURTEEN

After my release from my second stint in prison I met and married Amanda, my second wife, and she convinced me to give up the safecracking and head cracking. I realized how stupid the stealing and robbing was, and I never looked back on it again. My wife Amanda and I opened a business, which I shall describe in just a bit.

♣ ♥ ♠ ♦

Prison was no picnic. It was a tough place. I was about 10 stone 6 (that's 146 lbs to you Americans) in those days, but I had lightning-fast fists to go with my lightning-fast temper.

♣ ♥ ♠ ♦

I continued to play poker and was still beating up the private games, and it was becoming a problem for some of the people I played. In an effort to avoid playing with me, they would move the game and wouldn't tell me about it. I found out, though. The game was run by a guy named Marat. Everyone called him "Chef" because he used to do the cooking at a local hotel. There was money to be made there. The game was Seven Card Stud. The venue was a dodgy little smoke-filled room in the back of some run-down establishment, right out of the movies. I was waiting for the game to begin when Marat got on the phone with someone I didn't know. I couldn't understand him. He was talking in Turkish or Greek or some shit -- I didn't even know what language he was speaking. Eventually, he hung up the phone, came over to me and said, "David, no one is coming to the games because they see your car parked outside. I'm sorry, you have to go." I was gutted. Soon, word got around, and I was *un*invited to the other private games around town as well.

Sean Ellison, a friend who ran a roofing business, told me we should try our luck in Leeds, where he had heard of a poker room at a Staki's Casino. By car, it was only about an hour up the road. We got to the casino and sure enough, there was a poker room. The problem was that they were playing games I'd never heard of before. The games were Omaha, not just the 4-card game, but a 5-card and a 6-card version as well. The player on the button could decide how many cards we would play. Even though years later this would become one of my very favorite

games, at the time I had never heard of it. Fortunes can quickly and repeatedly change in the course of one, normal 4-card hand. The 5-card or 6-card version really throws a twist into things. Usually, only the most experienced, well-staked players had the belly for the 5-card or 6-card version. Mind you, I said, "Usually."

♣ ♥ ♠ ♦

It didn't take a fucking genius to figure out they had decided to take their money back and were waiting to jump us. I fired my gun off in the air. That late at night in the close quarters of an alley the gun sounded like a cannon going off.

♣ ♥ ♠ ♦

I decided to just jump straight into the 6-card Omaha game. Within thirty-five minutes, I had tripled my money, and I thought, "This is incredible. I'm busting this game up." The tide turned quickly, though. An hour later I was flat broke -- not a farthing left to my name.

While I was in Leeds, though, I started to win a lot of money. I found out about another game, played on Tuesday nights, in a place called Derby. The Derby game was more complicated. It was a crazy game there, played by crazy gamblers, but it was similar to the game I had played in Leeds. I did ok there: some nights I'd win, some nights I'd lose.

From there, I played the same types of games in Nottingham, where I had much better fortune. The game was in a huge building in a rough area of town; half the building was a gymnasium and the other half was where we played poker. I had great success there. I think I won 36 times out of 40. This was a game where I'd walk into the building with a gun in my pocket and a bat on my shoulder.

In Leeds, during the first few weeks I played there, I became friends with Gary Whitaker. Gary knew where all the games were played, even a private one that was played at his mother's restaurant in Doncaster. He'd drive me around town to the various games in Derby, Nottingham, and other places. Sometimes, we'd stay gone several days at a time.

Once, Gary and I drove to three different towns where I busted three

CHAPTER FOURTEEN

different games. We started off in Nottingham, then Bradford, then Sheffield. In Sheffield, one of the guys in the game who had gone broke invited me to come back to his house and play some more. We got to his house about 6 or 7 in the morning. I busted him in just a few hours, and Gary and I walked out of the house around 10 a.m. We'd been up all night and now the sun was beating down on us. Feeling flush from my winnings, I looked at Gary and said,

♣♥♠♦

"Where should we go now?" From there we drove straight to a bookie, where I managed to win another £70,000. Within a couple of years I was banned from the bookies in England as well.

As I said earlier, when I got out of prison for that last time and got married to Amanda, I tried to do the nine-to-five bit and opened a jewelry store and pawn shop. I ran it for two years while my wife carried on with her full-time job, which was quite a good one; she was a laboratory technician. I hated running the store, though. I felt like a prisoner in that place. I didn't give up poker, though. I actually started up my own game behind the store. Often, we'd start the games at night. Sometimes, they'd run all night and into the next day. We'd still be playing in the back while my wife was serving customers in the shop.

We did a lot of things to keep the games going, particularly when someone would win big and try to leave with the money. Once, a guy named Phil won a ton of money and started to leave; that was bad for the game. I asked him to stay on a bit, but he said, "There's nothing more to drink." So I went to Amanda, who said we still had some champagne left over from our wedding day. So we got the champagne out for Phil, who drank and played until he lost everything. Amazingly enough, he left quite happy. Another time, there was a guy who also won a substantial

david ⬧ ULLIOTT

sum and tried to get out with it. I didn't like the guy, so I told him to go ahead and leave, but leave through the back door. Amanda had locked the front, I told him, and had taken the key with her. The guy gets to the back and sees this giant vicious dog looking through the window. The dog was licking his lips. All the dog was really doing was drooling over the food at the poker game, but the guy didn't know that. So, he came back and sat down just long enough to lose all his money. The business itself, the jewelry and pawn shop, that is, was and is quite successful. My now ex-wife Amanda still runs it.

♣ ♥ ♠ ♦

One guy named Charlie T, who had also won a lot of money, got his head busted with the butt of a shotgun during the course of the robbery, and, of course, they came straight for me.

♣ ♥ ♠ ♦

I always played around tough crowds. At one time in my life I had a friend I traveled around with named Tony Booth, a professional boxer, who has a book out called *Boxing Booth*. In the book he tells a funny story about the time he saw me carrying a folded newspaper: He said, "What have you got there?" I opened the newspaper and showed him a cleaver I had hidden inside. Then I showed him that I had a pistol in one pocket and a stun gun in the other. He says to me, "So where the fuck are we playing tonight?"

On another night, Tony and I ended up in a game in Manchester. The game was run by a guy named Dave Gardner. There was a really nice guy from Liverpool in the game who was a bit of an alcoholic. He had not won a hand all night. I was heads up with him on one hand and made a big bet. Before the guy could call, he grabbed his chest and fell on the floor. I looked down at the guy on the floor, started to scoop the pot, saying, "Well, I guess I've won this." But before I could rake in the chips, the guy's eyes started to flicker and he told his brother to call the bet. My bet was a stone-cold bluff, and the guy won the pot just as he died.

As the ambulance took the guy away, Tony and I were walking out the door and I said, "Fuck me. How lucky am I? I just got beat by a dead man."

CHAPTER FOURTEEN

Tony just looked at me and said, "What about that poor fucking bastard. He hadn't won a hand all night and when he did, it killed him."

As you can see, my life was quite the rollercoaster ride. I traveled about playing in some pretty rough games in Leeds, Bradford, Nottingham, Birmingham, and Northampton. In those games, if you won you had to worry about getting out with your money and your balls. Frequently, I carried a gun in my pocket. I used to play some at Derek Baxter's game. He was one of the most famous poker players in England. He was getting on a bit in years but was still a quite an icon in English poker. He banned me from his game for carrying a gun. I was pissed at the time but it turned out for the best. The very next week his game got raided. I was very fortunate in that instance. I could have gotten busted at an illegal game with an illegal firearm. I don't even want to think about what might have happened then.

I played in complete dumps, too. I played at a place called Pappas, located in an alley with an entrance that was an old, rusty fire escape. There were dead rats all about and the place smelled of piss. It was damp and filthy—fucking disgusting. Even the mice wore overalls. The owner was a tall, thin drink of water. He was Pakistani, about 6-foot-6 and weighed all of about 110 pounds. Rail thin. He had this big scar on one of his legs. At one point he disappeared for a couple of months and when he came back he said he had been shot in the leg. I told him that he had to have been the best fucking shot ever taken in Pakistan, because this guy had the skinniest legs I'd ever seen. When he went to the duck pond, the ducks threw crumbs at him. Most of his clientele were players from Pakistan and India. We weren't playing for a lot—maybe £500—but I was busting them all. Still, they kept coming. Every time I would bust one, another one would take his seat. This went on for a long time. That night I fought more Indians than John Wayne. At the end of the night I had all their money and they were none too happy about it.

Gary and I had started to leave through the kitchen door. I turned the light off and waited for my eyes to be accustomed to the dark. Then I quietly opened the door and listened. I could hear them down in the

♣ ♥ ♠ ♦

alley mingling and whispering. It didn't take a fucking genius to figure out that they had decided to take their money back and were waiting to jump us. It was about six o'clock in the morning, quiet and dark. I fired my gun off in the air. In the close quarters of an alley the gun sounded like a cannon going off. Gary didn't even know I had the gun on me. The sound of the shot scared the piss out of him. Fortunately, it scared the Pakistanis, too. They were scrambling and flailing about, knocking over dust bins as they ran like rats from a sinking ship.

We got to the car and Gary's face was white as a sheet and his eyes were big as saucers. The poor guy just about had a heart attack. He said to me, "Ok, what now?" I blew the smoke away from the gun barrel and said, "Let's find another fucking game, baby." And off we went.

In Birmingham, I played at the Rainbow Casino, a very rough place where very-high-stakes poker was played, and I won a *lot* of money. While there, I'd heard of a private game run by a guy named Steve Au-Yeung, the guy who would eventually give me the name "Devilfish". I decided to take the money and go down to the private game. Twenty yards from the house I had a change of heart. I thought to myself, "What's the point? I've got all this money. The players there are all going to want to borrow from me to stake their game." So I did a U-turn and went back to the hotel and went to sleep. That turned out to be very fortunate for me.

Twenty minutes later, we learned, four guys had busted into Steve Au-Yeung's game wielding shotguns. It was chaos. People were running about, climbing over the walls, out the windows, doing whatever they could to get away. One guy named Charlie T, who had also won a lot of money, got his head busted with the butt of a shotgun during the course

of the robbery. In those days it was common for those kinds of busts to be inside jobs. Some employee of the casino tracks those who are winning big. He picks up the phone and tells his thug buddies and the shakedown busts out. These people thought I was at Steve Au-Yeung's game with a lot of money, and they had come looking for me.

Steve was a guy who loved to give nicknames to the people he played. One night he saw me looking a bit dodgy, with my dark shades and fucking mean look on my face, and said, "You *look* like a devilfish." I didn't know what a devilfish was. I was thinking of a shark or something of that nature. Later, I looked up a picture of a devilfish and realized it was not such a compliment. It's an ugly motherfucker, but a devilfish is very dangerous when attacked, so I decided the reference must be to my ferocious style of play and not to how I looked. I always likened my play to the way Mike Tyson fought. Every single time Tyson threw a punch he didn't just want to knock his opponent down, he wanted to kill the guy. That's the way I play every hand. I want to put my opponent down for the count. I have mellowed a little over the years, but to this day, if I get a couple of chips into the pot, I don't like to give them up.

♣ ♥ ♠ ♦

Don't get me wrong. I no longer need a duster for fighting. After all, these days I am rarely in trouble more than say, four days a week.

♣ ♥ ♠ ♦

The Devilfish name didn't actually stick until I made it to the States. I had actually forgotten all about this Devilfish bullshit the minute I left Steve Au-Yeung's house.

In January 1997 I decided it was time for me to try my luck in Las Vegas. My first tournament was to be at the Four Queens Casino, and I finished heads up against Men "the Master" Nguyen at The Omaha Tournament. At some point, one of Men's supporters stood up and yelled, "Go on, the Master." At that point my only supporter, my friend Gary, stood up and yelled, "Go on, the fucking Devilfish." I beat Men Nguyen that night and the headlines the next day read, "Devilfish Devours the Master." I went home a winner.

david ULLIOTT

Three months later, however, I was back playing at Binions, and my fortunes changed for the worse. The money I had won was almost too much for me. I relaxed and started to play sloppily. I went broke, losing over $200,000. I borrowed $70,000 more and proceeded to lose that as well. Fortunately, I met a friend, a sweet old white-haired guy named Bobby Lores, a bail bondsman from Texas who, I understand, is alive and well and still running a game. He took a shine to me and loaned me $2,000 to buy-in to the 1997 pot-limit WSOP Hold'em Event. I won over $180,000 and my only WSOP gold bracelet.

On the final hand of that tournament, I held the A-4 of hearts, suited. The flop came down 3-5-7 with two hearts. My opponent had pocket 7's. With the flop he now had three 7's. I needed a 2 or a 6 for a straight, or any heart for a flush. He called all-in. I'm sure he thought he had me stone dead. I missed on the turn and it made for pretty grand drama. I got my deuce on the river. The next day's headline was, "Miracle Deuce." People actually forget the other outs I had. I could also have won with a 6 or any heart. I was actually a slight favorite to win, but the media played it as a "Miracle Deuce."

♣ ♥ ♠ ♦

This $100,000 represented over half of everything I had to my name. Only a truly crazy bastard would have even considered something so insane. So I said, 'Sure, let's do it.'

♣ ♥ ♠ ♦

I had *Devilfish* engraved onto the bracelet. I also got the idea of making two large rings with *Devil* and *Fish* engraved on each. I used to always carry a duster—that's 'knuckle-duster' or 'brass knuckles' to the Americans. In England, if you get caught carrying a duster, it's an automatic jail sentence. With these large rings, I could have my duster with me out in the open and it would be legal. Well, not completely legal, but certainly nothing worth a jail sentence. Don't get me wrong. I no longer need a duster for fighting. After all, these days I'm rarely in trouble more than say, four days a week.

CHAPTER FOURTEEN

After winning the $180,000, I paid off my debts and started to win big cash games. Then I met Mansour Matloubi. He was an Iranian poker player who was quite active in the 1990s. He won the 1990 Main Event, the first non-American ever to do so. Matloubi had this idea of pitting me heads up against Lyle Berman in a pot-limit Omaha game. Berman was considered the top heads-up Omaha player in Las Vegas at the time. Berman was agreeable, but wanted me to come to the table with $100,000. Remember, this was after I had paid off a lot of debt, so this $100,000 represented over half of everything I had to my name. Only a truly crazy bastard would have even considered something so insane.

So I said, "Sure, let's do it." T. J. Cloutier sat behind him as we played. I won $168,000 from Berman before he decided to quit.

After I beat Lyle Berman, I had close to $300,000 in front of me and Puggy Pearson walked by. Pearson, who died in 2006, was an old-school big-time gambler who had won four WSOP bracelets in the 1970s. He had this big tour bus, named "Roving Gambler", that he traveled about in, with an inscription on the side that read:

"I'll play any man from any land any game he can name for any amount I can count."

I had heard about Puggy and his tour bus but never actually saw it. So once I saw Puggy, I gave out a shout to him, "Hey Puggy, it's your turn. Come on, let's get this on." In his southern drawl, he said, "Devilfish, let me show you something. Come with me." So Gary watched my money and Puggy took me to his tour bus. He showed me the inscription, which was as I remembered, but also showed me the last line, which was written much smaller. It said, "Provided I like it."

"Devilfish," he said, "I don't like it."

Since then I have had about twenty high-stakes heads-up Omaha matches, and have only been beaten once, by Sammy Farha, in one of the three heads-up matches we've played. Sammy is a gambler, and I love to play him. Getting money out of Sammy is a tough thing to do.

david ULLIOTT

With my rough past and poker success, the reputation I carry at the tables still only helps me about half of the time. The younger players and amateurs, who I call 'monkeys,' are scared to death of me. They can be easy marks for me. The other half of the time, however, it's a different story. I also carry a big target on my back, and the monkeys all want to beat the Fish. They all want to beat me with rubbish and show their shit hands to me at the end of a bad beat. All the

♣♥♠♦

big names have targets on their backs. When you enter a tournament with 5,000 players and 4,500 of them are monkeys, it's very common for one of them to get lucky and take you out. It's like running across a mine field. You can zig-zag for a while, but one of the players is bound to get lucky, and he can take you out. Every time I play in a tournament now, I tell all the big players, "Let's chop down all the trees at the start, so the monkeys can't get in."

Besides the monkeys, there are a lot of female players who are getting into the game. As a rule, I don't think the women play as well as the men. There are exceptions, of course. In England we have a woman named Lucy Rokach, who is a bit more of a Rottweiler than a woman. She eats raw meat (and her opponents) for breakfast. You take a pot from her and she is going to come after you with bad intentions. So, there are some good ladies out there. Top to bottom, however, women are just not as aggressive as men, and the big players are very aggressive.

When I sat down at the first table at the World Series of Poker, this year, there were three women there. I asked them, "Who the fuck is doing

the cooking, the ironing, the washing and the cleaning?" They were not amused. So just for grins I added, "Women have small feet so they can get closer to that kitchen sink. And they always get married in white so they can blend in with the kitchen."

I do my best to take the luck out of the game. Early on, you have to avoid the monkeys. I like to keep the pots small and not put all my chips at risk too early. In the later stages of the tournament the blinds are so big that you *need* to have some luck on your side. It's in the middle of the tournament, when you have some chips to use to maneuver, that the skill comes into play. That's when you can steal some pots without the good hands. To win, you need to build a chip stack. You don't always need the cards if you have the chips.

People ask me sometimes, "When are you going to slow down?" I am getting on a bit, but I still out-party everyone I hang with. I have a 21-year-old girlfriend who has been with me for over a year, and I am still addicted to the action. It's hard for me to think about slowing down. So people say to me, "Why don't you buy property on a beach somewhere and retire." Hell, I might buy the property anyway. But there is no way I'm thinking of retiring. I play when I want to, and I feel no pressure if I don't feel up to it.

Maybe I have some sort of a death wish. I don't know. I still hang around the town center with some of the roughest characters you can imagine. Some of my friends are pikeys, a pretty tough lot. I still go down and watch the bare-knuckle fights. I just like hanging out with the rough people. My life is a little crazy, but I like to drink and party, too. What can I say? That's me.

I play the guitar and the piano. I love bands like AC/DC and the Rolling Stones. I play a lot of Eric Clapton. "Please note, I didn't say I played *as well* as Clapton, I just said I like playing his songs."

I have six sons, one daughter and three grandchildren. I enjoy being part of their lives. I have a beautiful home and a Ferrari. More luxuries than most people would ever hope to have. I am truly blessed.

david ULLIOTT

Devilfish Poker, www.devilfishpoker.com, my latest business venture, keeps me out of trouble when I'm not playing poker. We are doing very well right now, even though we're not yet able to accept American customers.

I live my life by this simple philosophy, "Life is a blast, but it does not last. Live it long and live it fucking fast." That's the Fish, baby. ♣

You can visit Dave at DevilFishPoker.com. Dave is very fond of supporting charities that promote the health and welfare of children.

CHAPTER ✦ FIFTEEN

CHAD BROWN

Whether auditioning for a movie role, facing an intimidating batter from the pitcher's mound, or finding himself heads-up at the final table in the World Series of Poker, Chad Brown is always focused on achieving his goal. In time, Brown placed poker as a higher priority than promising careers in modeling, entertainment, and professional baseball. A highly skilled cash-game player, Brown hit his stride in tournament poker in 2006, accumulating enough points to win Bluff Magazine's "Player of the Year Award."

He continued his strong play in 2007, finishing fifth in the $1,500 Pot-Limit Omaha 8-or-Better event, and then second to Erik Seidel in the $5,000 World Championship No-Limit 2-7 Lowball event. Brown used his acting experience to land roles hosting several poker television shows, including "The Ultimate Poker Challenge."

An avid fitness and nutrition buff, he has written a series of articles for Bluff Magazine regarding the importance of a healthy lifestyle and the positive impact it can have on one's poker game.

I was 15 or 16 when I began playing poker with friends in the back rooms of Italian cafes. I was a consistent winner, even though the games were fairly casual. My career aspirations as a youngster had nothing to do with poker, but I soon began to count on poker winnings to supplement my income.

My father used to run a Seven-Card Stud game out of our house in the Bronx, New York. When I was around 12, he taught me some of the basics of the game. More important, he taught me the value of watching and evaluating my opponents and their style of play. For instance, he would tell me to watch how an otherwise good player might change his style when he got angry. When players become angry, they

♣ ♥ ♠ ♦

often begin to play poorly. His advice was to be careful around these types of players when things are going well for them, or they'll take your money. But when they start to lose their cool, it's your turn to take the chips.

He also taught me to understand that even the best players in the world are going to get beat, and one thing that separates good players from bad ones is how they deal with their losses. When my dad got beat and began to feel frustrated, he had the discipline to get up and walk away. He would tell me that to become successful, I needed to find a style that works, and play that style all the time. That was a valuable lesson, and I benefit from it today. I have a reputation among my peers for maintaining a calm demeanor at all times.

The games played at the cafes were more than Seven-Card Stud. They varied by dealer's choice. We played forms of Omaha and Criss-Cross and

a wide variety of other games. I learned early that I had a natural ability to understand the differences in odds and probabilities in the various games. This ability paid off in spades, especially in the days before there were websites with odds calculators. Players had to rely on their own abilities. I remember circumstances when I'd raise and re-raise at times that seemed odd to other players. People thought I was plain lucky when I'd take down the pot, but I knew instinctively when the odds were in my favor, even though it may not have appeared that way to my opponents.

♣ ♥ ♠ ♦

I allowed them to think I was lucky. Even at an early age I knew better than to explain to them why I was playing the way I did. 'Yep, I got lucky on that one,' I'd say, 'maybe you'll get lucky next time.'

♣ ♥ ♠ ♦

I allowed them to think I was lucky. Even at an early age, I knew better than to explain to them why I was playing the way I did. "Yep, I got lucky on that one," I'd say, "maybe you'll get lucky next time." In today's poker game I see players chastise others and draw attention to bad play in moments of anger. You may hear a player say, "You raised holding pocket fours with an A-Q-J on the flop after I bet the pot? Are you a complete idiot?" To me this is crazy. You'll never see me teach a guy to play better while I'm trying to get his chips.

There were times when I'd win $300 to $400 per night on weekends in the cafes, but those days my mind was never on becoming a professional poker player. I wanted to become a male model, or even better a professional baseball player, and I had legitimate shots at both careers.

I started modeling clothes in print ads— magazines and newspapers, and so forth. I also began taking acting classes, because there were opportunities in television commercials as well. The first commercial I made was for Jordache jeans, and other commercials came along also. During that time I began to take an interest in acting as a career. Modeling had become boring. The magic behind the ads was with the photographer, not the model. The model was just the look. Acting was a creative art.

I also began playing sandlot baseball in New York. This was serious

baseball, and required an invitation to play. My coach, Sid Pack, had had a great deal to do with the early development of the brilliant major leaguer Rod Carew, and having Sid work with me as an outfielder and pitcher was a big deal. I played for Columbus High School, one of the best high school programs in New York. We played for the city championship in my freshman year. We had a shot at the big prize in my senior year as well, but we lost a heartbreaker just prior to the championship game.

♣ ♥ ♠ ♦

I took the audition from a casting director named Whitney Burnette, who told me, 'Chad, you are hands down the best person for this role but I have to tell you – you are not going to get it.'

♣ ♥ ♠ ♦

I was pitching that day and we were ahead 5-2 in the fourth inning. With the bases loaded and two outs, my center fielder misjudged a line drive. What should have been a routine out (or at the worst a drop-in single) to close the inning ended up as an inside-the-park home run and we were now behind by a run. In the next inning we had a runner on second base with two outs and our best hitter at the plate. But we made another mistake—the runner got picked off by the pitcher. We weren't worried, though, because we still had a few innings to catch up, or so we thought.

The next inning, we got hit by a rainstorm of monsoon proportions. There was no way we were going back on that field. The game was called after five innings, and declared official. We had lost 6-5. The team that beat us went on to win the championship.

Pitching has parallels to poker. As a pitcher, handling the batter is all about strategy. When a hitter comes to the plate, the pitcher is always trying to read what pitch the batter is expecting. If a hitter is expecting a fast ball, he will time his swing differently than if he expects a change-up or a curve. And depending on whether he believes the pitch will be high and inside, or low and outside, he will stand differently at the plate. As a pitcher, you are always calculating what the hitter expects, so you can surprise

him by throwing something different. Poker is similar; you are always trying to read what is going through the mind of your opponent, and you are betting accordingly.

Following high school I played baseball at the University of Miami. In my freshman season, I sat on the bench, which was pretty much new to me. I had always been a starter, and one of the star players. Sitting on the bench was foreign, but my coach told me that I would be starting in my junior season. Still, I couldn't see myself sitting on the bench for two years. I

♣ ♥ ♠ ♦

found it to be a humbling experience. So, after six months at Miami, I left the team and went back to New York, where I joined a semi-pro league called the Westchester Baseball Association.

While I played, I started acting school and began modeling again. I was good enough in baseball to receive a minor league contract offer from the New York Mets farm system. But at roughly the same time, I got an acting audition for a role in the soap opera, "The Edge of Night" a soap that was popular at the time but is no longer on the air. So I had a decision to make—acting or baseball. It turned out that the decision was made for me.

I took the audition for the casting director, Whitney Burnette, who told me, "Chad, you are hands down the best person for this role but I have to tell you—you're not going to get it." I thought, this does not compute. "If

CHAD BROWN

this was a film, I'd have no problem with you," she told me, "but you are just starting out, and this is a soap opera."

I'm a practical person, and that logic made sense to me. In fact, I found the experience encouraging. Soap operas are hard work, because you have literally 24 hours to prepare for the next day's scenes, and that process is repeated every day. It's tough for a new person to handle that kind of pressure, but this casting director thought I could be a good actor and told me so. On the baseball side of things, I considered the fact that I was being offered an A-level contract. If I did well, I'd be moved up to AA and then, in time, to AAA before being called up to the Major Leagues. And the jump from AAA to the Majors is huge: a fair amount of AAA ballplayers never make that jump.

♣ ♥ ♠ ♦

Although he didn't say it directly, he was implying that I should consider steroids to help me develop physically on an accelerated timeline. What he was asking was impossible to accomplish without performance enhancing drugs.

♣ ♥ ♠ ♦

I asked one of the baseball scouts what he thought of my chances. He said I needed to add 20 to 25 pounds of muscle to my frame in the next couple of years, and show a great deal of improvement as well. And then maybe . . . just maybe, I'd have a shot. I knew the score—I'd been around. Although he didn't say so directly, he was implying that I should consider steroids to help me develop physically, on an accelerated timeline. What he was asking was impossible to accomplish without performance-enhancing drugs. I wouldn't even consider this option.

As I thought about it, I realized professional baseball was potentially an eight-year commitment, with no guarantee of a pay-off. In fact, it was far more likely that I wouldn't make it to the big leagues at all, and the minor leagues paid very little. The odds were stacked against me. I could find myself released and starting life all over again at the age of 30.

Even successful baseball players have a limited career. Actors can practice their trade for their entire lives. My decision was made, and I dropped out of baseball. I continued to play poker side games and began working with

an acting coach, who was a good mentor to me. I found a nice role in a soap opera, "Another World." I knew I'd have to head west, unless I wanted to become a stage actor, and I was not keen on that. In 1990, I moved to Los Angeles, fully expecting to become a bartender or waiter while I tried to jump-start an acting career.

But when I arrived in Los Angeles, I saw something that surprised me—casinos! I had no idea. I knew casinos were in Atlantic City and Las Vegas, but Los Angeles? Poker was legal here? I began playing in back rooms with amateurs, having no idea if my game was strong enough to compete with the poker veterans in the casinos.

The first game I found was a stud game in the Commerce Casino. I began playing in a $30–$60 cash game and won! I don't remember how much exactly, maybe $2,000. But I won. So I continued to play and started winning regularly. I found that there were a lot of players who were making obvious mistakes, and I started to exploit those mistakes.

My acting career began to accelerate at the same time. I landed a movie role alongside Woody Allen's ex-wife, Louise Lasser. It was called "Blood Rage." There were other jobs as well, like a role on "Maximum Bob," a TV show with Beau Bridges. There was a part in a show with Ahmad Rashad called "Caesar's Challenge"; the show was filmed in Caesar's Palace and I was dressed up as a Roman centurion, playing a role that was essentially the equivalent of a male Vanna White. I also had roles in the Showtime film "Miami Hustle" and the movie "Basket Case 2."

♣ ♥ ♠ ♦

The product was legit but the CEO was corrupt. After three years, the company went under. The options that I was to use to finance my production company were now worthless.

♣ ♥ ♠ ♦

I've always been both practical and goal-oriented, so when I was offered another opportunity outside of acting I considered it, even though I was finding work as an actor. In January 1995, one of my best friends was offered a job as a COO of a publicly held company. He offered me a job as

Vice President of Sales, with a stock options package as an incentive. The job required a move to Florida, but the potential upside was terrific. If the company became a success, I would make millions of dollars.

I balked. I told my friend that the corporate life was not attractive to me, and that I was not driven by money; I preferred to do things I enjoy. I had been slowly building an acting career, and this job represented a detour and a distraction that I didn't feel good about, so I passed. My friend insisted; "Give me a three-year commitment," he said, "I believe we'll both make millions on this deal. After that, I'll partner with you on a production company and allow you to control your own destiny."

♣ ♥ ♠ ♦

I made the final table, which was the assurance I needed to lock in the award – or so I thought at the time. When I got back, the editor called me and said, 'Chad, I am sorry. I made a mistake. It doesn't count after all.'

♣ ♥ ♠ ♦

It was hard to walk away from that offer, but I was still not totally convinced, so I made a promise to him (and to myself); if I didn't land a lead role in a major film by June, I'd do it. Nothing happened at first, but a week before my friend's deadline, things really started to heat up.

I got called to audition for a new situation comedy. I got my third call-back and was told that the star of the sitcom would be reading with me. The casting director said I'd be reading the role of a weatherman, a nice guy, but dumb, a little like the Ted Baxter role in the "Mary Tyler Moore Show." I walked in and found that the star was Kevin Pollack, a pretty big name. I read well and found out afterward that the role was down to me and one other actor.

The same week I auditioned for that sitcom, I made a screen test for a Rob Reiner film alongside Bette Midler. Both opportunities felt like I was going heads up at the final table of a tournament and failing to win. It was exciting, but in the end it didn't pan out. I wasn't discouraged, though— anything but. I knew I'd been close, and believed it was a matter of time before I'd have a breakthrough. In the meantime, I kept my word to my

friend. Off to Florida I went.

I didn't play poker in Florida, and I put all acting on hold. The company, a publicly held research firm, manufactured medical equipment. Its main product offering was a $100,000 noninvasive solution for herniated discs. The product was legit, but the CEO was corrupt, and after three years, the company went under. The options that I was to use to finance my production company were now worthless.

So I went back to California and made a call to reestablish a relationship with my former agent, who had by now moved on to a much larger, more prestigious agency. He was excited to see me again, and I thought his relationship with me would help me gain a contract with the larger agency. Three or four months went by, and nothing was happening. I was around 38 years old by now, and did not have a large body of work under my belt. Casting directors were looking for people who were young or had a name. I took a few parts, but I was starting to realize that an acting career may not take off for me.

I was playing a little poker along the way, and in 2002 I finished third in an Omaha Hi/Lo event and won a Seven-Card Stud tournament at the Bellagio, taking home over $80,000 combined. At that time, poker tournaments were starting to gain in popularity. In 2003 Chris Moneymaker won the Main Event, and poker exploded across the nation. Poker was becoming a 'legitimate' sport and was finding a large television audience. I began to envision shows on poker and endorsements, as well as other things that held entertainment value. I'd already had good poker experience. With my acting background and experience in television I saw career opportunities in the poker explosion. I knew I could be a marketable commodity in this emerging world.

I decided to pursue poker full-time. I made the final table in 2004 at the WSOP in Seven-Card Stud, finally going heads up against Ted Forrest. I finished second but I'd gained a lot of exposure. This tournament was televised, and people saw interview clips of me reflecting on my acting and modeling career. A Hollywood producer saw the interview and called my manager (who, ironically, was no longer working with me) and told him he was making a poker show and thought I'd make a good host.

CHAD BROWN

The show was "The Ultimate Poker Challenge." I was cast as the host, and the show became the highest-rated nationally syndicated poker show, and later spawned two spin-off programs. I also hosted "Poker Parlor" and "Cash Poker." The irony didn't escape me. I had played poker to bring in a little money to tide me over while I was pursuing a television career, and it was poker that was helping me secure my best television job.

Although I was already at world-class level in cash games, I had to adjust my style to the nuances of tournament play. I also had to develop my No-Limit Hold'em game, which I had not played a great deal up to this point. I had a great year in 2005, and made it to a number of final tables. The following year I peaked and was named *Bluff Magazine*'s 2006 Player of the Year, a prestigious honor and an accomplishment I'm very proud of.

Winning the Player of the Year award is a good example of how I use focus to reach a goal. When I realized that I was in contention for the award, no one on the poker circuit had more drive than I did. In September 2006 I saw that I was leading in points, and I told my fiancée Vanessa, who is a fine poker pro herself, that for the rest of my year it was all about winning that award. To give myself the best shot, I would play every remaining qualifying tournament. I learned about a major tournament in London, but I wasn't certain whether or not it counted toward the standings.

♣ ♥ ♠ ♦

I had been slowly building an acting career and this job represented a detour and a distraction that I didn't feel good about, so I passed. My friend insisted; 'Give me a three-year commitment,' he said, 'I believe we will both make millions on this deal.

♣ ♥ ♠ ♦

I called the editor of *Bluff Magazine* to ask him about it. I said, "There's a $10,000 buy-in at this tournament. Does it count toward the award standings?" The editor assured me it did. So at the last minute, Vanessa and I dropped everything and flew to London to play in that tournament. I made the final table, which was the assurance I needed to lock in the award—or so I thought at the time. When I got back, the editor called me

CHAPTER FIFTEEN

and said, "Chad, I am sorry. I made a mistake. It doesn't count after all." I felt a little deflated, but I had made $150,000 in the tournament, so I wasn't too disappointed.

However, I still did not have a lock on the Player of the Year honor, so I began searching for the next qualifying event. I flew back to Atlantic City for a $5,000 stud tournament. For a tournament to count, it has to have a minimum $5,000 buy-in, and at least 100 players must be entered to compete. I thought, "No problem here." Stud was a popular game in Atlantic City, and the buy-in was indeed $5,000. But when I arrived, I found that only 30 players had registered to play.

♣ ♥ ♠ ♦

So I flew from London to Atlantic City for a live stud event and ended up sitting in my hotel room the entire time playing an online tournament – and I won it all – $225,000!

♣ ♥ ♠ ♦

That same day, I made a decision to blow off the stud tournament and enter an online event that also did not qualify for the *Bluff Magazine* award. PokerStars was having their biggest H.O.R.S.E event of the year, a $5,000 buy-in online tournament. I was a big favorite in that game because of the wide range of games I play. Only 30 players had registered for the live Atlantic City event, and there was much more money to be made in the online tournament. I would have played for less money in the live tournament if it qualified, but since it didn't, I went for the cash. So I had flown from London to Atlantic City for a live stud event and ended up sitting in my hotel room the entire time playing an online tournament—and I won it all, $225,000! But I still did not have the award locked up.

From Atlantic City I hopped on a plane and flew to Vegas, where there were two tournaments that qualified for award points, one with a $5,000 buy-in and the other with a $10,000 buy-in. I made the final table of the $5,000 tournament and effectively locked up the award. My mission was complete.

I feel very blessed to have had good options in life. Although I'm

dedicated to poker now, I have not turned my back on acting altogether. My friend James Woods, the actor and a fine poker player himself, recently spoke to me about a part in a movie he is directing in 2009. And I've been speaking to another director about a role in a movie where poker is part of the storyline.

Away from the tables, I do not operate other business interests. I prefer to focus on poker and keep myself open for entertainment opportunities. My fiancée and I are also becoming involved in charity work. Vanessa recently won a tournament representing our new charity. Many poker players do a great job for charities, and both Vanessa and I feel strongly about doing our part.

This game is always changing and evolving. In tournament poker, the young guns of the online world are rapidly changing tournament strategies. The days when a single person can become recognized as the true master of the game may be over. Even Phil Ivey will tell you that everyone has a bad run, and anyone can be beaten. Although poker is a sport, there is certainly some luck involved. An amateur could never walk onto a golf course and beat Tiger Woods in a game of golf. But certainly an amateur poker player can get a good run of cards and beat a bracelet winner.

On an entire body of work, guys like Phil Hellmuth or Phil Ivey would probably be known as the best overall players in the world. And for a career, those guys deserve to be recognized for that achievement. For me, no matter what the future holds, I know that in 2006 I bested tens of thousands of players and was on top of the poker world, and no one can take that away. ♠

CHAPTER FIFTEEN

You can visit Chad at DowntownChadBrown.com and play poker with him at Poker Stars (www.pokerstars.net). Chad supports the No Limit No Profit Initiative (www.nolimitnoprofit.org), which supports innovative programs and research aimed at decreasing worldwide poverty.

CHAPTER ✦ SIXTEEN

daniel Negreanu

Daniel Negreanu is one of the most successful and entertaining players in the world of high-stakes poker. Always friendly, funny, and talkative, the Canadian-born Negreanu also has a killer instinct and amazing list of wins that makes him one of the most respected players of all-time.

Daniel has collected four World Series of Poker bracelets and is also the all-time money leader on the World Poker Tour, not too shabby for a young man who has yet to celebrate his 35th birthday.

He is a popular player among his peers, known for an almost eerie ability to read his opponents. Negreanu was named Favorite Poker Player at Card Player's Player of the Year Awards in 2006. Now living in Las Vegas, he is one of the most recognized faces in poker, with regular television appearances as a player on ESPN, Late Night Poker, Poker After Dark, and High Stakes Poker, as well as a commentator for the EPT and the APPT.

Daniel plays at PokerStars.net

It's hard to pinpoint the precise moment that led me toward a life playing poker for a living, but looking back, there were definitely some moments in my childhood that led me down this path.

I can remember going to the mall with my brother and my parents and just staring at people. I guess all kids do that, but there was more to it for me than just staring at things that were new to me. I was, at just five years old, trying to figure people out. I was a people watcher then, and I'm a people watcher to this day.

I can remember staring at a couple sitting at lunch. The guy, I could sense, had money and was with a beautiful girl. I could see, because of how much attention he gave her, the way he leaned toward her and constantly wanted to hold her hand, that he loved her very much. The girl? That was a very different story! She didn't love him at all. The more he showed her affection, the more she'd roll her eyes at him. She was distant, and totally annoyed by this guy.

A few minutes later, some friends joined them. All of a sudden this woman's eyes lit up. Her right leg stretched out closer to the new guy who'd just sat down to join them. I was five years old, but remember thinking to myself, "She's only with that rich guy for money, but she doesn't like him. She likes that other guy."

Now that was a pretty easy read, but maybe not so easy when you're five! Since then, I still do that sort of thing when I go to the mall. I can't help myself, I've always been intrigued by people and want to know what makes them tick. It just so happens that doing that kind of thing is excellent training for the poker table. You do the same kind of thing when you play poker. Your goal is to get inside your opponents' heads and figure them out.

I grew up in Toronto in a pretty typical European-style household. My father worked as an electrician and my mother, who is Romanian, stayed home and took care of the kids. My brother is five years older than me and we are polar opposites in almost every way. He's tall, strong, and can fix anything, while I just dial 1-800-Handyman.

CHAPTER SIXTEEN

In addition to people watching, my other childhood interest was numbers. I didn't play video games in exactly the way the other kids did. I used to play RBI baseball, but back then the computer didn't track the stats for you. I'd play the games just to keep track of the stats myself. After a while I'd memorize the numbers, for example, if a guy was 4 for 11 I knew his batting average was .364. I'd keep pitching stats, batting stats, you name it, I'd track it. My mom used to wonder, "What are you doing with all these papers?" when she'd see them all stacked up and scattered around my room.

If it wasn't video games, it was wrestling tournaments. I had a mini ring with my "Macho Man" Randy Savage dolls, Hulk Hogan, Ricky Steamboat, Jake "the Snake," the British Bulldogs, and all sorts of other wrestlers. I'd get a piece of paper and create a 64-man tournament with all my wrestlers. I'd flip a coin to see who wins the match, then, being a kid, I'd have Steamboat body slam Jesse Ventura and keep him down for the three count. I'd do this with all the matches until we got down to a winner.

♣ ♥ ♠ ♦

My first taste of a poker game was through my buddies at the pool hall. One night after a tournament I got invited to a house game. I showed up with $10 and a six pack of beer.

♣ ♥ ♠ ♦

Eventually, I didn't even bother with the wrestlers or the ring. I was just fascinated with bracket tournaments and developed my own point system, based on results from the bracket tournament. It was pretty crazy. I had a book full of tournaments that I ran, with player-of-the-year races and everything.

As I became a teenager I started to play a little snooker at the pool hall. There was nothing cooler to me than entering a bracket-style tournament, where I actually got to play! I'd play the pool tournament every Tuesday, and although I wasn't the best player in the room, I was probably the most competitive. Eventually, we'd travel on Monday to another pool hall for a tournament, play the regular tournament on Tuesday, and then

daniel NEGREANU

travel again on Wednesday to play a tournament across town. I just loved it.

My affinity for people, numbers, and competition eventually brought me into poker. I'd never played the game as a kid, and my first taste of poker was through my buddies at the pool hall. One night after a tournament I got invited to a house game. They were playing all kinds of crazy wild card games like Kings and Little Ones, Follow the Queen, In Between, 7/27. I showed up with $10 and a six-pack of beer. I wasn't legally old enough to drink back then, being only 17 years old, but nobody seemed to mind. Drinking a few beers wasn't a big deal in my house, and my parents would let me have a beer with dinner or when hanging out by the pool with my father.

♣ ♥ ♠ ♦

It didn't take long before I lost my $10 and ended up chilling on the couch, just hanging out. I didn't have a clue what I was doing at all. That game started to become a regular thing, though, and I was determined to figure it out, because of my competitive nature. There was one guy in the game, an Asian kid named John Seto, who seemed to win almost every night. I'd watch him, and he'd just sit there the whole night and maybe play four or five hands the whole night! How can you win if you don't play, I thought? Well, when John played a hand, he always had the best of it. He only played the premium hands, and it didn't seem to matter much to the other players at the table. They were too busy trying to figure out what they had or too busy worrying about themselves to be bothered by the fact that they should be running for the hills when Seto entered the pot!

I learned a valuable lesson from Seto: don't play if you don't have the best of it. Be patient, and wait for good hands. I started to do better

when I played fewer hands. Then one night we all got a wake-up call. This chubby, cologne-wearing, jewelry-wearing, big-haired Italian friend of ours, Benny, showed up and took complete control of the game. He was always betting big, pushing everyone around, raising the stakes, and that first night he walked out with a $600 win. By far the biggest win the game had ever seen. Benny was just crazy aggressive and bullied the table. So on one hand you had Seto, who plays like a rock, and on the other end of the spectrum was Benny, the loose cannon who would pound you into submission.

♣ ♥ ♠ ♦

My life started to really revolve around poker. I'd show up to school at about 11:00 am with a deck of cards and some poker chips, just in time for lunch so I could get a game together in the cafeteria.

♣ ♥ ♠ ♦

Watching the combination of Seto and Benny play was how I initially developed my strategy. I'd play good cards, like Seto, and bet like a wild man when I got them—just like Benny. It took me a little over a month to really start to figure it all out, but eventually I started beating those guys. I was 17; these guys were all in their mid to late 20's.

My life really started to revolve around poker. I'd show up to school at about 11:00 a.m. with a deck of cards and some poker chips. Just in time for lunch, so I could get a game together in the cafeteria. The lunch break would end, but the poker game didn't stop. We'd usually move the game to an empty classroom, so the teachers wouldn't bug us to go to class.

I eventually got suspended from school because of one kid who stole money from his mother to pay me the money he owed me. The kid owes me $300, steals a check from his mother, and I'm the one that gets kicked out of school for cashing it! Didn't seem fair to me, but I didn't mind. The extra free time I had allowed me to study what I really wanted to focus on anyway: poker. I got some books and started to take the game even more seriously.

daniel NeGReanu

Eventually, I graduated from my house games to some quasi-legal poker games in a private club called Check n' Raise. That's where I met Howard Goldfarb. Howie was a hero at our club, just coming back from Vegas after finishing second to Dan Harrington at the World Series of Poker. Man, just the idea of going to Vegas and playing in the WSOP gave me chills. I knew that's where I wanted to be, and I was determined to get there one day.

I was now "The Kid," the youngest player on the underground scene in Toronto, playing at the Bridge Club, the River Room, the Raisin' Room, and all sorts of underground clubs. It never really felt all that dangerous to me. Sure, I'd been robbed a couple times, but it never really scared me. One night at the Bridge Club I was playing in a stud hi/lo game when a group of five guys with masks and shotguns came in yelling, "Everyone on

♣ ♥ ♠ ♦

the floor and empty your pockets." I was worried. I didn't bring any money to the club at all, because I always played "on the sheet," meaning that I'd settle up at the end of the week if I lost. I didn't think the thieves would buy my story, though, so I had to think fast. Nick, a tall good-looking poker hustler was next to me, and he had like five grand laid out in front of him. I looked over at him as we lay face down under the table, and grabbed about a thousand from him so it would look like I had some money too. He nodded at me, so I did it.

Within about 10 minutes, the thieves had left and life returned to normal. We were all back playing again the next night.

You can get cheated in any poker game, but I only got cheated once (that I know of) at the Chimo hotel in Toronto. By this time, we had legal

charity casino games all over Toronto. On any given day, there would be 60 tables full of players playing either $10-$20 or $5-$10 limit Hold'em. I absolutely crushed those games. None of these people had any clue what they were doing. For the first month, in an eleven-handed game, I was the only player who would ever fold before the flop! Back then, I remember them laughing at me, "Ha ha, how can you fold without even seeing the flop?" In the end, I was the one laughing, though, as I'd routinely win close to $1,000 a day. Eventually, some hustlers from Detroit and other parts of Canada heard about these games and came by for a taste of the action.

♣ ♥ ♠ ♦

I was now "The Kid," the youngest player on the underground scene in Toronto, and I played at the Bridge Club, the River Room, the Raisin' Room and all sorts of underground clubs.

♣ ♥ ♠ ♦

There was Detroit Don, Blacky Blackburn, and a guy known simply as "Tex." I was "invited" to play in a private pot-limit Hold'em game with these guys. A much bigger game than I was used to playing, but I'm as competitive as they come, so I wanted in. The game was $10-$25 pot-limit Hold'em, and I lost $13,000 that night. That hurt. I had worked hard to build that bankroll, and I blew all that money in one night, to a bunch of cheats, no less. Oh well, lesson learned. That was the last time I ever played in any private games.

At first, when I was a teenager, my mother told me in her thick Romanian accent, "Daniel, go to school. Forget about the poker." She didn't love the idea of me playing poker for a living, but when I showed my parents my books and how seriously I was taking things, they started to warm up to it. Obviously, after I had some success my mother was very proud of me. My father, unfortunately, passed away before I started to really make a mark in Vegas.

When I turned 21, there was only one place I wanted to be: Las Vegas. I'd planned on going there in 1996 and becoming the youngest ever WSOP champion. My first problem was that I didn't have the $10,000 buy in, so I

daniel NEGREANU

played in a super satellite. The satellite gave away eleven seats to the main event, and with 13 players left I was looking good. A player went all in, I went all in with my pocket aces, and another player also called, with AK. This was it, AA against JJ and AK. I was on my way to the big dance! The first card I saw was a Jack. I was devastated. Me, playing in the WSOP, just wasn't going to happen. Huck Seed won it that year, and I couldn't bear to watch the event. I wanted to be *in* the event, not a spectator.

♣ ♥ ♠ ♦

The game was $10-$25 pot-limit Hold'em and I lost $13,000 that night. That hurt.

♣ ♥ ♠ ♦

I went back to the WSOP again in 1997, played some satellites, but again, fell short. I was yet to play in any WSOP event, and instead spent long nights grinding away in the $20-$40 limit games. When I'd go broke in Vegas--and it happened again and again--I'd head back to Toronto with my tail between my legs and rebuild my bankroll. I never gave up, but it was wearing on me, for sure. Eventually, I "figured it out" and started beating the $20-$40 game in Vegas pretty regularly. In 1997 I had a good late run in tournaments too, winning back-to-back limit Hold'em tournaments on my way to the Best All Around Player award at Foxwoods. I had more money than I'd ever had before, too—over $60,000.

But that money too didn't last. At the Rio Carnival of Poker in January 1998 I blew a bunch of money playing $75-$150 limit Hold'em, made a ton of bad loans, and by the time the WSOP 1998 rolled around I was again struggling to stay afloat. I won three tournaments leading up to the WSOP, but I also staked the wrong people, and still had awful money-management skills.

By this time I started to get to know some of the Vegas locals. One guy, a poker dealer who had recently quit dealing to play poker, was especially friendly. His name was Mike Matusow. Anyway. I ran into Mike in a $200 buy-in satellite for the $2,000 pot-limit Hold'em event at the WSOP the next day. It ended up getting down to me, Mike, and Todd

Brunson. They asked if I wanted to do a save, meaning everyone gets $500 and we'd play for the other $500. Considering that my bankroll at the time was about $2,800, I obviously took the deal. Heads up against Todd, my K-J beat his K-Q and I'd won the satellite. Todd then throws me his $500 chip and says, "Here, I'll take a piece of you in the tournament tomorrow." Well, I hadn't even planned on playing the tournament, but if Todd Brunson had the confidence to throw a total stranger $500 to play the event, I figured, why not!

♣ ♥ ♠ ♦

This was my first ever WSOP event. I would have been ecstatic just to make the money. Before I knew it, I was in the money . . . then, down to two tables . . . then, at the final table! At that table was some guy named Chris Ferguson, who later went on to do pretty well at the WSOP. I ended up playing heads up for the title against an Englishman named Dominic Bourke. I'd never played pot-limit Hold'em heads up before, and didn't have a clue what I was doing. Dominic clearly did know what he was doing, but it all came down to the coin flip of all coin flips. We were all in, almost dead even in chips. My hand was Ah Qh and his hand was Jc 10c. The flop came, Qc Jh 3c, and that's when all the chips went in. The turn was a black card, a spade. Phew. The river was another black card, a six, and I swear I couldn't see if it was a spade or not. I looked up at the crowd watching, and saw people raise their hands and cheer. Then, and only then, did I know that I'd won. I remember collapsing on the ground. I couldn't believe it. At the time, I was the youngest bracelet winner ever, at age 23. It wasn't the main event bracelet I'd hoped for, but I was still very proud of myself.

daniel NEGREANU

After the tournament I celebrated with Todd Brunson's girlfriend at that time. She was there to watch me play the final table, and also to make sure I didn't run off with the money! Her name was Jennifer Harman. I already knew who she was, having seen her playing the big games all the time. In fact, she had got a big chunk of my money at the Rio earlier, in January. We hung out at the bar, drank beers, and just talked. We've been best friends ever since.

♣ ♥ ♠ ♦

By this time I started to get to know some of the Vegas locals. One guy was especially friendly, a poker dealer who recently quit dealing to play poker. His name was Mike Matusow.

♣ ♥ ♠ ♦

By this point, I was starting to become a little more well known in poker circles. It was the first year I would ever get to play in the big one, and I was super excited. While I was sitting at a random table waiting for it to start, I overheard Howard Lederer and Huck Seed talking. I guess they were doing a pool for the event, where they needed to come up with a list of players to win the big one. Huck looked over at me and said to Howard, "What about this kid?" Howard stared over at me, then asked Huck, "Who is that?"

"That kid just won the $2,000 pot-limit Hold'em tournament. He's like 23, and he's probably awesome." I couldn't believe my ears! Huck Seed, the World Champion, called me awesome! I can't describe how I felt just then. I felt a little bit like, "I'd made it." But the event didn't go too well for me. I was nervous, and totally outclassed. Mike McGee eventually busted me on Day One in an embarrassing hand. He was so aggressive, he had me totally confused. I lost all my chips to him on a board of A-A-6 and all I had was a pair of eights. Yuck.

From that point on I became a Vegas regular. I didn't play limit Hold'em very often anymore, and that had been my bread-and-butter game. Instead, I traveled the tournament circuit and played the mixed cash games. I played all the games, at limits anywhere from $200-$400 to $400-$800. The games were tough (this was pre-poker boom), mostly

just professionals in the game, with the occasional drop in. I'd go broke from time to time, even then, but I always had confidence in myself to rebound.

By the year 2000, all the traveling to tournaments across the country really started to wear on me. I didn't travel as much, and spent more time in Vegas. It was my worst year in poker ever. Truth is, I hardly ever played poker, and even when I did, I was always drunk. In December of '99 I'd won the U.S. Poker Championships, and also won a decent amount playing three-handed Stud 8 or better with Phil

♣ ♥ ♠ ♦

Hellmuth and Jon Hennigan. I now had money, and no longer had the hunger.

I'd go to the Bellagio and blow twenty or thirty thousand and didn't really care all that much. Eventually, as expected, the money ran out. In 2001 I went to Ted Forrest and asked him to back me in the cash games. With someone else's money, and also now that I was back to the grind, I certainly wasn't going to take it lightly. I refocused myself and started to do really well. Ted gave me $2,000 to go to L.A. with, and by the end of the month I had turned it into $60,000. I went back to the Bellagio and started playing the $400-$800 games again. I no longer had Ted as a backer, and started to climb to the next level. By 2003 I was playing $4,000-$8,000 mixed games with the best in the world—and winning. That limit was still a bit out of my comfort zone at the time, though, so I mostly stuck to the $2,000-$4,000 limit.

By late 2003 I had it all figured out and the idea of being broke again was totally out of my system. When I was younger I just didn't care at all, but had come to realize that I was still being foolish. I realized not only that I should have more money, but that I should get my priorities in order. I should stop being a screw-up.

The timing was pretty good, too. In 2004 I tore up the tournament scene, putting together a year that would be tough to duplicate. At the WSOP I won my third bracelet on my way to Player of the Year honors. Immediately after the WSOP, I won the $10,000 buy-in event at the Sands, against one of the toughest fields I'd ever faced. Later in the year I won the $10,000 WPT event at the Borgata, then did it again in December, winning the $15,000 WPT event at the Bellagio. That made me the all-time money leader on the WPT, *Card Player*'s Player of the Year, and the WPT Player of the Year. The year 2004 is certainly the highlight of my career, and for the rest of my career I'll be looking to match that same kind of intensity and drive to do it all over again. It's tougher now, with so many more great young players out there, but that's not going to stop me from trying!

What would I tell someone trying to become a top player these days? It's different now than it was when I started out. These days, the best way to learn the game is to sign up for a training site online, and then practice playing online. You'd be foolish not to take advantage of all the available information you can find online.

I'd like to be remembered as a great all around player that succeeded in both tournaments and cash games. I'd like to be remembered as a guy who loved poker and always looked out for the best interest of the game before my personal interests. Also, I'd like to be remembered as a guy who obviously was having a lot of fun at the poker table. ♠

CHAPTER SIXTEEN

Daniel Negreanu plays poker at PokerStars.net. He supports the Lili Claire Foundation, which helps enhance the lives of families and individuals living with neurogenetic disorders such as Williams Syndrome, Down Syndrome and autism (www.liliclairefoundation.org). The foundation helps ease the challenges these familes face by providing suppport services through partnships with UCLA and the University of Nevada School of Medicine. The foundation was created by David Resnick and Leslie Litt Resnick.

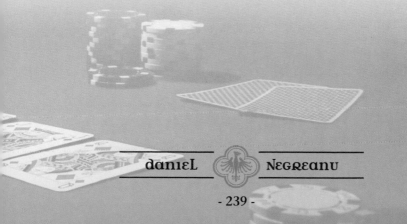

daniel NEGREANU

CHAPTER ✦ SEVENTEEN

PHIL IVEY

PHIL IVEY

Phil Ivey has more than 30 World Series of Poker money finishes, an incredible feat for a young man in his early thirties. Phil won his first World Series of Poker title at the age of 23, beating Phil Hellmuth and Amarillo Slim. Two years later, in 2002, he won three more WSOP titles (tying a record with Ted Forrest and Phil Hellmuth for three bracelets in one year), two Bellagio tournaments, one World Poker Open tournament, and two Commerce tournaments.

In 2005, he won $1 million at the Monte Carlo Millions tournament, finishing first. The very next day he won an additional $600,000 with yet another first-place finish at "The FullTiltPoker.Net Invitational Live from Monte Carlo."

In 2006, Phil was named Player of the Year by All In *and* Bluff *magazines. In 2008, he won his first-ever WPT Championship, capturing the title at the Los Angeles Poker Classic. It was Phil's record-setting eighth appearance at a WPT final table, and the feat moved him into the top ten on the all-time tournament money list.*

Phil is married and currently resides in Las Vegas.

I was born in Riverside, California, in 1976 but moved with my family to Roselle, New Jersey, when I was just three months old. I grew up in a large household with lots of family around me. There were 14 or 15 of us in the house; my parents, my sister, and lots of cousins. You could say I had humble beginnings but we always got by. I particularly relied on my grandmother for support.

♣ ♥ ♠ ♦

My grandfather first introduced me to poker; I was eight years old at the time. He pulled out a deck of cards and patiently taught me to play Five-Card Stud."

♣ ♥ ♠ ♦

My mother worked in insurance. My father worked in construction when he was working, which was usually about six months out of the year. Our family played a lot of games together: Monopoly and Parcheesi and others. I also played a lot of basketball. My sister was eight years younger than I was, and because of this gap, it was later in life when we began to be close.

My grandfather first introduced me to poker, when I was eight. He pulled out a deck of cards and patiently taught me to play Five-Card Stud. We played for coins from a penny jar, and he taught me how to bet. I was completely hooked.

At night, I would approach my grandfather and say, "Hey, you wanna play?" He'd always be up for a game. He'd say, "Do you want another beat down?" I never actually beat him, though. Later, I found out that he was actually cheating and I knew why; he wanted to teach me a lesson about gambling. He didn't want me involved in poker for anything more than fun. My mother didn't want me to play poker for a living either. In fact, I'm not sure she likes it, or that she supports my decision to be a pro even now. Although my grandfather didn't like it, he supported my decision, because I think he knew that I had my mind set on doing it, and he probably thought, "Oh well, I cannot stop him because he has such a strong will."

I grew up loving all manner of competitive challenges, whether it

CHAPTER SEVENTEEN

was cards, sports, or video games. I liked outdoor sports—especially hoops—but I never took them very seriously. Outdoor sports took up too much time, and I knew early on what I wanted to do when I grew up. Even in middle school, when friends, family, or even teachers asked me what I planned to be, I told them, "I'm going to be a professional poker player," an answer that was met with mixed reactions. By the time I was 16, I was already a familiar face at a regular home poker game held by a friend of my dad. I even had a fake I.D., which I used in Atlantic City. I was pretty focused on poker in high school, and I played in private games all over the State of New Jersey. It was obvious very early that I had a gift when it came to gambling. I was counting the days when I'd turn 21 and be able to hit Atlantic City and Las Vegas.

♣♥♠♦

Even in middle school, when friends, family, or even teachers asked me what I planned to be, I told them, "I'm going to be a professional poker player," an answer that was met with mixed reactions.

♣♥♠♦

After high school I began to get a little restless. I didn't want to wait another three years to play legally in the casinos. I got a job as a telemarketer, soliciting products where a piece of the profits went to a police foundation. I was that annoying guy who called you at home looking to sell you something! I was good at it, too. I was able to save some money, which I planned to use to play poker in Atlantic City. So I used my fake I.D., took my entire $500 bankroll, and headed for the Tropicana Casino in Atlantic City. The fake I.D. read "Jerome Graham" and even though the dealers probably knew I wasn't 21, I had money, so few questions were asked.

Now out of high school, I played the poker tables morning, noon, and night, with few breaks. I definitely displayed a strong work ethic. It was common for me to play 14 or 15 hours a day or more. I was there so often and so long that people began to wonder if I even had a place to live. I became known as "No Home Jerome," a nickname that was very befitting at the time.

PHIL IVEY

In addition to the Tropicana, I played other spots in Atlantic City, such as the Taj Mahal and the Showboat. One day when I was 20 I took a bit of a risk and played in a $10-$20 game and met a professional poker player who told me he was making over $100,000 a year as a gambler. He said he was doing it like a job, ten hours a day, five days a week, and that he had been doing it for the last 10 to 15 years. His story made quite an impression on me. I mean, I loved poker, and now I saw a path that I might take in life. The path to being a professional poker player was laid out in front of me, and I intended to follow it. Back then, I was observing everything about the game—analyzing every hand, every situation. No detail was too small for me to overlook. I thought about poker strategies so much that I had trouble falling asleep at night! Had I played every hand perfectly that day? What worked, and what didn't work in the hands that I had played that day? What were the players looking for? Why did they play hands certain ways? I made tons of notes; and I even kept a small journal with my thoughts and observations. How did other players play hands? The bottom line was: how could I play hands better? The notes in my journal helped me understand the players better and allowed me to make better judgments in tough situations. I have no idea what became of that journal.

♣ ♥ ♠ ♦

Now out of high school, I played the poker tables morning, noon, and night with few breaks. I definitely displayed a strong work ethic. It was common for me to play 14 or 15 hours a day or more.

♣ ♥ ♠ ♦

Although I was good around my home games, I certainly didn't win in Atlantic City right away. At first, I lost more than I won. When I'd lose I'd go back to the telemarketing job to earn enough of a bankroll to go back to Atlantic City. The plan was that someday I would just be a professional poker player. For a couple of years, I went back and forth from poker to telemarketing. If I kept winning, then I didn't have to go back to work. Eventually, I didn't have to go back to work at all! Even though I'd lose at times, there was never a point where I was not

certain I was better than everyone I faced. What these other players had on me was experience and discipline. I watched the better players carefully and learned through trial and error. I was confident, determined and patient. I knew it was only a matter of time before I would turn the tide and begin to win.

As you can imagine, I developed my game a lot through trial and error in those days. The process of going broke off and on was painful, but it taught me a lot about the game. One of the things I learned early on was the value of managing my money. ♣ ♥ ♠ ♦

I was never afraid or too proud to move down in stakes if the situation called for it. If I had $30,000 to my name I'd take $15,000 and go play $75-$150. If I'd lose, I'd move down and play $30-60 with $10,000 until I'd built the bankroll back up. If I lost that and had to move to even lower stakes, I'd do that too.

Some of the younger players today don't understand this, and I think it may hurt them in the long run. Some of these guys make names for themselves, then get staked. If they went broke, they'd beg for money from their friends rather than go get a job and build up their bankroll the hard way. I never did that. I never borrowed money. Even if I wanted to, I didn't know anyone well enough to do it. When I needed money, I just went back to work.

Eventually, I turned into a winning player, and by the time I was 20 it made sense for me to move to Atlantic City to be closer to the games. Traveling back and forth was tiring, and less travel meant more time at the tables. The day I turned 21 I walked into the Tropicana Casino and told the shift manager that my name was Phil Ivey, and not Jerome. The shift manager, Kate, just smiled and said, "Damn, I just knew you weren't 21; you looked so young, but you had a great fake I.D., so what was I

supposed to do? You still don't look 21, but I guess I have to believe you now." Of course, I was a great customer and I helped keep their tables going, which made more rake for them. So, 'No Home Jerome' quietly retired and Phil Ivey, the professional poker player, was born.

On my first trip to Las Vegas, I played at the New Orleans Hotel and Casino. I was scheduled to stay only long enough to play in Mike Sexton's "Tournament of Champions." Although I was eliminated from the tournament in short order, I didn't see the outside of the hotel for two weeks! I made many trips to Vegas, and I started to follow the tournament circuit. Eventually, I won some tournaments, including my first WSOP title in 2000—the $2,500 buy-in pot-limit Omaha event—at age 23. That paid $195,000 for first place, and I had faced down Phil Hellmuth, who finished fourth, and played heads up with Amarillo Slim Preston, who I also have a great respect for. Two years later, at the 2002 WSOP, I won three titles. Right after that, I turned 27 and married my long-time girlfriend Luciaetta. With my confidence brimming after that history-making performance, I came back home to Atlantic City with a bankroll of close to $400,000. I began to play $400-$800 limit, and although I didn't realize it at the time, I was a little out of my league. I ended up losing almost all of it. I saved my last $40-$50,000, and started playing in the $75-$150 cash games in Atlantic City. Eventually, I found my stride and rebuilt my bankroll to around $200,000 playing $75-$150, and then jumped back up in limit and beat the $400-$800 games soundly enough to increase my bankroll to around $600,000.

♣ ♥ ♠ ♦

One of the things I learned early on was the value of managing my money. I was never afraid or too proud to move down in stakes if the situation called for it.

♣ ♥ ♠ ♦

That's when I decided to make another move. I had met Larry Flynt, and I knew that he had his own high-stakes poker game in Los Angeles, a $1,500-$3,000 limit Seven-Card Stud game. I decided to move west and give it a shot. I had never played in a game with stakes like that. In fact,

CHAPTER   SEVENTEEN

the highest limit I had ever played was $600-$1,200. I brought nearly $600,000 to the table—my entire bankroll—and lost almost all of it in the first weekend!

True to my philosophy, I took a step back and started playing $80-$160 at the Commerce. Immediately, I started really killing those games. I rarely lost, and after a few months I brought $600,000 to the Larry Game again, and again I lost $550,000 of it in one weekend! I stepped down in limit one more time, and went back to the $80-$160 game at the Commerce. After about a year of this back-and-forth, I finally started beating the Larry Game, and that was a huge accomplishment.

♣ ♥ ♠ ♦

That's when I decided to make another move. I had met Larry Flynt and I knew that he had his own high-stakes poker game in Los Angeles, a $1,500-$3,000 limit Seven-Card Stud game.

♣ ♥ ♠ ♦

Barry Greenstein, a three-time WSOP bracelet winner himself, was among the people I eventually became tight with. It would be Barry who would later introduce me to "Big Game" in Las Vegas.

I loved the lifestyle that Barry was living in Las Vegas and wanted that lifestyle for myself. Over the years, I built up quite a substantial resumé in both tournament and cash game play. Barry once remarked that I was the best tournament poker player in the world, and the only player to successfully transition from tournament poker to beating the Big Game. I'm talking about the Big Game that's held in "Bobby's Room" at the Bellagio; that was my next stop. Beating the Big Game was the next step in the progression upward for me. The Big Game featured mixed games ("mixed games" means a combination of games like limit Hold'em, Seven-Card Stud low, Seven-Card Stud high-low split, pot-limit Omaha, limit Omaha eight or better, and many more games), and I forced myself to learn all of them. I mean, I hadn't mastered any poker games other than Seven-Card Stud—the game of choice in the Larry Game. I was behind the curve in the mixed games, and that made me a mark.

The Larry Game was played only on the weekends, so I started coming

to Vegas during the week and began playing in the Big Game. I opened another chapter in my life when began playing with the best all-around side games players in the world. Guys like David "Chip" Reese and Doyle "Texas Dolly" Brunson populated that game. At first, the boys in Bobby's Room at the Bellagio welcomed me with open arms. But I wasn't losing much in the mixed games during the week, and I was killing the Larry Game on the weekends, so my bankroll continued to grow, even as I paid tuition in the Big Game. Eventually, I figured out the mixed games, and I began to beat the Big Game. At that point, the boys at the Bellagio weren't quite so happy to see me anymore!

The success that I've enjoyed has been a blessing. I believe I have a gift but my success is not just based on that. It has come with a lot of ups and downs and a great deal of very hard work. I enjoy a reputation for being cool and fearless at the table. That reputation serves me well. In large cash games, it is not uncommon for me to play 3-5 off-suit as aggressively as I would pocket aces. And my opponents know this. I'm not afraid to make my opponent make a decision for all his chips.

People frequently ask me what amount of money is at risk before I begin to be nervous: there is no amount of money that makes me sweat. You must remember that I don't come from money. To me, when I'm gambling, it's what I do—it's who I am. I don't get nervous when I'm betting big money. I just try to make good decisions. I feel that no matter how much I lose, I can always recoup it—without exception. I might have to play a little smaller or a little harder, but I always know that if I lose it, I'll get it back. That's how I've always felt, my whole life. So if I have it and I'm able to bet it, I will.

When I first started playing $400-$800 back in the day in Atlantic City, Henry "The Toy Man" Orenstein used to beat me all the time. That man kept me broke for six months. But I would drop down and build it back up in the $75-$150 game for a week in order to get back in the $400-$800 game. I'd play, and he'd break me again! This kept on happening. I don't think I beat him one hand in six months. But I never gave up. I kept on coming back. I knew I'd get there.

CHAPTER ✦ SEVENTEEN

In order to be one of the best poker players in the world, it's important to be able to put everything on the line—that's gambling. To be really good at poker, you can't be too tight or too cautious with your money. No one is saying you should play recklessly, but too much caution can cost you as much as being too reckless. The overly cautious player will lose just as much as a reckless player—just more slowly. Because you're always gambling for big amounts of money, you have to have a certain disregard for money. You have to believe that you will get it back if you lose.

♣ ♥ ♠ ♦

I play the major tournaments and have enjoyed success there. The television coverage from tournaments is where most people know my reputation. But outside of the big WSOP and WPT events, I generally stay away from tournaments and stick to what I love best—the big cash games. The tournaments are great for television, but if you really want to find the best poker players in the world, you'll find them at the big cash games, like the $4,000-$8,000 game at the Bellagio.

People tell me I have an intimidating stare. Sure, I look at my opponent when I'm trying to figure him out. And I don't wear sunglasses. I know that bothers some people, but if they can't deal with someone looking at them with big money on the line, then they shouldn't be there. If they have tells, it's their responsibility to hide them. Lots of top players don't wear sunglasses. I tried to wear them once at the WSOP and misread my hand. I did not hesitate to toss those sunglasses in the trash.

I'm not really as private a person as I am portrayed. I just don't like to be bothered when I'm playing poker, and most of the time, I'm playing poker. That's the thing. I don't like to take time away from my poker for

anything except my wife, my family, my friends, and whatever else that's really important to me.

My wife, Luciaetta, is wonderful. She helps me out with everything I'm unable to do because I'm playing poker all the time. She takes care of me, and is definitely a help when I lose. When she's there, I feel like everything will be fine. Without Luciaetta, I wouldn't be nearly this successful. She'll never know how important she is to me.

People ask me whether I'd approve of my kids playing poker professionally. I'd rather they not do it. This is a tough business and although we all know the success stories, I've seen this profession break a lot of people. And Las Vegas is filled with temptations outside of poker that can ruin your life if you're not careful. Poker is a great hobby, but being a professional is a very different story. But how can I stop them if that's what they want to do?

I know that if I play poker and I put in the hours, I'm going to win in the long run. For me, it's just a matter of time. It's like a job. If I ever lose, I just have to go back to work. And of course, I will. You can bet on that. ♠

You can visit Phil at PhilIvey.com and play poker with him at www.fulltiltpoker.net. Phil Ivey contributes to a variety of charities that support the health, well-being, and education of children around the world.

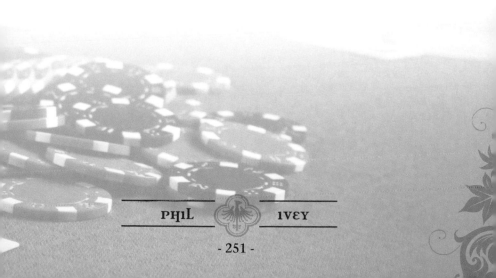

PHIL IVEY

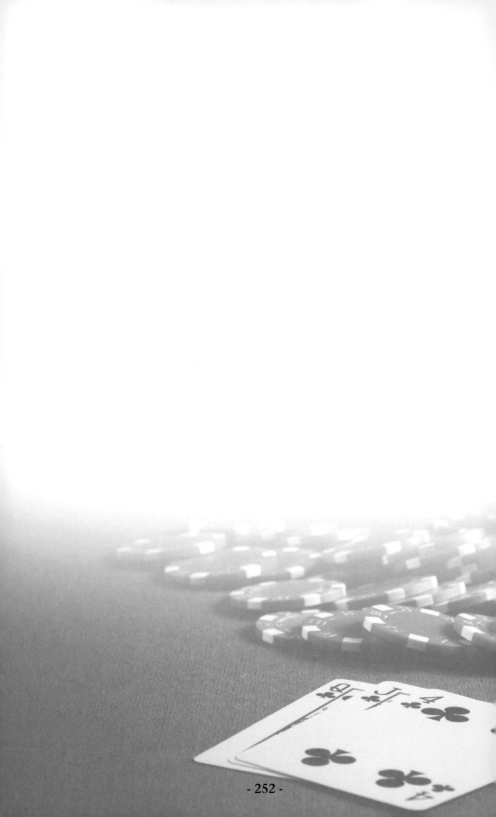

YOUNG GUNS

♣ ♥ ♠ ♦

CHAPTER ✦ EIGHTEEN

TOM DWAN

Tom "Durrrr" Dwan is part of the online revolution that has propelled many players into the national spotlight of high-stakes poker. At just 22 years old, Tom's impressive cash winnings, both live and online, have earned him a reputation as one of the brightest stars in the game, a title Tom reluctantly accepts, despite his disinterest in celebrity status.

His cash winnings are even more impressive when you consider that Tom was denied a seat at the WSOP in 2006 and 2007 because he had not yet turned 21. When he finally hit the legal age limit, he immediately cashed in, making the final table at the 2007 WPT World Poker Finals at Foxwoods and earning the tidy sum of $325,000 for his efforts.

Equally comfortable playing six hands at a time behind the computer or sitting at the final table of a major event in front of television cameras and large crowds, the plainspoken New Jersey native sees poker not as a road to fame, but as a vehicle to finance his other interests.

Professional gambling is not the kind of career that most kids grow up dreaming about, and I was no exception to that rule. As a New Jersey native from the small town of Edison, I was brought up in a normal, middle-class setting. By the beginning of high school I was a pretty typical teenager; I was a decent student, played a few sports, and found myself on a path I assumed would lead toward college, and a career.

My initial frustrations with academics began young, when I first realized that I no longer held interest in a small portion of what my instructors were teaching. When material was taught that I saw no future use for, and also wasn't interested in, I'd pay little attention. Though I managed to retain decent grades, I began to notice myself veering away from the traditional scholarly course. Without any other options at the time, however, my education progressed uninterrupted through the next few years.

As a 17-year-old high school senior, I played my first-ever game of Hold'em during a family gathering. The setting was casual; the table included a high school friend and four or five of my family members, with a $5-$10 buy-in and a basic understanding of the rules. It was an informal game that no one took too seriously, and I spent much of the evening learning the basics from the two people who originally taught me poker: my dad, Thomas Dwan Sr., and my uncle, Anthony Codella.

I was never coached or trained, other than that original five minutes, in Hold'em, or any other poker games. My family is responsible for first teaching me to play, though surprisingly, their knowledge in cards never exceeded the recreational level. After that first family session, I started playing Hold'em occasionally with friends in harmless, $5-$10 buy-in house games.

My first online game came about during an unexpected turn of events due to some inclement weather. A snowstorm interrupted my plans to see a movie one afternoon with friends, and our ensuing boredom led to our discovery of Empire Poker, where we played in free sit-and-go tournaments the rest of the day. After a few days intermittently watching

some of the cash buy-in games, it seemed that I should have an ability to succeed in an online cash setting. I soon invested $50 and officially began my career in small-stakes poker.

At this point, I was still at the novice level. It wasn't long before I began bringing in money, however, as I noticed more and more poor decisions being made by other players. Initially, I thought it was almost too easy, and grew skeptical of online poker. I was more focused on my impending graduation, basketball, and hanging out with friends at this time. Poker was on the back burner, and a career in high-stakes gambling was nowhere in sight.

♣ ♥♠ ♦

I noticed more and more poor decisions being made by other players. Initially, I thought it was almost too easy, and grew skeptical of online poker.

♣ ♥♠ ♦

My parents were not initially supportive of my online habit, which had taken the place of my getting an actual job toward the end of senior year. I had begun playing more and more regularly as the weeks progressed, now for $.25 and $.50 blinds, and it became clear that poker was more of a legitimate moneymaking venture than I had originally anticipated. By the summer, I had made about $15,000, and that was enough to convince my parents that I didn't need a job, while still having money to rent a shore house with friends.

My online playing name has always been "Durrrr." I really tried (for all of about 90 seconds) to come up with a name that was sure to stick in players' heads, and wouldn't immediately intimidate my opponents. No one is afraid of a guy named Durrrr, and certainly no one wants to lose money to him. It was a name that fit from the very beginning.

I first realized the perks of having a disposable income during the summer before heading to college. Even at 18, it was a luxury to visit the Jersey shore, go out with friends, and virtually buy anything and everything I wanted, without worrying about the cost.

Once at Boston University, my poker playing continued to increase. Though my online time was somewhat limited by schoolwork

TOM dwan

and my social life, I was still able to earn another $40 to $50 thousand relatively quickly. While my fellow freshman classmates were scraping by on limited budgets, I was able to do pretty much whatever I wanted. I was enjoying dorm living, constantly going out, and getting better and better at poker. Life was great, except for my academics, which clearly suffered because of the lifestyle I was absorbed in. I wouldn't say that poker is the reason I was failing out of school, but I became less scared to miss a class, or turn in a project late, than most of my peers. I still attended and did work for the classes that interested me. However, when I didn't find interest in the material, I would end up skipping class and going to a movie, or whatever else was happening.

♣♥♠♦

My online playing name has always been "Durrrr." No one is afraid of a guy named Durrrr, and certainly no one wants to lose money to him.

♣♥♠♦

By my second semester at Boston University, my earnings had ballooned to nearly $150,000. I didn't want to drop out of school at this time, but I realized it was a growing possibility, since I wasn't motivated to endure the less interesting parts of school. This troubled my parents, who were clearly worried about my declining motivation to complete my degree. Obviously, my parents wanted me to stay in school, because they thought it was in my best interest.

In seeing the magnitude of money I was making, I eventually came to the realization that I could perhaps succeed in an unconventional career as a gambler. My parents finally gave up the fight to keep me in college, and although they would still like to see me get a degree, they continue to support my career choice. I don't foresee finishing school in my immediate future, though I would never rule it out. It just didn't make sense to me to waste time studying inane topics when I could be earning substantial amounts of money that could later be used to finance new business ventures or fund other personal interests.

Despite sacrificing college for a card game, I have never been as obsessed with poker as many players tend to get at such high stakes.

Poker will, undoubtedly, always be part of my life, though never again at the forefront like it has been the past few years. I averaged about 40 hours a week this past year and a half, because the games during the end of 2007 until early 2009 seemed endless, and ever-increasing in both stakes and mistakes by my opponents.

I don't see myself keeping that kind of pace for very long, as it has already died off in the last few months. I hope to play no more than ten to fifteen hours

♣ ♥ ♠ ♦

a week during the next few years. Granted, I will continue to take part in all the major tournaments, but poker will never be my main focus in life. For me, there are so many more exhilarating and worthwhile things to do than play poker, and when I think back on my most thrilling experiences in life thus far, playing cards does not top that list. At some point, I'd like to play poker for an average of say 5 hours a week, although realistically for the next few years, 10-15 is probably a more accurate guess.

I've always been a little unconventional compared to other high-stakes players in poker. Though many believe that reading your opponent is a huge factor in winning, I think it's highly overrated by most recreational players. That said, poker is a game almost equally about the cards you get and your opponents' actions, including their overall thought processes and their current frames of mind.

In live games, I think there is definitely an advantage in being able to read players, though even the most amazing players will pick up only on something useful, on the basis of movements or gestures maybe 10-15 percent of the time. Live tells are certainly a factor, but for me, not

TOM dwan

an overwhelmingly decisive one. There are more important elements of poker than studying tells, such as being able to read your opponents' ranges and knowing how often they bluff or value bet.

Though a player cannot consistently win by using intuition alone, I have also played against people who exclusively use mathematical probabilities in their technique. I find it unwise to ignore the more complex logic and unique individual aspects of poker, and those who neglect this factor end up losing much of the time. Math has a definite place in poker, like any game, and being oblivious to it will obviously be very costly, but it is important also to be conscious of your opponents' tendencies and moods.

There are far fewer chances for good decisions based on reads in big-money cash games, where players are more often highly skilled. Players who are really good are going to be really good at all aspects of the game, regardless of what they might try to claim. They will know the math, they will know the complexities of their opponents, and they will surely understand the intricacies of each situation, using their experience as an advantage.

♣♥♠♦

Another big part of poker success lies in watching the best people play. As I mentioned earlier, you can learn a lot by watching mistakes online, and remembering the outcome if a situation repeats itself. Watching people's successes can also be beneficial, both online and live. I wouldn't say that I model myself after any one player in particular, but there are plenty of great players that I can learn from while watching, such as Phil Ivey and Patrik Antonius.

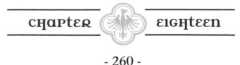

CHAPTER EIGHTEEN

One of the main elements in becoming a good poker player is the time commitment involved. Learning poker requires a tremendous amount of time, what with the countless variables, card combinations, and varying skill levels that players are up against. Even players at the highest level, some who have been playing as long as fifty years, continue to adjust and learn the game's nuances. That's what sets poker apart from other casino games.

Despite the apparent benefits of having decades of experience in poker under your belt, I've never found my young age to be a disadvantage in my playing. The poker world has people from all different generations, and the cards continue to fall the same, regardless of age. It's all about how you play the cards you get, and I think good players understand that.

♣ ♥ ♠ ♦

I wouldn't say that I model myself after any one player in particular, but there are plenty of great players that I can learn from while watching, such as Phil Ivey and Patrik Antonius.

♣ ♥ ♠ ♦

Trash-talking is one of the more annoying aspects of high-stakes poker that many players try to utilize. Though there are several exceptions, the trash-talkers tend not to be the best players, spending too much of their time trying to get into their opponents' heads. This tactic surely boosts television ratings, but truly talented players, who refuse to allow a break in their concentration for what someone else is saying, often have the most success. The same goes for players who are able to block out large audiences or television tapings.

Outside of Las Vegas or casino settings, not many people know who I am. It still seems strange to me that notoriety has come with my playing this card game, though I don't believe it has changed me in the slightest. I do not relish the attention or fame I receive from playing poker. It's not who I am. Fame in poker is almost a mixed blessing: well-known players often have big targets on their backs, and a lot of added pressure to perform well again and again, in a game that clearly has its ups and downs. It can be a little humiliating losing large amounts of money at the

TOM   dwan

highest stakes, because even non-poker friends can hear about how much you lost shortly after it happened. However, there are some advantages to being known, and often somewhat feared, by inexperienced opponents. Oftentimes, opponents that I don't know very well, who are either taking a shot at a bigger cash game or playing me for the first time in a tournament, will make very illogical plays against me.

♣ ♥ ♠ ♦

Though there are several exceptions, the trash-talkers tend not to be the best players, spending too much of their time trying to get into their opponents' heads.

♣ ♥ ♠ ♦

The plain and simple fact is that no one wins all the time. No one would play poker against someone who wins that consistently. I have found that the most successful players are the ones who can rebound quickly from crushing losses, not taking it personally and not crumbling under the pressure of losing insane amounts of money. For me, I care a lot more about "how" I lose than about how much I lose, at least until the sums start representing a significant portion of my overall poker bankroll and/or net worth. I have had over a dozen occasions, lifetime, where I lost more than a third of my bankroll (only one or two of those when my bankroll was under $5,000 or so—I used to be a super-bankroll nut!). I've also had about three situations where I lost more than half of my bankroll, one of them extremely tough to deal with. Starting sometime in April 2007, until around November of the same year, I lost over $2 million, while having under $3 million at my 'peak' point in April. Huge swings like these can be scary, especially to a 20-year-old kid who was already somewhat unsure of his skill (huge downswings will do this), and conscious of how family and friends were perceiving his actions. But at this point, I simply moved down a lot in stakes, and played a ton of hands until I gradually made back my losses, and then added on some future wins. The ability to deal with these losses, both over the course of a day and over thousands of hands spanning weeks or months, is a requirement

for any successful high-stakes poker player.

As a newer player, there are a lot of mistakes to be made before fully understanding the game. Just because you've won a hand does not mean you played well, and the same goes for losing. As I said before, I've lost plenty of hands knowing I played them right with the cards I was dealt—and I've won many that I then I had realized I played wrong. A large percentage of poker players are very bad at recognizing a poor decision if they've won the pot, as those players are too consumed with stacking their chips and feeling happy. Being able to acknowledge a bad play, even one that wins you money, is one of the most important parts of a complete poker game.

There are plenty of genuinely enjoyable moments in poker, like when you finally break through and beat a player who has traditionally run well in heads-up competition. You have to take the good with the bad in this game. Only really dedicated players will take their losses with a grain of salt. Losses will obviously be more devastating for newer players; but the more money you accrue, the easier these losses become.

♣ ♥ ♠ ♦

I lost over $2 million, while having under $3 million at my 'peak' point in April. Huge swings like these can be scary, especially to a 20-year-old kid who was already somewhat unsure of his skill.

♣ ♥ ♠ ♦

Poker can be enjoyable for me even when I'm losing money, which is a facet of poker that often takes time and experience to realize. With the right combination of good sportsmanship, good company and good card playing, even the most competitive of games can be pleasant. To me, this is how the game should be played.

It's difficult for me to imagine where I would be had I not started playing online poker during that snowstorm five years ago. I probably would have graduated from Boston University in 2008, continuing on to graduate school somewhere, or looking to start my own business. I'm glad, by now that poker has easily enabled me to launch two of my own

companies, without having to search for start-up capital, or change the way in which I want to run them to meet an investor's demands. Having this freedom and ability to take many risks that most people can't is one of the main reasons I got into poker. My success at the tables has greatly increased my chances of success elsewhere, and I remain pleased with my decisions thus far.

Though I don't view poker as my true calling, my experiences in this lifestyle have opened a lot of doors for me, and have introduced me to some incredible people, and to connections for my future. Many of my far-fetched ideas from high school seem completely realistic now. Four or five years ago, they felt nearly unreachable.

Poker has been good to me, and there's no denying that. Regardless of my successes at the table, this game does not define me as a person now, nor will it in the future. I have very little concern for how my name will be remembered in the history of the poker world. Hopefully, my record will speak for itself. I'm not the type of player who needs the bracelets, the sponsorships, or the magazine covers. It's not the competition or the high-stakes that make me play. Poker—for that sixth hour and beyond per week—is simply a catalyst for me to amass the funds I will need later to finance the other interests I have in life. That being said, I do find the game of poker to be deeply stimulating intellectually, and I appreciate all the things it has taught me about life. It's definitely a more rewarding, and often more satisfying, job than I would've guessed five years ago. ♥

CHAPTER EIGHTEEN

Tom "Durrrr" Dwan

TOM dwan

CHAPTER ✤ NINETEEN

ANNETTE OBRESTAD

Annette Obrestad

Annette Obrestad is one of the shining new stars of poker. She has won over $2.5 million in cash games and tournament play, but cannot legally put a quarter in a slot machine in Las Vegas until September 2009, when she finally turns 21.

Beginning her poker career online, Annette went on a tear. In 2006 and 2007, she won over $500,000 on PokerStars, $200,000 on UltimateBet, and $136,000 on Full Tilt Poker. In her biggest accomplishment to date, Annette notched a win in the World Series of Poker, Europe in 2007, making her the youngest person ever to win a bracelet.

In the WSOPE, she bested a field that included many of the other top poker professionals in the world. She used her trademark aggressive play to accumulate chips, made the final table, and eventually went heads up with John Tabatabai. In the end, triple sevens won the day for the teenage sensation. Annette Obrestad had won the World Series of Poker Europe main event, cashing in for over $2 million just a few hours after turning 19.

I was a pretty normal child growing up in Norway. I was living with my mom and going to school, hanging out with friends, and doing things that girls like to do. One of the things I enjoyed was bowling. I started bowling when I was 11 years old and fell in love with the game. When I got a little older, I joined a club and played for several years. I built my bowling average up to 160, which was pretty good for a girl my age. I also watched bowling on television. While watching a televised bowling tournament one day, a banner started to scroll along the bottom of the screen. Like a lot of people, I usually don't pay much attention to commercial banners.

♣ ♥ ♠ ♦

I filled out the online form which included checking a little box that verified I was 18. I was only 15 but more than capable of clicking the little box and agreeing to their terms and conditions.

♣ ♥ ♠ ♦

This banner, however, was for Multipoker, an online poker room. I'm not sure exactly what the banner said to catch my attention, but I visited the site and opened an account. It was pretty easy. I filled out the online form, which included checking a little box that verified I was 18. I was only 15, but more than capable of clicking the little box and agreeing to their terms and conditions. My online career was born.

I started playing Seven-Card Stud sit n' go's with play money. I had always liked computer games and, like a lot of teens my age, I had spent hours on the computer. When I started playing poker online my mom didn't think too much about it. To her it was just another online computer game, even though she knew it was poker. I was winning money, but the sums were so small that it never really worried her. By the time she really figured out what I was doing I had already started making more money than she was making at her full-time job. It was pretty tough for her to be upset with me at that point.

I was born in Stavanger, Norway, just about nine miles from Sandnes, where I live today. Stavanger and Sandnes are part of a conurbation,

CHAPTER nineteen

making the city area the third largest in Norway. Stavanger is commonly referred to as the Petroleum Capital of Norway. I grew up doing well in class until high school, when I became bored and my grades slipped into mediocrity. My parents were divorced when I was four years old, and I grew up with my mom. I also have a half-brother who is 12 years older than I am and married, ironically to a woman named Annette. It gets a little confusing at holidays. They have a child, making me a very proud aunt.

Once I opened up an account on the Multipoker site, I found out about Hold'em. Soon after that, I started playing freerolls on UltimateBet. One day I got lucky and won an online tournament, which awarded me nine bucks. I used that $9 to start a bankroll, and I have never deposited a dime into an account from money I have not won playing poker.

♣ ♥ ♠ ♦

One day I got lucky and won an online tournament which awarded me nine bucks. I used that $9 to start a bankroll and I have never deposited a dime of money I have not won into an account.

♣ ♥ ♠ ♦

I dropped out of high school six months prior to graduation. I was enjoying a great deal of success, and just didn't see the need for school. The school system in Norway is quite a bit different from that in the United States. I was studying to be an interior decorator. Even though I was only six months from graduation, I still had years of study ahead of me to actually become an interior decorator, and by this time I was pretty much set on being a professional poker player. My mom was supportive. By this time I had won more money than my mom had made in the preceding two years, so it would have been hard for her to argue with the decision even if she had felt strongly about it.

When I was first building my bankroll I played really tight. I didn't make big moves, and never bluffed. I just played basic ABC poker all day. That got me to a certain point, and by then I knew I could beat the low-

ANNETTE OBRESTAD

stakes games. But then, for quite a time, nothing much happened, and I just felt as if I were stuck. I realized that in order to move up and be able to beat the big guys playing the higher buy-in tourneys, I had to change my game. So I began experimenting with raising some of the marginal hands that I usually didn't play, and decided to improve my post-flop play even if it meant looking like a donk for a while. After making many funny moves and a lot of mistakes, I finally got the hang of it, and I think that's when I really started winning a lot.

♣ ♥ ♠ ♦

I was outplaying and earning more than thousands and thousands of people and my bankroll had grown to over $20,000. I remember thinking, 'Wow, I am really good at this. I can really do this.'

♣ ♥ ♠ ♦

I remember a defining moment when I was around 16 years old. I had been playing online a good while, and I started perusing my rankings and winnings. I was outplaying thousands and thousands of people, and my bankroll had grown to over $20,000. I remember thinking, "Wow, I'm really good at this. I can really do this."

I really hit the radar when I became ranked on Pocketfives. The ranking made people stand up and take notice. I was building a fan base. It was shocking. I hadn't thought people paid that much attention. A *lot* of people follow this game.

I get asked about one particular event fairly regularly when I am playing live tournaments. And yes, it's true; I once won an online tournament and never looked at my hole cards. . . well, almost never. Here's how it happened: One Sunday, I was having a really bad day and feeling a little blue, and decided to have some fun. I wondered how long I could last in a tournament if I played blind—playing without looking at my own hole cards. I had always believed that if I played smart and focused on how others were playing that the cards I held really didn't mean all that much. I decided to put that theory to the test. I entered an online tournament and pasted a piece of tape on my computer monitor

over the spot where my hole cards were, so I was unable to see them. I began playing and watching my opponents for weaknesses in their games. I ended up winning the tournament. I thought it was hilarious, and ended up posting the experience on a poker forum. The news started spreading over the internet like wildfire, and has easily become the question most frequently asked of me.

♣ ♥ ♠ ♦

It was really an interesting thing to do. You have less information because you have no idea what your cards are. You have to pay extremely close attention to how your opponents are playing. How are they playing pre-flop? How much do they open with? Basically I was looking for weakness or tentativeness in another player, and then it was bet, bet, bet, and hope they fold. In this case, it worked. I'm not sure it was worth the uproar it caused, but it happened.

The first time I played in a live tournament I didn't tell anyone who I was. There were probably a lot of people there who recognized the name, "Annette_15," but no one knew my face and I wanted to keep it that way. It was pretty amazing to watch people look at me, this young girl, sitting down "with the adults" to play poker. I think everyone there thought I must have been really bad. At least that was the vibe I got at first, and that was fine. I wanted to project an image of a sweet, innocent girl who knew nothing. I hoped it would give me an advantage. Once play started, however, it did not take long for people to figure out who I was.

At first, the players at the table thought they were just going to run over top of this little girl and take all her money. They learned pretty quickly that that wasn't going to happen. So I never really got to play anonymously at the live games.

After I won the WSOPE in 2007, I invested in a house, where my mom and I now live. She comes with me to tournaments sometimes—when

she can take time off work. She likes to play the slots. When she doesn't travel with me, she continues to work. She loves her job—doesn't make much money but enjoys what she's doing. I still see my dad a little, but I don't spend as much time with him as I should. He knew I was starting to make money playing poker online, but had no idea I was playing in live tournaments, much less the WSOPE. When he learned that I not only played, but won, he called me up and said, "Hey! What the hell just happened?"

♣ ♥ ♠ ♦

And yes, it's true; I once won an online tournament and never looked at my hole cards... well, almost never.

♣ ♥ ♠ ♦

The day after I won the tournament, my phone rang nonstop for over twelve straight hours. It was journalists wanting comments and interviews, and I wasn't prepared for that. I felt bad blowing so many people off, but I had no idea what to do or what to say. I was 18 years old, and reporters were not supposed to be part of my life. I even wondered, "What am I getting myself into?"

Once I had signed my contract with Betfair, interviews were a requirement, so I became more comfortable with them. Betfair is the worlds' largest internet betting exchange. The company is based in Hammersmith in West London, England. Getting a contract with them was a huge deal for me. It's highly unusual for a player to be asked to sign with them unless they have won multiple bracelets.

I would love to be able to spend my 21st birthday in Las Vegas, but I'm scheduled for a poker tournament in London that week, so I'll miss out, but you can bet that Las Vegas is high on my radar. A lot of people who follow me are wondering how I'll do in Vegas, and you can include me in that group as well. Peter Eastgate just broke Phil Hellmuth's record as the youngest player ever to win the Main Event at the WSOP, and some people are naturally curious about whether I can break Peter's record. Honestly, if I didn't get asked that question so often, I'd never think about

it. So many people are competing for the title that the chances of me coming in and winning it on my first try are extremely small. I play the odds a lot, and I know that those odds are not very good. I'm not going to put that kind of pressure on myself. I simply don't need it. Sure, I'll play the Main Event and give it my best, but I'm not going to Vegas with unreasonable expectations. I want to enjoy the experience. I'm young. And there are a lot of tournaments ahead of me.

♣ ♥ ♠ ♦

Maybe someday I will live in Vegas. The prospect of living there is attractive, but not in the near future. I still have a couple of years on my contract with Betfair, and I have many European tournaments to play.

♣ ♥ ♠ ♦

I was 18-years old. Reporters were not supposed to be part of my life. I even wondered, 'What am I getting myself into?'

♣ ♥ ♠ ♦

Vegas will be a place for me to work at refining my tournament skills against the best players in the world, and I believe I will stick to the tournaments and avoid the big cash games. I don't think of myself as a cash game player. I'm a tournament no-limit Hold'em player—that's what I do, almost exclusively. I'll play a little Omaha cash game every so often, but tournaments are what I really enjoy. I don't play H.O.R.S.E. and I get really bored with limit games, so I won't have as many cracks at the bracelets that the others have—at least not at first.

Sometimes, I'm asked whether I would ever take a crack at casino games like craps or blackjack. The answer is, "Absolutely not." Why would

ANNETTE OBRESTAD

I do that? You can't beat the house in the long run, no matter how hard you try. I see some great poker players win big money at the tables and then blow it all in the casino. I just wonder how so many smart people can do something so dumb. I just can't understand why anyone would put themselves through that ordeal when they know, going in, that they will lose. They'd be better off burning the cash than betting it.

I love this game. I know I'm young now, and have a lot in front of me, and I don't know yet exactly what I'll be doing five, ten, or twenty years from now. I do know that I will always be a poker player, up until the day I die. ♦

CHAPTER nineteen

Annette Obrestad
2007 World Series of Poker Europe Main Event Champion

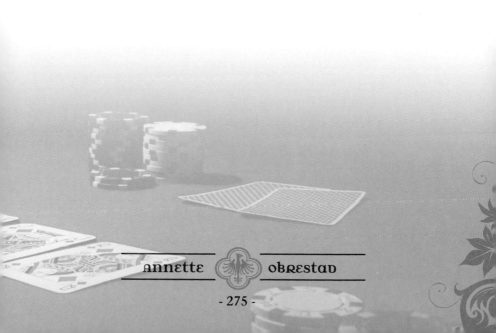

annette OBRestad

CHAPTER twenty

peter eastgate

PETER EASTGATE

In 2008, Peter Eastgate became the youngest World Series of Poker Main Event champion in history. It was only his tenth live tournament ever. He had paid full entry into the event, a prudent decision. Peter was just 22 years, 10 months, and 28 days old at the time of his victory. (The previous record had been held by Phil Hellmuth, Jr., who was 24 years, 10 months, and 5 days old at the time of his victory in 1989.)

Eastgate was born in Denmark and is a Danish citizen, but now lives in London. He is yet another "young gun," an internet prodigy who later made a successful crossover into live tournaments. Although he specializes in short-handed no-limit Hold'em games and high-stakes heads-up cash games online, Peter has a few live tournament cashes to his credit as well. Peter has finished well in a number of live European events too, including the Irish Open and the Scandinavian Open.

When I was in high school, I was like many others my age – I didn't really know what I wanted to do. I was raised in Dalum, a suburb of Odense, Denmark, and I had a very normal upbringing. My family is wonderful. Right after graduation, I had a nice opportunity to travel a bit, taking some time to work as well, while I decided on my future. The jobs I had were low-paying ones. Believe it or not, I was once a substitute elementary school teacher.

♣ ♥ ♠ ♦

Online, I could have several tables going. I could fold two hands but still be involved in plenty of action with the other two.

♣ ♥ ♠ ♦

I went to college for just half a year, studying economics at Aarhus University in Denmark. While there, I started playing poker with friends in live games. One of these friends told me about playing online, and I found that I really enjoyed it. I was just 18 at the time. I played on several websites, but not one in particular. I had a number of online nicknames, but my most famous was probably "See Me No More."

In those days, I didn't read books on poker to improve my play. I was just playing for fun, one table at a time, and my progress was slow initially. But as time went by, I began learning more and more, and became more and more comfortable with my online play.

One of the aspects of online play I enjoyed most was being able to play multiple tables at one time. There is not nearly as much action in a single online game. If you fold a 5-2 off suit, you sit and watch the other players play. Online, I could have several tables going at once. I could fold two hands but still be involved in plenty of action with the other two. Sometimes, I'd play up to six or seven tables, but most of the time just four or five. When you're playing multiple tables, you can learn the game far more quickly, because you're exposed to many different hands and situations in a short period of time.

There's convenience as well. You don't want to play? Don't play. When you're ready to play, there's always a big cash game available. It's ready when you are.

CHAPTER twenty

My parents were skeptical about my playing poker online. Even when they began to be more comfortable with it, they let me know that they wanted me to do other things as well. But like most parents, they wanted me to be happy. As long as I was happy, they were happy, and I knew, pretty quickly, that poker was making me happy.

A lot of the people who have done well in poker have been inspired by the big names they see on television. I have a great deal of respect for these players, but it was not their success that motivated me. For me, the online players and those who wrote poker blogs were the people who most influenced my play. The really good online enthusiasts have very analytical minds, and have written compelling theories and strategies about the game. Frequently, I'd see or read something I liked, and I'd work to incorporate that strategy into my own game.

♣ ♥ ♠ ♦

My parents were skeptical about me playing poker online. Even when they started to become more comfortable with it, they still let me know that they wished me to do other things as well.

♣ ♥ ♠ ♦

It was the summer of 2006 when I first realized that I could make enough money playing poker for it to become my career. Prior to that year I was just a young player who was addicted to the action at the tables. But now, my game had escalated beyond the lower stakes. I started beating the medium-stakes games regularly, and by the end of the year I made about $300,000. Seeing that in 2005 I had pretty much broken even, this was a huge turning point for me.

The difference between 2005 and 2006 was experience. I played a lot of hands-hundreds of thousands! I learned from my mistakes and learned not to repeat them. A number of good Danish pros have become my friends. I enjoy talking to them about swings. We like to discuss our experiences, and the conversations have helped me a great deal. There is good camaraderie among the Danish pros on the tournament circuit.

PETER EASTGATE

I qualified for the 2008 World Series of Poker Main Event via the Ladbrokes Poker website, and traveled to Las Vegas as part of Team Ladbrokes. Early on in the Main Event I encountered hundreds of amateurs who had all dreamed of playing in the WSOP Main Event. For them, it was like a fairy tale. So many people entered. One thing I noticed was that the tournament attracts so many bad players strictly because they want to be part of the event. They know they have no shot to win, but they enter anyway. In Europe you don't see nearly as much of this. Most of the players you encounter in the big tournaments in Europe are pretty good poker players.

♣ ♥♠♦

The difference between 2005 and 2006 was experience. I played a lot of hands – hundreds of thousands! I learned from my mistakes and didn't repeat them.

♣ ♥♠♦

I had not made much of a mark in tournament play prior to the WSOP Main Event in Vegas. In fact, before the Main Event, my greatest accomplishment had been making the final table at the 2007 Irish Poker Open, finishing ninth. It's not as if I didn't enjoy success, though. I managed to do very well building a bankroll from winning online.

A lot of people ask me how an online player can win in a live tournament, and vice versa. In online play, of course, there are no visible "tells." In live tournaments, during the early rounds, I do see tells as a factor, particularly against weaker players. But as you advance in the tournament and face better and better players, those tells become fewer and farther between. Every professional player, after all, is good at hiding his tells. And really, when you do see a tell from a good player you have to wonder if you're seeing a true tell or are just being tricked into believing what your opponent wants you to think. So, for me, tells are not that important a factor in my game. At the final table, in fact, I can't say I was picking up any tells at all. I was doing what I do online; I was watching the betting patterns and looking for weaknesses in my opponents' game.

CHAPTER twenty

One factor that may have played some role in my success was that because I had not played in a lot of tournaments and was not a fixture around Las Vegas, it may have been easy from some of the players to overlook me, or look past me. Not that I think anyone showed me a lack of respect, but I don't believe that many of the players thought of me as a real threat. Certainly, many of them underestimated me.

When I entered the Main Event, I didn't allow myself even to dream that I'd win. At 22, just being at the Main Event was an accomplishment. I wanted the experience, and of course I wanted it to last as long as possible. As I kept playing and advancing, I still never set a goal to win it. It wasn't until I reached the final table that I allowed myself even to consider that victory was a possibility.

♣ ♥ ♠ ♦

There's a lot of responsibility that comes with winning the title, and I'd like to be a good ambassador for the game.

♣ ♥ ♠ ♦

When I play poker I'm known for staying calm and collected at all times. It's just who I am . . . externally. Inside, however, I'm feeling it. In the first three or four days of the tournament, I was playing a little below my average. I wasn't sure if I'd survive to the next day, and I went all in just twice. After that, however, I never had my entire stack threatened. There were moments when players had me covered, and I was mentally prepared for them to make a move to try to knock me out.

The most important thing I did to prepare for the final table was to adapt to the pressure—by thinking about how much was on the line and how high the stakes had become. I wasn't nervous or afraid. If I had finished ninth, as I had at the Irish Poker Open, it would still have been quite an accomplishment.

At the final table of the Main Event I went heads up against Ivan Demidov. I had never played against him before, but I had watched him play some on Day 5 and also on Day 7. So I felt I knew a little about how he

PETER   EASTGATE

played. I knew he was capable of some very misleading moves, and in fact he did try some tricky things when we played heads up. Unfortunately for him, I had a number of very strong hands, and there was no possibility I would fold.

♣♥♠♦

When the tournament finally ended, I was relieved that it was all over. The WSOP had begun long, long before. Playing was a huge physical drain, and I was worn out. So I was just happy that I could relax a little now and celebrate.

After the tournament, my phone started ringing nonstop. Some people believe that I must have partied like crazy, but that just isn't true. I was exhausted from playing two days straight in an extremely tense and competitive final table. On the first day we played 15 hours, starting at 10 a.m. The next day we started at 10 p.m. The timing really messed up my daily rhythm.

People did begin asking me for autographs. I need to work on that. (I've had a person or two comment that my autograph doesn't look much like a signature.) One of the common questions was how I would handle fame. My answer is always the same; I'll remain the same person. My personality has not changed, nor will it. Peter Eastgate, after the Main Event, is the same person Peter Eastgate was before the Main Event. I pride myself on remaining a humble person who is thankful for the success I have enjoyed.

I know that the $9 million championship prize is a lot of money, but I have to say that I don't feel that the money defines me. Certainly I was

proud to win, but the amount of money I win is not the only measuring stick I will use for accomplishments in life. In fact, I think my attitude about money gives me an edge over some players. I've won a lot of money online and I've lost a lot of money online. I know what both are like. I believe some players are thinking much more about the money on the line when they are making a decision about a hand.

My friends are still my friends, and they still treat me the same. A few days after winning the Main Event I went home to London. I got off the plane and everything felt the same. Most people there hadn't known who I was before, and most still don't know who I am. That's fine by me.

I'm sure there are doubters out there who wonder if I'm really a good player, or if I just got lucky. I expect there to be some pressure on me to show that I can continue to play at a high level, but I have a lot of confidence in my game, and I'm not too worried about whether I post big results next year. I still think of myself as more of a cash-game player. I find the cash games to be more challenging, and I'll continue to do that a lot.

There's a lot of responsibility that comes with winning the title, and I'd like to be a good ambassador for the game. The statements you make are heard by millions of poker fans, and you have to be aware of what you say. I believe in sending positive messages, and will try to conduct myself as best I can.

I enjoy poker thoroughly. I'm passionate about it. I think if people I loved wanted advice on whether to pursue poker as a career, I'd encourage them to pursue it only if they love it. I'll tell them not to leave their job right away, because this game is filled with bruising ups and downs.

Poker has afforded me a very good income and lots of opportunities. Seeing new cities and experiencing new cultures has been hugely exciting. I get to travel the world and do many things that I probably never would have done, were it not for my involvement with this game.

I don't necessarily know what I will be doing six months from now,

PETER EASTGATE

much less six years. I'm still young, and I don't feel pressure to decide anything on a timeline. For now, I will continue to enjoy the game that has enriched my life, and I'll do my best to be the best ambassador for the game I can be. ♥

You can visit Peter at TeamEastgate.com and play poker with him at www.pokerstars.net. Together with some of his friends, Peter established Friends of Eastgate, (www.friendsofeastgate.com) which raises money for different children's organizations around the world.

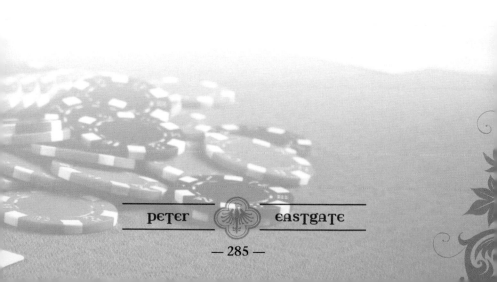

PHOTO CREDITS

CardPlayer Media: All photos on cover with the exception of Johnny Chan and Erik Seidel; all photos in Table of Contents with the exception of Doyle Brunson and Erik Seidel; all photos in Introduction; 3, 10, 15, 17, 18, 19, 25, 32, 33, 39, 46, 47, 48, 53, 55, 59, 65, 73, 78, 79, 81, 85, 86, 88, 91, 92, 93, 97, 99, 100, 102, 103, 106, 107, 111, 113, 116, 118, 120, 121, 123, 124, 125, 131, 133, 137, 139, 140, 141, 149, 150, 156, 157, 158, 161, 163, 166, 169, 170, 171, 175, 178, 181, 183, 184, 187, 189, 191, 193, 194, 195, 208, 211, 212, 213, 214, 217, 225, 227, 232, 235, 237, 239, 240, 241, 245, 251, 254, 255, 259, 260, 265, 266, 267, 271, 273, 275, 276, 277, 282, 285

Larry Grossman: On the cover, Johnny Chan and Erik Seidel; In the Table of Contents, Doyle Brunson and Erik Seidel; 2, 12, 13, 19, 22, 27, 31, 33, 34, 59, 63, 68, 79, 93, 108, 125, 128, 141, 142, 171, 173, 182, 183, 230

Doyle Brunson: 3, 4, 9

Jennifer Harman: 43, 45

Howard Lederer: 47, 57

David Ulliott: 201, 204, 211

Chris Ferguson: 155

Poker Brat Clothing Company: 77

Getty Images: 58

World Poker Tour photograph courtesy of WPT Enterprises, Inc.: 226

UltimateBet: 105